MW00980187

Out OF THE DARKNESS & Into the Light

Answers for STROKE using Traditional Chinese Medicine & Glyconutrients

by
Ruth E. Lycke

authorHOUSE™

1663 LIBERTY DRIVE, SUITE 200
BLOOMINGTON, INDIANA 47403
(800) 839-8640
WWW.AUTHORHOUSE.COM

First published by AuthorHouse 11/01/05

ISBN: 1-4208-8811-0 (sc)

Printed in the United States of America
Bloomington, Indiana

This book is printed on acid-free paper.

Cover Photo: Picture of Tianjin, China taken out from the hospital window

Foreword

Here is an exciting and informative adventure of the human spirit. This gripping book can truly help to disprove Rudyard Kipling's statement that *East is East and West is West and never the twain shall meet.* East meets West in this book in an exciting way.

Here is an American woman who has had the pluck, the determination and willpower to dare to do what many Americans would have said was impossible. In the process she has discovered a path to hope for stroke victims who had no hope.

Her quest for wellness truly took her on a global adventure that should be read worldwide.

I recommend it with all my heart.

Joe Batten, MS, CPAE Speakers Hall Of Fame
Author, *Tough-Minded Leadership, The Master Motivator* and Many More

Contents

1

A Typical Monday

I've found that as life goes by we get busier and busier. Days turn into weeks that turn into years and all while we are apparently not looking. We plan and plot, schedule, scheme, and devise clever little ways to keep it all sorted; as we try to fit in one more thing. This pretty much describes the life both my family and I led. It was a typical Monday like every Monday before; you know...more things to do than time available.

As the clock radio clicked to 5:00 it blared with the announcer's voice and Steve (my husband) hit the snooze button to enjoy his typical 5 minutes of transition time before crawling out of bed and beginning his morning ritual.

The alarm came to life again at 5:05 and the beginning of the day seemed to come all too early as Steve slid the covers back and clicked the button on the clock radio back to its armed position for the next attack tomorrow morning. I heard his deep sigh as he shuffled off to the bathroom to begin his day. Shower, shave, and dress before the shuffling off to the kitchen for coffee and breakfast. He would bask in the glow of kid-less silence that occurs in our house only prior to six a.m. when he can sit and read and slowly sip his coffee.

Meanwhile, back in bed I'm enjoying the warmth of the blankets as I pulled them up tight and squinted looking for the TV to respond to the remote in my hand. No luck, I had to reach out further before the TV came alive with the morning news. I retreated back beneath the blankets to listen and postpone the start of my day a bit longer. I knew very well that my time to move would come all too soon and once I started moving there would be no opportunity to slow down.

Before I realized it Steve came back in the bedroom and gave me his traditional peck on my forehead and then disappeared up the stairs to begin the process of rustling each of the kids from their unconscious slumber to a state of pandemonium.

I heard the front door close as I flipped back the blankets, which inconveniently awoke Pepper our new 1-year-old miniature pincher. I stumbled through the morning shadows and made my way to the bathroom. The light, when flicked on, was all too bright for morning and I was tempted if even for a minute to shut it off and head back to bed, but morning, and the sound of children arguing drew me ever closer to that place in life we like to run from… reality.

I threw on a pair of old faded jeans and a clean white shirt and made my way to the kitchen to check on the condition of the troops. As I turned the corner and entered the kitchen I bumped into Roy, 14 as he was escorting two of our four dogs, (okay, okay four is a bit much but we won't go there now) Scoundrel and Motley outside. Pepper joined the trail of wagging and spinning as they scurried outdoors to make their literal mark on the world.

I reached for the intercom; pressed the buttons, and paged Elizabeth, 9, she was awake and dressing. David, 13, on the other hand had fallen back to sleep and only came to life when I spoke with him repeatedly and threatened to dress him myself. He vowed to get dressed and head downstairs immediately.

As I turned I found Roy posted outside the downstairs bathroom waiting to get in and take a shower. It was obvious that Bundit, our 17-year-old Thai exchange student, was still in the bathroom enjoying his solitude. By 7:45 the daily miracle had occurred and all the kids were dressed, books in hand, coats applied in various fashions and they were lined up waiting for the school bus to arrive. At 7:55 the bus squeaked to a halt in the road and the troops boarded, they were off to school and wouldn't return until 4:00 that afternoon.

Freedom at last!

With the kids at school and Steve at work it was time to begin the things that I had scheduled as important for the next several hours.

Things flowed normally throughout the day as I went about hurrying here and there, parceling out little tidbits of my time like I was serving a cheesecake. I finished up the duties I could squeeze in and retuned home to dress for a school board meeting. Serving on the board seemed like a natural thing to do with three kids in school and I must confess I always enjoyed leaving the troops in Steve's capable hands while I sprinted out the door. Honestly I think it was the 10-minute drive alone that I really cherished as I headed out for the meeting early that evening.

3

The school board meeting had been set to start at 5:30 so that we (the board members) could finish and attend the athletic banquet set to start at 7 p.m. that same evening. The meeting progressed rapidly and one by one we dealt with the issues that were laid out for us but we didn't wind up until after 8 and the banquet was already in full swing. I stopped briefly before leaving the meeting to offer my congratulations to Pat our elementary principal who announced her engagement that night. Her announcement seemed like a pleasant way to transition from business to the fun that lay ahead.

As I headed up to the high school gymnasium the banquet had finished and the award presentations were well underway. I quietly entered the gym and took a seat at the far end of the festivities on old wooden bleachers next to my cousin Kathy. As I listened and watched the awards were given out, I jokingly told my cousin that if any trophies were to be passed on to the school board it was her turn as a fellow board member to receive them. I sat there only a short time when I began to feel a bit flushed. I took off my gray wool suit jacket and continued to observe the proceedings. Each of the coaches touted their sport and a parade of letter winners and participants followed. I became increasingly engrossed in the affair awaiting my cousin's daughters name when I became violently ill. While holding my mouth with my right hand I grabbed my cousin with my left and bolted toward the gym door. As we approached the doorway I began to feel my right side getting weak. While leaning heavily on my cousin we continued to head to the bathroom, careening into the trophy case and a garbage can on the way.

We finally made it to the women's bathroom where I grasped the sink and clung to it to keep from falling down. I was still throwing up and didn't want to try moving again and it was glaringly apparent to me that I needed help fast. I asked my cousin to dial 911. It was the best way I knew to stress to her the nature of my current condition and I didn't know if I could speak or be understood for much longer. My eyes were blurred but I became keenly aware that someone else was present. She asked my cousin if my condition was acute and again I repeated in a desperate and more intense tone:

DIAL 9-1-1

"OH GOD HELP," was my quiet inner cry! I didn't like making a scene but I was in serious trouble and I knew it. I continued to cling to the sink when just seconds later someone behind me was speaking. The voice was very calm but gave me the impression she knew what she was doing. I didn't dare look or take my eyes off of the sink, the room was starting to spin and it was all I could do to hang on. She said she wanted to lower me to the floor but my background as a paramedic combined with the fact I was still violently ill made me hesitant to do anything that would jeopardize my airway. With her assurance and air of confidence I relented and down on the floor we went.

It was cold and hard but just as she had promised she stayed at my head and kept my airway clear. It was at this time that I distinctly remember being slid out of the bathroom and into the hallway where I became conscious of the presence of at least two additional people, the high school principal and a first responder. I knew both of these individuals quite well and felt an overwhelming desire to apologize for the inconvenience I was now causing. It was obvious that more was happening around me, a discussion ensued about whether or not to cut off my turtleneck shirt. I joined in to let them know that I had taken off my jacket, which I considered the pricey part of the outfit, so I really didn't care. As far as I was concerned they should do whatever needed to be done.

Everything seemed to be a bit hazy but they continued to reassure me as they worked. Other people were intentionally kept out of the hallway as they then began to load me on the stretcher and lifted me into the ambulance. Once the door was closed the noise faded and the atmosphere began to feel very close. As we began the trip to the hospital in town it became very apparent to me that when I let go of that sink, I released more than a physical structure. I put my life in the hands of someone who could look out for me regardless of what the people around me did or didn't do.

Meanwhile, as I was being tended to, my cousin Kathy ran to the church next door to the high school in an attempt locate my husband, Steve. He just happened to be there with both Roy and David at a Boy Scout meeting. Kathy urgently interrupted the meeting and explained to Steve that I was being ushered out of town in an ambulance and he might wish to follow. She said she would take care of our boys and with that Steve immediately left and began the 15-mile trip to town. He was on the heels of the ambulance all the way and was caught off guard only once when halfway into town the ambulance stopped and two paramedics from a second unit got on board. They had driven out from town and in order to save time met us half way.

I vaguely remember their arrival as they stopped long enough to establish an IV line before we continued. I guess at this time, I didn't quite grasp the severity of my condition because all I could think of was how much the IV hurt and how if they had used the large vein they could have had a better site without pain. I quietly prayed they wouldn't have to restart it at the hospital. These were all inconsequential things but for some silly reason they were the only things I could focus on.

2

Darkness Begins

The road hummed and the siren wailed as ambulance traveled the 15 miles into town in record time. The back doors flew open and a number of hands grabbed the stretcher and popped the wheels and lifted as the wheels clanked as they hit the ground. No sooner had the wheels hit the ground then I found myself bursting through the emergency room doors and a flurry of activity erupted.

The doctor and nurses that met us pointed us in the direction of X-ray and followed. I watched the lights and tiles on the ceiling blur by as I entered the CAT Scan room. The commotion continued as I was lifted again and placed gingerly into the scanning unit while the doctor anxiously awaited the results. The symptoms I described were in turn relayed by the nurse at the scene (that's right the calm voice that spoke to me in the bathroom just happened to be an off duty ER nurse) to the doctor in the ER. The symptoms had given him a pretty good idea that he was dealing with a stroke of some sort and the CAT Scan would confirm the diagnosis. If it was what the doctor thought, he could then rapidly administer a clot busting medication and the prognosis for full recovery was great!

No such luck!

The doctor took only minutes to reach his conclusion – there was bleeding in the brain stem area that was totally inoperable and he wouldn't touch it. Immediately my husband Steve, who arrived on the heels of the ambulance, was consulted and asked to make the decision as to which of three hospitals he would entrust my life. Faced with such a choice he turned to the Doctor and asked, "If it were your wife…"he stammered, "What would you do?"

The doctor replied without hesitation and immediately they went to work preparing me for transport. My eventful arrival in the emergency room was about to get a lot more exciting. The last thing I remember is hearing muffled sounds and not being able to keep my eyes open. I was stabilized, medicated, intubated and loaded onto a life-flight helicopter for the 20-minute flight to a hospital that specialized in strokes.

From the moment I entered the emergency room they were concerned that the brain would stop bleeding on its own and with medication and rest I might survive this ordeal. I would later find out that only a small number of strokes are bleeding strokes and only a fraction of those occur in the brainstem. It would be a miracle if I survived this one.

As soon as the blades of the helicopter stopped I was transferred to an awaiting gurney and the flurry of activity began again. New tests were ordered, doctors were called and I slowly made my way from their emergency room to residency in the intensive care unit.

Steve drove the hour to the next hospital not knowing what he would find when he arrived. Would I be alive or dead? Conscious or unconscious? He was relieved to find I had survived the trip and been transferred to the intensive care unit.

There was very little for Steve to do except fill out forms. Once all the paperwork was completed he was allowed to go to the intensive care waiting room and begin the monotonous job of waiting and watching for change. With nothing to do but pray and wait, hours turned into days. The next several days the routine continued, watch and wait. As the each day slowly passed, family and friends came by to pray and offer Steve some sense of hope, a word, and a touch... but there was little hope to be found and the prognosis was poor. I had been placed in a drug-induced coma, hooked up to a ventilator, given an NG tube for feedings, an IV for medications and wires that seemed to be everywhere.

Steve seemed to sum it up best,

"There you were, laying so still, not moving a muscle. A machine breathing for you, tubes connected to everything, wires hooked to more machines, all watching and waiting for God to act. I just held your hand, not knowing if today would be the last day that I felt its warmth."

Not wanting to shock the kids with the trauma of ICU, ventilator, tubes and monitors, and my obvious comatose state, Steve kept them at home. I was completely dependent on others for everything. It was just God and me!

I guess I should have realized how bad off I was, after all my older sister that I hadn't seen in years, came when I was in ICU. Just like her to get the upper hand and visit me while I was in a coma and couldn't talk back. You never think that you could be so active one day and cease to exist in this world the next and you certainly don't feel that this world will be able to continue in your absence. Yet, there I was, a once active and full of life individual with everything to live for, hanging onto physical life by a thread. My time here on earth seemingly controlled by a machine clicking with each breath of air that it forced into my lungs. There was nothing that anyone could do but watch and wait. The bleed occurred on a Monday night and it was assumed by the doctors that I would die sometime on Tuesday.

It never ceases to amaze me how wonderfully we have been created. That even in the midst of this outwardly still body a flurry of mental activity goes on. My sense of sound became acute and I battled at first with the reality of the event. I was apparently in a hospital and it had to be real the sounds were just too good to be a dream, but how and why? "Rest, just rest," was the overwhelming voice that God echoed in my head. Verses that I had long since memorized came to the front of my mind. I knew comfort was mine, calmness, soothing rest, and peace. The mental battle that I was having with God was replaced by a gentle reassurance that all was well. I felt certain that there would be a time to fight… just not now.

It wasn't until four days later that I started tugging at my ET tube and it was then that the doctors determined I was strong enough to take the tube out. I still had an NG tube running from my nose to my stomach for feeding and I would have to prove I could swallow before that was removed. Ha! Easier said than done.

The entire scenario that had been played out while I was resting (unconscious) was relayed to me later by my best friend of more than 20 years, it reaffirmed what Steve had been feeling for the past few days.

"Even after you came out of the coma." She shared, "it just was overwhelming. When I left ICU I just walked down the hall and cried. Then I sat in my car and just prayed and cried. It was so sudden and unbelievable."

Unbelievable was right the whole thing felt like a big dream. Over the next several days doctors came and went and I really don't know what they said or for that matter who they were. I was told later that I was visited by every specialist there was... eye, ear, internist, urologist, cardiologist, neurologist they all came through giving their thoughts and opinions and of course they all had a fee attached. All in all I don't think that there was one portion of my anatomy that didn't get the "once over".

The only specialist that really mattered never left my side, he was with me during the event of the bleed, carried me to the bathroom, held me close as I was life-flighted to the hospital, guided the hands of the doctors and watched over me through it all, the Great Physician. (Psalm 139:7-12)

How comforting it is... that day and night are alike to God. He can see through it all and navigate them as one. God was with me just as if I were awake, even while I lay in a coma, and again as I drifted in and out of consciousness He was constant, never wavering. People would come and go but He remained steadfast. Individual and group prayers became palpable, I could feel them, and as God gave me strength I began the search for understanding.

As I slowly re-entered the everyday world I became more aware of the endless number of people who seemed to come through my door. When you are groggy and have no true concept of time you swear you only close your eyes for a minute. The fact was my eyes were so messed up after the bleed and subsequent stroke I kept them closed almost all the time. I suffered from a form of double vision and often kept my eyes closed to decrease headaches.

I vaguely remember the speech therapist visiting later in the day on day 5, Friday, to conduct a swallow test. It was finally decided after many attempts and crooked smiles in between, that I could have the NG tube removed. I was thrilled to be making progress the idea of having that tube pulled was … well… not exactly on my "top 10" list of fun things to do. Upon reflection, I really remember very little about Intensive Care other than feeling an overwhelming calm in the midst of being very confused. I must confess, however, the nurses in ICU were fabulous. I found myself having someone who responded to the smallest request with the utmost care, consideration and speed. In short I was so well cared for and unfortunately unconscious for most of it.

Toward the end of the day on Friday, my brother, his wife and two very dear friends entertained me in my room in ICU. One of them, Carolyn, smuggled up a plastic dish of chocolate ice cream with fudge sauce. It was wonderful! I still couldn't move so I attempted to eat what she shoved in my direction. Let's just say that as a result of that experience I have developed a newfound appreciation for babies who are only 6 months old and are trying to eat cereal that is trust upon them by exuberant new mothers. Eating is definitely a learned and acquired skill that should not be taken lightly.

This bunch came to entertain me but they said I had them cracking up with laughter. I don't know if I was really that funny... they couldn't understand me because of the speech problems... or they were so relieved I was going to live that they would have laughed at anything. Regardless, I would have liked to have the whole thing on tape so I could have taken it on the road. It was just a joy to be alive, conscious and in the company of friends. It had seemed like an eternity since I had last been able to communicate with friends. But I knew that someone other than family and friends had never left my side.

I stopped to consider the hand that held mine through this seemingly horrible time. God was gracious and ever present and brought to mind that advice that my mother always gave in every situation. Look for the humor in this most dreadfully frightening experience and find it! You see (no pun intended) the stroke left me with double vision. Frustrating as this may sound at first until you realize the fun in it. If I could have only seen <u>three</u> things then I could at least aim for the one in the middle but with my double vision I saw two of everything and only had a 50/50 chance of picking the real object I was looking at. Could be depressing right? This is where it pays to look at things differently... I got twice as many flowers, boxes of candy, cards and visitors. It was a bit difficult when it came to drinking water though.

While in ICU I didn't watch any TV but I did think about a show that titles itself SURVIVOR... they (the members of cast and crew) don't have a clue to what <u>real</u> survival is, the price you pay, and the toll it takes from you and those closest to you. Surviving a stroke is one of those twisted realities. I'll never forget the doctor coming in my room and stating how lucky I was to have survived.

"You were one of the lucky ones," he said, "you lived! After all it could have been worse, you could have died."

Obviously the doctor had never experienced a stroke first hand or he would have seen the lack of understanding that dripped from his words. I must admit I had only a glimpse of all that God had in store and I found myself mystified, why me? Most people would have been content to simply survive the stroke. I had an urgent desire to know why me? Why this? Why now? What do I do with it... my survival that is?

3

Survival

Reality Sinks In

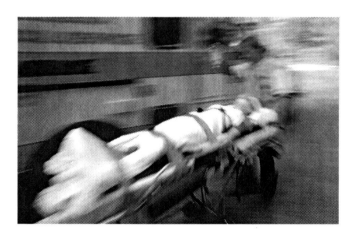

I remember when I had my first child and the doctor gave me some very good advice. "I have good news and bad news for you" she said, "which do you want to hear first?"

"The good news," was my reply.

"Well the good news is…" she continued, "things should return to normal."

"And the bad..?" I reminded her.

"The bad news…" she paused, "this… is normal!"

Strokes are a lot like that advice. Good and bad seem to come hand in hand, or so you feel. The good news… you're alive! The bad news… things will never be the same. The doctors, therapists, nurses and others will do handstands to avoid answering a direct question about strokes. After years of experience, research and study I have come to one conclusion… never say never. All the "experts" know for certain is that no two strokes are alike. They are as unique as fingerprints. There are similarities but every person and therefore every stroke is unique. The fact remains that nobody knows much for sure, as a result I found myself facing one overwhelming emotion when I left ICU for the floor… fear!

Fear is a very powerful and potentially devastating feeling. It resides deep within and is seldom understood by others. If I had something to face that I understood and comprehended I would be prepared to do battle. But this was different, I found myself facing one of the most challenging inner demons… fear! And not just any fear, fear of the unknown! No matter who I asked or sought advice from no one could tell me exactly what I could expect, what the future or even tomorrow held, their response was… we'd see.

I found myself being transferred from ICU late on a Friday night and was taken to a room on an adjoining "medical" floor. The nurses dutifully filled a cart with my hospital "possessions" and I was lifted onto a gurney and began the process of moving from one nurses' station to another. The transfer from my bed to the gurney left my mind and body dizzy and swimming. I looked up only once as the gurney made its way down the hall. I was instantly filled with regret as I realized the motion, and my eyes trying to sort it out... were wicked enemies. My stomach lurched and I quickly closed my eyes tight again. It wasn't until I was placed into a new bed that I gave in to my curiosity and glanced at my surroundings, being careful to keep one eye closed due to the double vision. I was thrilled when they turned out all of the lights and I could rest without the glare of bright lights in the night lit room. It was quiet and remote. I later learned I was at the very end of a medical ward. When all the activity of the move quieted down and all the nurses left I just laid there, eyes shut tight, trying to sort it all out. I knew they said I had a bleed and I'd been in a coma for days but where exactly was I and why was I here? My head was swimming; I had more questions than answers and struggled with even trying to think straight. I know I shouldn't complain but the late night move didn't seem to help me either! After all, I was graduating... being upgraded and moved all at the same time yet this transfer was to begin one of the first of many sleepless nights.

Not only had the motion played havoc on my stomach, but also the move signaled a change in a number of things. This would be the first night that I had not been in a drug-induced coma, and my first night outside of ICU. So much had occurred for me in that ostensibly little transfer. At this point time had little or no meaning to me and I soon discovered that because I was placed at the end of the hall, far away from the nurse's station, people had a tendency to forget about me. This may not mean much to most but consider this:

- I suffered a brainstem bleed
- I collapsed and was transferred to an emergency room

- I was put to sleep with drugs and flown to another hospital
- I suffered a secondary stroke affecting my right side because of the bleed
- I had been in a coma for over 4 days
- I awoke days later in an intensive care unit in another city
- I could not move my right side
- Due to the location of the bleed I had limited movement on the left side
- My children had not seen me
- I had not moved in 4 days
- The nurses in ICU paid attention to everything
- I could not position my bed
- I could not use a call button
- I was transferred to an understaffed medical floor at night on a weekend

Well, I was confused and concerned about each part of the move and for the first time in my life, I was scared. I had gone from a boardroom to a hospital room in a different city via a drug-induced coma. It was difficult to figure out what was real and what was a dream. After all, this whole stroke thing was a dream wasn't it? I could really move. I wasn't experiencing weakness and numbness and a total lack of feeling in portions of my anatomy… I'm just dreaming! Certainly I'll wake up soon!

But that's when it all came crashing down, I was awake, this was reality and not just some awful nightmare. All of those warm fuzzy feelings of surviving a terrible ordeal weren't just feelings they were cold hard reality. I couldn't move, or feel. I could not even easily understand the words that came out of my own mouth. I just wanted to cry but who would wipe away the tears? It was dark… I was cold… and so alone.

This was a nightmare! The feelings I began to experience swirled up inside of me, anger, resentment, disdain, and hatred. Every negative feeling I could imagine, I sensed! I was finally awake in the middle of this nightmare and where was God? Why had he allowed this to happen to me? I felt so alone and vulnerable.

It never ceases to amaze me how God brings things to mind when we need them, I had gone to the funeral of a beloved friend earlier in the year. She had been confined to a wheelchair for over 50 years! I had known her as a dear friend for close to 25 of those years and had cared for her and helped her on more occasions than I can recall. I couldn't remember her complaining even once. We often talked about the challenges she faced daily. How her life had taken on new vistas as a result of her accident. Somehow she came to grip with her disability and chose to overcome it rather than letting it get the best of her. It was at this time in my life that I realized two of the most important lessons in life.

1. The only thing you do when you cry for yourself is to blur your vision.
2. Our character is not shown simply in the fact that we endure, but in the <u>how</u> we <u>choose</u> to <u>overcome</u> adversity.

The next week on "the floor" taught me some very valuable yet tough lessons. It took more than a year to filter them and uncover the jewels hidden within. In the first days after the coma I found myself engaged in a continual struggle to discern reality. Even the clock on the wall was my enemy. I struggled to understand the simplest concepts of day vs. night. This is when a 24-hour clock would have been helpful. As soon as the idea for the 24-hour clock hit me, I realized I was seeing things differently. I knew then that there was a reason I survived and yet suffered such awful consequences from the bleed. It wasn't just for me but for others too! What an eye opening thought!

It was like one of my high school tests all over again but I wouldn't know the answers. I would have to uncover them one by one. It was what my mother had taught me so many years ago discover, learn and apply! The feelings of pain, frustration, anger, and moments of hopelessness... all took on a new meaning. With each episode when I seemed to struggle and suffer another blow to my ego, it became apparent it was to bring hope and understanding to others. I saw the reason for surviving the stroke clearly for the first time.

A verse that I had held close to my heart for years took on new meaning 2 Corinthians 1:1-4.

"Praise be to the God and Father of our Lord Jesus Christ, the Father of compassion and the God of all comfort, who comforts us in all our troubles, so that we can comfort those in any trouble with the comfort we ourselves have received from God."

I was no longer learning for just myself, I was learning and experiencing things that I could use to help others. My background in nursing, as the head of a clinic, and my work as a paramedic was there to give me insight into the little things that people are forced to deal with. I began to have clear understanding into things that typically bring frustration and anger or are overlooked by so many as simply trivial problems.

I discovered that getting moved out of ICU and onto a medical floor in the middle of a Friday night shift is not a good idea. I left the ICU, where if you coughed they checked on you, to being looked in on maybe once every couple of hours. It seemed to skip the notice of the staff that I had been flat on my back not moving for almost a week. I was exhausted! Not only did the stroke effect and paralyze my right side but because of its location in the pons area of the brain stem, my left side had also been affected. It was a struggle to change TV channels or even to lower the foot of my bed. I had to be fed, which meant that I ate when my husband could get off work or if one of the aids could find the time to help me.

If I was lucky, I saw a nurse at the beginning of the shift and at shift changes. I called on the call box only to get ignored or put off. I soon realized that I was viewed as the one who hassled the staff and, although it wasn't said, at times I felt as if I were intentionally avoided. I made a point of talking with the nursing supervisors and the patient advocate all because I knew I was seeing things differently and I didn't want others to suffer or be misunderstood. Now for the next step; Could any of this dreadful event be funny? I know that my mom had always given me that advice, but in this situation, with my circumstances, certainly she couldn't have meant that I look for humor in *everything*?

Yes, everything! There was no gap in her logic and talk about humor... you know the one where they say if you question God's sense of humor look at the person next to you? Well, there were times when I was so depressed and questioned God's judgment so much that I just wanted to end it all, only to discover because of my stroke I couldn't get the resources let alone do anything if I got them.

God's sense of humor continued to amaze me... we make such an issue over telephones in our society, when they ring they control our lives and like a Pavlovian dog drools at the bell, we drop everything to answer a ringing phone. Picture this; each hospital room comes equipped with a phone right? Well I couldn't even see clearly enough to dial a phone let alone reach for one to answer it. It became a game to see if I could beat the phone enough to cause it to flip into my lap where I could use my left hand to bring it to an ear. All this before the party on the other end gets discouraged and hangs up. I began to think the medical staff was secretly in on the game trying to place it further and further out of reach.

I found that after spending countless hours flat on my back, unmovable, with eyes closed tightly, that God does respond to prayer regardless of the position you are in when you pray. You may still balk at the answer, but He hears you just the same. In fact, the last time I checked with God "NO" was still in His vocabulary. He and I had countless discussions and when I was weak and would struggle in looking for humor or maintaining my vision He was faithful in providing me a friend to confide in. Although I was in a city far away from family it just so happened that my best friend from college days lived there. Cindy sat with me for countless hours at night just talking and listening, no matter how slurred my speech. Without her ear and heart there are many times I feel I would have gone off the deep end. Although you need to talk and listen to God, it still helps to have people around in order to bounce thoughts off of them and see their face. It makes it easier if they have a Teflon coated exterior though, that way things you might say in anger do not stick.

I found myself one night, depressed with my current situation, totally self-centered and feeling sorry for myself. It was at this time that my dear friend Cindy entered the room. It was 10:00 at night and although everyone else was ready for sleep I was wide-awake. She found it much easier to visit at night after her kids were taken care of and I enjoyed the time for the two of us to just chat about what I was experiencing. I knew the commitment that she was making and the dedication that she was showing me by coming night after night. The hospital I now resided in was more than an hour from my home, which meant very few visits from home, but it was her backyard. Having someone who was close and would visit was wonderful. That night I was feeling ice cold. No matter how warm the room or how many blankets I had piled on, I felt ice cold. We talked for hours and although my physical body was still feeling cold, my spirit was warmed with the time that she gave to me.

The next day came and I found myself dealing with so much "input" it almost seemed overwhelming. It was then in the midst of feeling overwhelmed the doctor informed me of something called rehab. If I was selected, it meant another move to another portion of the hospital, if not I might find an outside facility that would take me. Boy! Talk about stress, they wouldn't take just anyone you had to be medically stable and evaluated. In the middle of all that I was dealing with, they wanted to see if I could pass a test! Because of where the bleed had occurred and the secondary stroke it affected everything! They call the brain stem the portion of the brain that controls "housekeeping" functions: nothing important just: pulse, blood pressure, breathing, temperature, stability, and eyesight. I was definitely a mess. It would be a miracle if they took me.

Without realizing it I began a form of what they term "rehab" while I was on "the floor". To say it was an experience is somewhat of an understatement. The first time I actually got in the wheelchair I got sick. The little gal who was to haul me to the rehab unit and back was definitely a trooper. She carefully placed a safety belt around my waist and then with the nurses help swung me up in bed. As my feet dangled over the edge I felt my stomach begin to churn. An instant later they grabbed the belt and rotated me into the wheelchair that they had locked into position beside the bed. My head began to throb and my stomach began to convulse as she quickly placed the wastepaper basket in my lap. She and the nurse cleaned me up and acted like nothing out of the ordinary had happened, but I felt terrible. After that I was ready to throw in the towel but not her, she didn't give up and we made that trek to rehab complete with a wastepaper basket and garbage bag just in case.

As she pulled into the rehab room she positioned my wheelchair beside a row of others and locked it in place. I remember sitting in the wheelchair that first day, tired and sick and feeling that if I could have run I would have. I felt it should have been obvious to everyone present that I didn't want to be there. As a "newcomer" I got the joy of sitting and watching as others entered "the players box". Some stood, others walked with walkers or canes or better yet balanced using the parallel bars. The rest of us sat in wheelchairs on "hold", it was embarrassing and tiring, I felt terrible and looked even worse. I had an IV bag, a catheter bag and one of those "semi-private hospital gowns". I have to give them some credit they had taken another gown and put it on me backwards in an attempt to cover up my backside. The entire look left little to the imagination.

Over 20 minutes passed before it was my turn. I don't know if they knew I hadn't been upright for more than 15 minutes or if they made me wait intentionally. Either way by the time I was brought to the front on the line I was sick, tired and sweating profusely. The wheelchair was pulled into position beside the parallel bars, locked, and I was then asked to stand! Can you believe their nerve… STAND! They have got to be joking I could hardly sit, the room is spinning with no hope of stopping and they want me to stand! The last time I remember standing was over a week ago before the bleed and stroke… stand, they really must be joking.

They weren't joking!

Sweat streamed from my limp body as two therapists hoisted me into an upright position. I made an attempt to grasp at the air as I came up out of the chair. One of the therapists, Kevin, placed his foot in front of mine to keep me from sliding forward, while the other held me in place with the safety belt. The one thing I learned about physical therapists that day is that they never joke (at least about therapy) and they have the patience of a saint. Not only did they hold me in place and have me stand, we did it at least 6 times. At last I was lowered, shaking and sweating copiously, to the wheelchair. I sat exhausted and silent in the return holding pattern waiting for my trip back to my room. I've never been so happy to see my bed, as I was that day.

I was exhausted and collapsed after being rotated from the wheelchair to the bed. I closed my eyes and don't even remember the lunch tray being brought into my room. I woke up startled when my husband Steve entered the room and shook my left shoulder. He pulled the cover from the plate to expose different colored piles of puréed food. I could swallow but was placed on a modified soft food diet.

Steve slowly spooned the food in my direction as I carefully chewed and swallowed each bite. I found eating to be tedious, slow, and exhausting. As I finished up I dozed off and don't even remember Steve leaving the room.

Late in the afternoon the speech therapist entered my room for her form of torture. It started simply enough, she introduced herself and began asking me a few simple questions. I never should have fallen for that old ploy... she was evaluating me and I didn't even catch on. She was trying to get me to respond with answers that were more than simple yes and no. I responded slowly, answering with what little voice that I had. It was weak, shaky, and horse sounding. The words were slurred but I tried to make my meaning clear. Looking back on it I'm surprised she understood anything I said.

The occupational therapist visited a bit later and was much subtler; she came to the room as well and started by having me do simple movements. Knowing what I know now it was a definite conspiracy and I was not paranoid... they were out to get me! In their own ways they were doing good things, but at the time I wanted nothing to do with them. I was still feeling sorry for myself. I spent a great deal of time struggling with feeling that I was being *used* by God to learn and feeling like I was used up!

It is one thing to volunteer for something and quite another to be volunteered. I know that I've told God that I wanted him to use me in the work to further His kingdom... but who knew He would take me so literally and use me in this way. I mean after all who should know best.... me or God?

I'm shutting my mouth now... as soon as I remove my foot.

I know I should have been excited when I found out I was selected for rehab, but I was scared stiff. There was a 20-minute video presentation on the TV showing all the things that they did and what to expect. The reality was starting to set in and it frightened me to death. One thing I was never prepared for after the stroke was the change in emotions and feelings. I had been able to keep a lid on feelings before the stroke but now the lid was off and feelings seemed to flow all over the place.

I remember sharing with Steve the night before I was to go to rehab how frightened I was – how much I needed him there. This was the one night that I did not want to be left alone. I don't think Steve had a clue. To him "rehab" was one more step on the road to recovery. To me it was the first rung on the ladder of life and that ladder seemed pretty shaky. I'd dropped pretty far and hard and the idea of opening myself up to a new challenge was frightening. Imagine the person who used to scoff at change and challenges, now afraid to take the next step.

I was extremely nervous about the transfer to another department and allowed myself to be talked into taking a medication that would let me relax more and get some sleep. Little did I know then that I would react to the medication negatively. I'm certain that Steve thought the medication would have its desired effect so at the first sign of my being groggy he headed home. The pleading that I had done earlier in the evening, regarding my fear was, in his eyes, unfounded. I rested for about an hour and then suffered a horrible night of sleeplessness. I reacted adversely to the medication and it had the opposite effect. I was up all night and Steve, disregarding my pleadings had gone home so I found myself alone once again but this time frightened! One thing that I have learned is that if someone feels they need you... they do! After suffering a stroke your entire world is turned upside down and the person you once were is not functioning correctly. I found it extremely difficult to trust what Steve said from that point on, but God was with me and held me close that entire night. I found that this one night was one of the most important in the entire stroke episode and set the baseline for my trust and belief over the next several years.

When morning came I was exhausted and fighting the after effects of the drug. I was finally transferred but the first day in rehab was spent in bed. I struggled with staying awake the entire day. The nurses in rehab were extremely understanding and let me rest.

After waking up later that day I discovered that in the rehabilitation unit we were encouraged to wear regular clothes and not a hospital gown. With this in mind I put together a list of things for Steve to get. Because I was struggling with the area of trust I made up a list of clothes with him that I thought was specific... not specific enough. I'd lost 40 pounds in the hospital in 2 weeks time so things didn't fit as well and I still wanted to look decent even though I felt lousy. Well, as luck would have it Steve found every old sweatshirt that I owned and had not worn in years. This included every pair of sweatpants that had been used as paint pants and to top it all off he bought me 2 new jogging sets that ended up being 2x size. I've never worn a 2x in my life! I was a size 14 before I lost 40 lbs. from the hospitalization and the stroke. I must confess that at this point I was very disheartened and frustrated. It seemed that everything I needed or requested was being replaced with something else. I didn't understand what was happening. I had to keep in mind that I was experiencing these things not just for my sake but also for others.

The last straw was when I requested a pair of glasses. Because of my double vision it had been suggested that I get a pair of cheap glasses, take out one of the lenses and tape over the remaining lens. This would allow me to block one eye and see only one image. Steve returned with a pair of men's glasses that were much too large. This is the only pair he said he could find. Faced with his refusal to get a different pair I had the nurse's remove one of the lenses and tape over the other. This provided me with a degree of help with my double vision.

As for the wrong clothes, incorrect sizes and glasses that were much too large… I chalked this all up to the fact that Steve had suffered too. When I had the stroke he found himself as a single parent, responsible for three kids, a functioning home, and a wife in the hospital. I decided to make the best of a bad situation. It would have accomplished very little to berate him for his attempts. It became glaringly apparent that in addition to a husband, I needed a wife! You know someone who could sense my needs and read my mind no matter how clouded. In my condition there was nothing I could do about it. I was however very grateful for friends that seemed to fill in the gaps in not only reading my mind but in looking out for the welfare of my family. They cooked meals, brought over treats for the kids, acted as drivers, kept an eye out at school, and even helped on the homework front. All in all I couldn't have asked for more, everyone was great.

After the transfer and drug induced drowsiness I found that in rehab my days were now strictly regimented and full. It appeared that I was scheduled to do something for 6-

8 hours each day. The old me would have scoffed after all I only slept for 5-6 hours before the stroke. The new me, however, was only used to 2-3 hour of activity and most of that was set aside for the attempt I made at eating. This was definitely going to take some getting used to... kind of like basic training... it's a mindset. Sure... I had all of one day to get used to the idea.

I learned very quickly that these professionals in rehab were very different from the nurses on the floor; they got no satisfaction unless you improved. This was very unlike the floor where I seemed to be in a holding pattern, the rehab staff was there to motivate and encourage and they took your progress or lack of it as a personal challenge. As a result they were right there with you, wanting you to perform better and better and exceed your own efforts daily. Because they were so involved personally it made them seem less like enemies and more like friends.

As for the actual rehab it was **Return to Basics 101**; learning how to walk again, talk again, move my arms again, and eat again. Everything that I had taken for granted just two weeks earlier was now next to impossible. I held on to the hope that I could, with a lot of effort on my part, return to what I once knew and did. Everyone was careful not to set expectations that were too high and yet they never said you couldn't accomplish things. They would have all made excellent politicians.

Have you ever noticed that they call medicine a practice... makes you wonder if they will ever get it right or if they'll just continue to practice. While I'm on the subject the doctors have continually said we'll try this or that. I assumed because the word "we'll" was a conjunction it implied "we will" meaning the doctor **and** me. Oh silly me, what was I thinking! Funny how **I** get to **try** it while *they* sit back and observe whether or not it works. I can't complain though, when it comes to doctors I was fortunate enough to have two doctors in the rehab unit that were responsible for my daily rehabilitation and as busy as they were they always seemed to have time for a smile, wink, and squeeze of the hand.

My first full day in rehab I worked hard to look "normal" and put on one of the outfits Steve bought. Not thinking about it just letting the aid help me get dressed. When I was wheeled of to breakfast for the first time I discovered that all the patients in rehab eat in a common break room. Upon my arrival I was fitted with a towel as a bib. Breakfast trays were dispersed and the eating frenzy began. Different patients were at different stages in their rehab. Some needed very little help while others required almost complete assistance. I started out being fed by the nurse who staffed the break room during meals. My breakfast consisted of juice and milk and oatmeal, all things that are liquid or easy to eat. What I wouldn't have given to have steak and eggs! I was returned to my room with time to take a nap before rehab. Breakfast took more out of me than I realized and I quickly fell asleep. Before I knew it I was being roused to head to the workroom to stand and walk. It wasn't until I took my first steps in rehab that the brutal reality of my new clothes came to light. I stood up and the pants went down. The physical therapist that was working with me was quick to grab the pants and pull them up again. He sat me back down in the wheelchair and realizing the emotional connection associated with a stroke he announced that we were done for the day.

I'd say I've never been more embarrassed but I would hate to set myself up for something in the future. Needless to say the outfit went home that evening and didn't come back until it was washed several times in hot water.

I was happy that the therapist ended the day when he did. He knew far better than I did the emotional strain that an event of that sort would cause. I tried to make light of the event but it cut to the quick. A short time later I was wheeled back into my room and found myself in the bathroom looking at myself in the mirror while waiting for the nurse. I looked pathetic! My face drooped, my hair was greasy, the glasses on my face were 2 sizes to big, and my clothes were much too large. It was all I could do to keep from crying out loud. I had always prided myself in looking decent whenever I went out. Now looking in that mirror I was reminded that beauty is definitely only skin deep. I vaguely remember that prior to this everyone who I saw said how good I looked. All I can say is that if this was good then I must have looked horrible! I know I'm learning for the benefit of others not just for me but you've got to admit there are some lessons it would be nice to skip!

I was used to getting up early so I found it was easier for the night shift to get me up and have me ready for breakfast at 7:00. Everyone in rehab was expected to eat in the dining room and there were shifts as it were. Showing up at 7:00 put me with the early shift and was most welcomed by the staff who had more people wanting the late shift. The night crew was responsible to get people to breakfast and even though some people were able to get there unassisted; still others had to get dressed and then pushed.

Almost everyone used a towel as a bib… talk about embarrassing! You were seated at the table and one of the girls would go around and drape a towel over your shoulders to catch food and spills. I must confess it did little for the ego. I realize I had to learn to eat all over again, and with my left hand, but the bib thing was more than degrading. It did not escape my attention that all these individuals were completely capable adults before the stroke and many of them took great pride in their appearance before the tragic event. I found that I was able to use my right hand in a limited way as a support as long as it didn't require movement, in other words I could block with the right and chase with the left.

I took turns sitting and eating with different people as the weeks went by. It's amazing that as bad as you think things are there is always someone to remind you it could and very often is worse. Sometimes Steve was able to stop by and have a cup of coffee while I ate. They (the staff) push you to try and do things for yourself. Meal times became for me a major event in my life, not only was I learning the basics again I was able to learn from observing others. I watched in fascination as one woman, thinking she was helping, proceeded to do everything for her husband. He was limited in his speech but he could get out yes and no, if only she would have been patient and ask yes and no questions he would have felt much better about himself. Too often I sat and watched good meaning people hurt rather than help the one they loved.

Breakfast was usually followed by a workout with the physical therapist for at least 60 minutes and maybe longer. I referred to it as a workout because I was always sweating at the end. This was usually done in the hall or in your room depending on what the focus of the exercise was for the day. The staff had become quite adept at reading your non-verbal signals and challenging you just to that point beyond what you thought you could do. Because of my double vision I used those glasses that Steve picked up for me, you know the ones that had one lens removed and tape over the other lens. This blocked one eye and allowed me to see using the other eye. It worked great except for the fact that they were so large that every time I looked down the glasses slid down. Oh, another opportunity to learn!

Speech therapy came next on the list of daily activities and the focus for me was speech, cognitive skills, math, and basically a little smattering of everything because the entire brain was affected by the stroke. I don't think it would have been as difficult but because the eyes were affected I could not read. This definitely put me at a disadvantage because everything would have to be read to me. This is fine until you realize that my memory was affected as well! What should have been easy became next to impossible. I couldn't look at a list of words and recite them, I had to go a step further and remember the list and then recite it from memory. I was not able look at a "sample" menu and total prices on paper the way the therapist asked, I had to memorize each price and add them in my head. Remember topping off my vision problems was the fact that my right hand, the one I used to write with didn't work and I still lacked feeling in my left fingertips so I couldn't write with the left hand either. All in all I was a basket case without a basket!

During my time in speech therapy I did everything from reciting tongue twisters, which by the way I couldn't do before the stroke, to adding up those prices on a menu, reciting lists and word problems. All the skills were practice again and again and I learned that repetition is one of the therapist's unwritten mottos. The hope was that this repetition would help me to relearn many of the skills that had been taken by the stroke. To be honest the repetition would not have been as tough to handle if it weren't for the vision difficulties.

I usually got a break around 10:00 for either 30 minutes or 1 hour before the occupational therapist showed up. I generally collapsed during my break using the time for rest, sprawling out on the bed and trying and catch a few winks before it was time to begin the next series of challenges. It was during one of these breaks that the hospital kitchen staff first sent up a snack consisting of cheese slices sealed in plastic and crackers individually packaged. This seems simple enough until you realize that with my current disabilities caused by the stroke I couldn't open them if I wanted to! I guess I could have attempted to tear them open with my teeth, but it was obvious to me that they had no idea who this was for or they would have known my disabilities prevented me from enjoying their food. I know to them I was simply a room number and a diet order that they were to fill. The speech therapist started staying until the snack was delivered and graciously opened it up.

I know this was an opportunity to express frustration and anger, or a chance to practice thankfulness and work through the challenge and find a solution. Yup! Another lesson to be learned, It was at times like these that I remembered the Disney movie "Pollyanna" and the "glad game". Sometimes it was difficult to find something to be glad about but it was never impossible. Often it just took a little time and creative thinking!

When the occupational therapist did arrive we worked on typical day-to-day dressing challenges such as; taking a shower, combing hair, brushing teeth, and putting on clothes. Each task that I had taken for granted and done with relative speed and ease was now next to impossible to accomplish. Not being able to see straight, only having the functional use of my left hand and right-sided paralysis made each task particularly challenging. Just getting to the bathroom seemed impossible and unless I had help it was! I was ever so grateful that the occupational therapist was kind and patient and obviously had a good imagination and sense of humor. Her attitude toward me spoke volumes and made my frustration dissipate. Anytime I was tempted to give up she would come along side me and use her smile to coax that extra little try out of me. She was a godsend!

At this point in time during my recovery process I had very little strength and even less stability. I was pushed everywhere in a wheel chair and getting out of the chair was impossible without help and a transfer belt. I only left the chair to use the bathroom or get in bed. The wheelchair had to be positioned perfectly next to the bed, locked, a safety belt placed around my waist and then the nurse or therapist would lift me up and rotate me, and then lower me to the bed. Once there the work was not over I needed to be positioned correctly and the sheets under me and on top had to be smooth and in place. Exhausting, isn't it? It was during one of these transfers that the humor in life and my now everyday happenings became a laughing matter. Dixie (one of my nurses) came to transfer me to the wheelchair on the way to my goal of reaching the bathroom. At this point I still had a catheter in. During the transfer I started tipping and Dixie quickly rotated me back to the bed and somehow I managed to land on top of her. There we both were, Dixie on the bed and me pinning her down, unable to move, both laughing hysterically when my other nurse popped her head in smiled and couldn't help from laughing herself.

"You two! You should thank your lucky stars." She said as she grabbed my belt, rotating me and freeing Dixie.

"Why?" Replied Dixie.

"Just be thankful that catheter was in or you would both need a bath right now!" She retorted. We all snorted and gave out another burst of laughter. It was times like these that made the horror of my day-to-day circumstances bearable. It is also my reaction of laughter that made me a fun patient to care for. Sure I had more than my fair share of opportunities to be angry and bitter, but why? What does that accomplish? It certainly doesn't make things easier to deal with, just the opposite it makes the circumstances and me a trial.

After a full morning of therapy I wanted to give up, collapse, and sleep but lunch followed in the dining room and the entire process began anew in the afternoon. I saw each of the therapists at least two times a day and with the double vision many days it seemed to be twice as frustrating.

I had lost a total of 40 pounds in 2 weeks, partially due to the coma and partially due to the medications they had me on. It is not a diet that I recommend. The side effects are horrendous. It caused me both to be both tired and dehydrated. The dehydration caused problems with my voice and the contributed to constipation. It seemed that nothing in my body worked right. My Internist seemed to think that the medications were fine because on paper my vital signs were perfect so why mess up a good thing. I was not physically or mentally prepared to do battle so I gave in to the doctors orders and took the medications without complaint, at least for now.

By the time I was done with therapy for the day it was time to eat supper. Steve would stop by after he finished work to check on my progress and watch me eat. I don't really know if he had much of an appetite after watching me attempt to shove food in the general direction of my mouth! It was more like watching a race as I chased food around the plate. Thank God for mashed potatoes! Not only do they catch food but also they help it to stick on your fork and spoon.

That brings up an interesting subject: SPOONS! I don't know how long the rehab unit had been operating before my arrival, but I developed a distinct issue regarding the spoons that came with the meal trays. Now you must consider that almost all of the individuals in the rehab unit have some problem with their physical body or they wouldn't be there. In fact, at least half have an eating difficulty related to a stroke... either paralysis on one side or paralysis combined with parathesia (lack of feeling). This tends to make eating a bit of a challenge to say the least.

I first noticed my spoon at breakfast.... the milk was poured into my cereal and allowed to sit. This made it extremely mushy. Keep in mind that I was right handed before the bleed and stroke and now I was forced to use my left hand for just about everything. It too was affected by the stroke and as a result was very weak. I picked up the spoon in my left hand only to notice that it was a soupspoon! Sooooo you say? What's wrong with a soupspoon?

Now... I don't know about you but I never used a soupspoon to eat soup... let alone anything else! Here I'd been given a soupspoon and I had less than half of my mouth that was working or had feeling! The challenge was to find my mouth with the spoon in an attempt to get food in it! Finding it without delivering food (half of my mouth didn't open) was a bit pointless. I know that they must have felt that by increasing the spoons size you would increase the chance of finding your mouth and getting more food in! It made a kind of twisted logic. Any problems were of course offset by the addition of a towel used as a bib to catch anything that didn't go in. I must have been feeling a bit better because this twisted reasoning gave me a new mission in life.

After breakfast you were supposed to fill out your request for the next days meals... I would make my proverbial scrawls and then ask one of the staff to write:

NO SOUP SPOON

This appeared in big letters across the top of my meal request form, and I had the staff write it everyday! It took over a week but a dietitian finally stopped by my room. When I asked why rehab patients were given soupspoons, she replied that she honestly didn't know. She immediately called down to the kitchen staff to get an answer...

"It's all that's left," was her reply after she hung up the phone.

"You mean that we get soup spoons because everyone else in the hospital gets regular spoons!" I inquired, "and there are only soup spoons left?" I was amazed. It was logical it just didn't make much sense.

She shook her head in agreement. It was then that I explained how most of these people that were in rehab today, were in other situations less than a week ago. I myself had dined at some of the most prestigious places in Europe including a five star restaurant in Amsterdam where utensils were brought with each course. To go from that to eating mushy cereal with a soupspoon and having a towel draped across me was beyond humiliating. I agreed that I was retraining my left hand to take the place of the right but I didn't need to be humiliated in the process of learning. Needless to say that was the last meal in which I used a soupspoon. Sure, I spilled occasionally but I was able to give up the "bib" and attempt to look a bit more civilized again.

It did wonders for my self esteem and in speaking with those who visited me during meal times they were much more comfortable as well.

I was able to see it was all in the guise of learning. Learning to adapt and overcome but the stroke and the hurt feelings, humiliation and stress were real. The things that I endured and chose to overcome are often stumbling blocks to others.

Let's take visits as another prime example! You would think that a person laid up in a hospital would love to have visitors. They do, but there is too much of a good thing. I found that it was either feast or famine. You either had so many visitors that you became physically exhausted... or no one showed up for days! There are days I would have paid a stranger to stop by just to talk. Not that I had all that much to say, I just enjoyed the interaction and talking with people who saw and dealt with the real outside world daily. In looking back on it... it would have been helpful if someone from the church coordinated visits so that you would have something and someone to look forward to.

We need something each day to keep us focused on the bigger picture, the eternal and not simply the day-to-day affairs. Let's be honest, the daily affairs in a hospital revolve around your vital signs and how many visits to the bathroom you made. Not that it is unimportant but there is a lot more to life than daily bodily functions.

Each day in rehab melded into another and there was little that distinguished one day from another. I know that everyone who visited me shared how good I was doing and how much progress that I was making but to be honest it was difficult to see or even comprehend. When you are living each day in the moment you don't have a good idea of comparisons. I was trying to learn to stand and walk, I didn't care if it was 10 inches or 10 feet. It was all too difficult to me! It wasn't until I was told that my T.E.D. socks came off permanently after I passed the 300-foot mark that I actually had a goal. I hated the T.E.D. socks and would have done anything to get rid of them. I walked 300 feet that week and made the doctor keep her word, NO MORE TED SOCKS! Now had they told me that sooner, they probably would have gotten results sooner. The one thing I have learned is people are motivated by one of two things:

1. To get something they want (toward)
2. To avoid something they don't want (away)

Everyone is motivated, inspired, or encouraged by someone or something, the key is to find that and use it to benefit yourself or others. I have found that I am a very aggressive person and typically work toward a goal. I saw the 300-foot mark as a goal and the reward was being able to be sock free. Once it was laid out and I saw it, it was only a matter of days before I met it.

A short while later a dear friend shared with me that she was having a birthday party on December 19th and I was welcome to attend. Well, I saw it as the motivation and challenge that I needed to get home before Christmas. That became my target date, actually the 14,th which was the Friday before the 19th so I could have the weekend with my family to begin the adjustment process. I think the doctor thought I was crazy but she went along with it while watching my progress. I had a goal that I set before me and understood that certain things had to be done to meet that goal. No one said it would be easy but I knew that if I didn't ask myself to meet it I would be content not to. In other words if you don't ask the question the answer is no, so why not dare to ask? It's amazing the things you can do if your expectation is to succeed!

4

Living in Shadows

I did it! I was actually heading home on December 14th after surviving a near fatal brainstem bleed and subsequent stroke on November 12th. A month in the hospital seemed like an eternity and yet I know to my husband and my doctor a lot of questions still remained. How would I handle being at home, what more on my right side would I regain, how would I cope with outpatient therapy? These were just a few of the questions that remained unanswered and there would be many more in the days and weeks to come. My trip home from the hospital would mark a milestone in my life, a chance to start anew, or so I thought. The question that kept haunting me was: 'What kind of life would I return to?'

The morning was spent packing bags and stripping the hospital room that had become my home from any and all memory of my stay. Cards and mementoes were taken down from the bulletin board on the wall and shelves were cleared of trinkets. Everything was placed into plastic sacks waiting for Steve's arrival and their place in the suitcase he would bring. Breakfast time came and I was pushed to the table in the wheelchair to have my last meal in the hospital. Excitement mingled with trepidation overwhelmed me as I received countless wishes of a continued speedy recovery from patients and nurses alike. Reality was creeping into my mind as each person smiled and offered their best wishes. When I had finished breakfast I was wheeled back to my room to continue the check out process and await Steve's arrival.

It seemed like an eternity before he came but the nurses kept coming in with forms to go over and sign. The time would soon come for the job of packing things up for the long drive home. It was during this wait that I discovered that many of the doses of my medication had been increased for my return home. Suspicious, I refused the medications. I was convinced that several of the drugs where not necessary and at least one was responsible for my continued dehydration and vocal problems. I reassured the nurse that I would be seeing my personal physician in a matter of hours and knew that as my doctor she would talk with me and recommend only the medications that she felt were necessary. The nurse complied and we continued with the lengthy out-processing procedure.

Steve finally came and he finished packing everything up and prepared for my long awaited departure. The nurses came to my room and said their final goodbyes as I was wheeled toward the elevator. It was hard to believe that I was finally going home but I couldn't justify staying any longer. I would have the double vision for at least another 6 months and it was the vision that was impairing my walking, or at least that's how I felt. I took my final ride down to the first floor; we exited and for the first time I got a good glance at the freedom that awaited me outside the doors. I sat and waited while the valet brought the truck up and Steve loaded my suitcase and flowers into the back seat. While he was loading I gave the nurse one last hug goodbye and thanked her again for all she had done. Now was the moment of truth, they pulled the wheelchair up to the side of the truck and flung the door open. As Steve edged me closer I grabbed for the handle inside the door with my left hand and began to pull myself up, boy did I feel shaky. It took a bit of maneuvering to get into the high seat but with a lot of help I did it, I couldn't help but think how much better it was using the truck than trying to lower myself into the car. Steve buckled my seatbelt and we were headed home.

The trip seemed simple enough, after all in was only a short 60-minute drive home and one I taken thousands of times. Sure that was pre-stroke and before the world was turned upside down but I could handle it. We hadn't even made it out of the parking lot before I knew the ride was going to be more than a challenge. With each turn of the car my head went spinning. I finally asked Steve to try and turn more slowly but it was no use. I closed my eyes for the entire ride home content in the knowledge that we were headed in the right direction. I opened my eyes only once for a peek on the highway but closed them again quickly when I detected fence posts seemingly flying by. I know we weren't going very fast but my brain could no longer adjust for the speed. I gained a new appreciation for how my forefathers must have felt as they traveled in covered wagons, nice and slow! Speed, it seemed, was my enemy and there was no room for building a friendship with it today.

I was happy when the truck finally stopped and Steve announced that we were home. I opened my eyes to take in the wonderful sight, home at last. I looked intently at the front door as it opened, I knew the kids were in school and had forgotten that Steve's mother had come all the way from Oregon to help him. I hadn't realized before this moment but we had 6 steps leading to the landing in front of the main door and today it looked like Mt. Everest! After an hour on the road and with no feeling in my bladder I felt it was a safe place to start. Steve wrangled the walker out of the truck and positioned it at the top of the stairs and with his help I managed to climb the stairs and head straight for the bathroom.

After conquering the bathroom Steve guided me to one of our recliners and I sat down. Boy was it low, I felt myself being enveloped by the chair as I sat back. Come to think of it I think collapsed is probably a better word, I was amazed at how low to the ground the chair was and how exhausting the trip was. I knew that it would take a lot of hands to get me out of the chair but I was content to say there for the time being. No sooner had I sat down then my lap was filled with wriggling creatures of the four-legged variety. Motley, our beagle and Pepper our minpin jumped up to greet me. Their excitement was duly noted when just then Scoudrel (who is not small) tried to climb up in my lap too. With a little coaxing I was able to encourage her to accept sitting next to the chair and not in it. They all seemed happy to greet me and although this was a pleasant welcoming was really looking forward to seeing the kids later in the day.

I had a few hours before we would head to town to meet my physician and so we sat and talked as I enjoyed the aura of home. I just sat back taking in the sights, smells and sounds. The Christmas tree was up (it was Friday, December 14th) and a few presents were under the tree. The children had made it clear to me that they expected me to shop for their presents and it was obvious that they were serious about their expectations.

Time seemed to fly by and before I knew it, it was time to head to town. We left early enough to stop by the medical rental store for a wheelchair. After our stop we headed to the doctors office. Steve pulled up to the door and came around the back of the truck getting the wheelchair out as he passed. He opened my door and I was greeted with a blast of cold air as I grabbed for the handle above the door. Holding the handle in my good left hand I swung toward the chair, as he turned me around and I quickly sat down. Steve pulled the chair with me in it to the doorway and then ran back to park the truck.

After he finished parking the truck we made our way to the waiting room and checked in. This would be the first time I had seen my doctor in months and the very first time she had laid eyes on me after the stroke. It was an odd feeling as we waited patiently. When my name was called Steve wheeled me to the door where the nurse greeted us. She remarked how good I looked and with that remark she led us down the hall to an awaiting exam room. When Doctor G arrived I definitely noticed the surprise on her face.

"How are you?" She began.

"A bit worse for wear," I remarked, "but I'm alive and that's all that counts."

"You look good" she continued.

"I've looked worse." I laughed.

We continued as I briefed her concerning my recent hospitalization and near death experience. I gave her a copy of the medical summaries that I had hand carried from the hospital and she quickly read over the most recent files. I explained the medications that I had been taking and the problems I was experiencing as a result. She quickly saw the problem and told me the medications she wanted to start me with. I assured her that I would have the prescription filled immediately on our way to visit the rehab center. The plan was to continue extensive rehab everyday and evaluate it after the holidays. We parted after setting up a follow up appointment for three weeks.

Steve had made an appointment at the Rehab Center for an initial evaluation and introduction of the rehab staff. We dropped off the prescriptions on our way and arrived early. He wheeled me into the waiting area where I soon became aware of each and every person there and their apparent disabilities, scanning them I found myself comparing them to my disabilities. I guess comparing is something you do without really thinking about it. Can they walk? Is their arm impaired? Are they there for something or merely waiting for someone. It's really very superficial because you can only see devices that they carry with them. I had no idea what they were thinking or for that matter what was really going on in their lives. Several minutes passed before we were taken back to the speech therapists office. Her name was Alyson and I was impressed with her disarming smile from the moment we met. She seemed to have a genuine kindness that filled her and she was pleasant and accommodating, trait's that earned her 5 stars in my book. After speaking with her I met the physical therapy and occupational therapy staff, it seemed there were too many faces and names to remember. I just know that they all seemed kind and concerned with how they were going to help me.

As we passed the front desk I was introduced to Peggy and I made a point to remember her name. She was the receptionist that scheduled the appointments and I was confident I would see her often and didn't want to risk offending her. She sat behind a large tall counter and only the top of her head was visible from my wheelchair vantage point. She was kind enough to stand and introduce herself and I knew from that instant we would hit it off. We finished up by scheduling appointments for the next week. It was the end of the year so I had benefits to use or loose. I was set to see speech therapy, physical therapy, and occupational therapy almost everyday. In a twisted sort of way I was actually looking forward to it, after all it was a great way to pass the time.

Once we had scheduled the rehab appointments and stopped to pick up my meds we headed home. We got were there just in time to see the kids as they piled off of the bus. They knew I was supposed to be home and they bolted for the door the moment their feet hit the ground. I had already prepared myself for the onslaught and taken my preferred seat in the recliner as I awaited their exuberant welcome.

It was so good to see them at home. Between their hugs and the dog's clamor for attention, all seemed right with the world. We spent the rest of the night chatting as each of the kids took turns filling my water glass. As time clicked by the reality of the day's affairs started to seep in along with drowsiness that accompanies such a busy day. I was helped out of the chair by Roy and Bundit and into the wheelchair to head to bed. Steve wheeled me back and my quiet joy began to change to concern as we made it to the bedroom. Greeting the family was one thing sleeping at home was quite another. I had grown accustom to the fact that if I need help in the night it was there. Steve on the other hand was a sound sleeper and not exactly cheerful when you woke him up. I managed to get from the chair to the bathroom with the help of the new rails that Steve had installed. It was just one of many changes that we were going to have to make to accommodate the "new me"

I made it to the bed with help and lay down as Steve pulled the blankets up around me. I was freezing, he turned the gas fireplace on and according to him it got to be about 85 degrees in the room. All I know was I was finally comfortable and fell asleep around 9.

5

The Continuing Struggle

Rehab continued on a furious pace with 3 sessions a day and daily sessions until the New Year. My progress was slow but by January I put aside the wheelchair and attempted to use jut the walker. The pace at the rehab center had also slowed to three visits each week at which I visited speech, physical, and rehab therapy. I made progress at a very retarded rate until my double vision subsided about 7 months later.

I found myself a year later still suffering from lack of feeling on the right side and walking short distances with difficulty. My balance was shot and I still needed support when I walked any distance. My double vision had cleared up but I continued to have vision problems where everything in my "horizon" moved when I walked. The constant bouncing in my line of sight made life miserable. I was checked by doctors and given the "good news" that my vision in my right and left eye was perfect. On the outside this sounded good until they confirmed that the right and left eye did not work well together. No glasses or surgery could help and I could not expect change because the "problem" was a result of the stroke. This was devastating to hear and yet a reality I had to deal with. As a result I could not focus on faces when I walked and found myself simply looking at shapes and movement. This limited my time on a computer to about 30 minutes and I found myself listening to the TV instead of watching it.

The vision problems were just a few of the daily "disabilities" that I had to deal with. The absence of feeling made walking difficult and I could not grasp or hold things in my right hand. Out of site was literally out of mind when it came to my hand and I only had a limited grasp response. Each one of "disabilities" loomed over me and I tried my best to overcome them. The problem that most impacted my life was that of urinary incontinence. The lack of feeling affected my bladder and I never knew if it was full or empty. This caused me to limit my traveling greatly or make certain that I used a bathroom frequently or at least had one close at hand. There is nothing more embarrassing than having an accident in public. Hard as I tried, the accidents continued and my travels outside the home became limited and almost non-existent. When I did go out I made certain to limit all fluids before I left and definitely didn't drink while I was out.

Within 8 months my rehab time and money were exhausted and I was encouraged by my doctor and therapists to enjoy what I had fought to get back. With nowhere else to turn I decided that their words were probably true and I started accepting most of my disabilities and began to arrange my life around them. I was tired most of the time so I slept late, took naps, and went to bed early. I found that I had a hot and cold body where one side was hot and the other cold. It became a joke when friends could actually feel the difference in my hands. I would spend my time under blankets or in front of our fireplace trying to get warm.

I found that I limited the number of school events that I attended. Church was out because I would either fall asleep or panic with my bladder problem. I felt like a shut in, deep in my heart I knew there had to be an answer but I was frustrated with not being able to find it!

6

The Decision

I woke up early on a September morning feeling tired, nauseated, and decided to stay in bed and rest. This was a definite change of pace for me because by this time it had become second nature to get up and at least attempt to attack the day, starting with being there as the kids were preparing for school, watching them board the bus, and then seeing to the dogs in the kennels.

You see, shortly after my stroke, we began operating a small kennel business that took care of pets for people who were going away on trips and vacations. We had planned it prior to my stroke and decided that after I came home it was a good focus for the kids and me. Besides, it was a small business and we limited the number of animals we would take in. With my 2 sons and daughter to help, it kept me active and the dogs, which could sense my disabilities, were not any hurry when I worked with them. It allowed me to maintain contact with people and have a sense of doing and being involved. This morning I was happy that there were no dogs to care for other than our own. I was definitely under the weather and feeling ill was not something that I enjoyed.

Staying in bed for most people is a pleasure. Even when they don't feel well they enjoy cuddling up in a blanket and sleeping. For me the entire episode was torture, my muscles were tight and wanted to lock up, my stomach was doing flips and my double vision had returned along with constant dizziness. It hurt to keep my eyes open for any length of time and I found even keeping them closed brought little, if any, relief. The 15 steps it took to reach the toilet might as well have been a hundred; I careened into everything on the way and spent my time trying to steady myself on furniture and walls as I attempted the trek. I had learned over the past 2 years how to use the objects around me to my advantage and to steady my walk but today the distance seemed almost impossible. Everything around me appeared to be in constant motion and numbness on my right side didn't make locating objects possible with my eyes closed. Bed seemed to be the safest place for me to stay and, after all, this was just a little bug and I'd feel better in the morning, right?

Morning came and went without any change for the good and I ended up spending the next several days in bed. The upset stomach and dizziness settled down after 2 days but the muscles locking up and the vision problems continued. I found myself listening to the TV and audio books to pass the time. I didn't dare drive and focusing on anything too small became impossible. After several weeks the muscle problems began to lessen but the vision problems remained. I found myself suffering with double vision for another 6 weeks. I assumed that once I got rid of the initial double vision after the stroke, it was gone for good. I found out the hard way that illness affects me differently after the stroke.

It was at this time after suffering through what should have been a simple stomachache that I determined to find new answers. According to the leading eye doctors, the left eye was perfect and the right eye was perfect they just didn't play well together. Glasses or surgery would not correct it.

"Just be content with the problem" they would say "after all you can still see!"

Obviously I was not content. This was just one of a number of medical challenges that I was faced with as a result of the stroke. Daily I dealt with a lack of all feeling on the right side of my body, only gross motor movements in my right hand, balance difficulties, limits in the distance I could walk, and a mask like feeling that covered three quarters of my face. All of my doctors were thrilled with the recovery that I had made and they all felt I should be excited with what I was able to get back. I know I should have remained content but after that bout with a simple stomachache I was not excited about what I had become or what I could look forward to. The stroke made all my movements difficult and at most times painful. My activity level decreased and my weight increased. I tried dieting but was limited by exercises that I could not do. Nothing seemed to work. My cholesterol for the first time in my life was going up and my physician suggested medication to lower it. After years of fighting to be "the same old me" personal frustration was starting to set in. I spent a week in rehab to re-evaluate my hand after 2 years and the results were dismal. In spite of the fact that I did exercises every day the test put me back at ground 0, where it had been following the stroke.

I was tempted, if even for a moment, to let the stroke and the resulting medical problems get the best of me. It was then that I knew I had to take control of my future and make choices that would lead me in a new direction. I took time out to pray and evaluate where I was. I knew I hadn't survived and come this far without God having a purpose. After all He says in Isaiah that He has plans for me to give me a future and hope!

I had started extensive online research as soon as I came home from the hospital after suffering the stroke. The reality of the devastating effects were the motivation I used to learn more about what had happened to me and what I could expect.

I prayed, opened my mind, and looked into everything; magnets, nutritional supplements, different therapies. Each of them were on the table to be explored! I had begun acupuncture treatments after the first year with some small results. I felt like my balance was better and the total lack of feeling had been replaced with intermittent pain on the sole of my right foot. To me, pain was better that numbness; at least it seemed to offer a remote sense of hope. Because of the expense involved and the fact that insurance saw this as "alternative" I was forced to limit my visits. I felt as if the answers loomed out there just beyond my reach but I remained faithful to pray and actively look. I learned a long time ago that it is difficult, if not impossible to steer a parked car! It was critical that I keep seeking a solution, praying all the while that one would surface.

The kids were faithful to help me at night with range of motion exercises and it was during one of these times that I asked Yiwei, one of our Chinese exchange students, about Chinese treatments and acupuncture. I had remembered the year before asking JinWei, our other Chinese student who was now at college, about acupuncture in China. Yiwei told me then that the Chinese medicines and acupuncture worked and had been used very effectively for thousands of years. I hadn't thought much about it after I chose to get acupuncture close to home, and it wasn't until this conversation with Yiwei that I began to think seriously about treatment in China. I asked her to begin doing an online search in Chinese regarding stroke treatment in China. At the same time I began looking intently into research being done on strokes and any types of studies that I might be considered for.

After weeks of searching and applying for dozens of studies I was accepted as a research candidate for a study that was being conducted in Alabama. Their research consisted of gloving the good hand and putting the affected hand through a series of tasks each day for a period of 3 weeks. In addition I would be required to use my affected hand for 90% of the things I did during that three-week period. I was thrilled I finally had been accepted into something.

A matter of days later I was asked by the American Heart Association to go to Washington DC as the survivor from Iowa during their stroke lobby day on capitol hill. I asked Yiwei if she wanted to go and see Washington DC and meet the senators and congressmen with me. She jumped at the chance and we spent 5 days touring the city before spending several days with the American Heart Association contingent.

Good things are supposed to come in threes and this was no exception, after returning from D.C. Yiwei found information online about a leading teaching hospital and university in China. I guess during the excitement of the trip to D.C. I had forgotten about her research. This was good news but I didn't know if the hospital in China would accept me as a patient. In fact, I hunted online to see if any other

American had sought treatment in China. The answer I came up with was a resounding no. As requested, I faxed copies of my medical history to the hospital in China in hopes that they would consider me as a prospective patient. I had the advantage of a Chinese contact, Yiwei's mother. She spoke to the leading physician at the hospital in Tianjin and relayed his information and questions to Yiwei in Chinese and who would in turn translate them for me in English. The number one question that the doctor forwarded to me was, 'what do you want me to do for you?' Wow! Was he asking for a list? If so I had one ready: restore feeling, balance, fine motor control, and if possible fix my eyes. The response that came back was surprising and intriguing. They would take me as a patient! They wouldn't promise anything because it had been almost three years since my stroke but they would examine and evaluate me to determine what they could do. Their warning to me was that I should plan to be in the hospital three months at a minimum. This hospital that she found was a leading hospital and university in traditional Chinese medicine, not just acupuncture.

Boy, now I had two choices on my plate, 3 weeks in Alabama or possibly 3 months in China. Now was the time to make the pros and cons list and make the tough call. At the outset it would cost as much to fly to China to find out if they could help as it would to spend three weeks in Alabama. After all I had no idea if they could help in China and if so how long it would take and how much it would cost. On the other hand if they could help the possibility existed that they would restore feeling, balance and fine motor control. That was a lot more than I could get with the study.

I had a long talk with my kids, if I went to China it meant being gone from home for a long time. They were going to have to be responsible for a lot around the house if I was gone for 3 months. They were now 17, 16, and 12 much older than the 14, 13, and 9 year old that were home when I had the stroke. I had a long talk with my husband because it meant borrowing money for the treatment and being a single parent for 3 months. When all was said and done I knew that if I didn't go to China I would always have regrets. I would be taking a big chance but I figured in the worse case they would tell me they couldn't help and I'd return and attempt the study in Alabama. Besides JinWei was returning to China this summer and I would have an opportunity to visit Changsha and see both her parents and Yiwei's parents. Even if they couldn't help with the stroke the trip would not be a waste, I would have a great opportunity to see family and a piece of China.

It was a go, the kids and Steve were behind me and everyone who found out was excited. I was especially eager to tell my stroke support group and members of the Iowa American Heart Association Advocacy Committee on which I serve. If indeed they have answers then hopefully I could bring those answers back and give other stroke survivors another option.

The next few weeks flew by, I had to get my passport renewed and apply for a visa. The passport came first; we expedited it and paid the extra for a fast turn around. The people in the courthouse and the post office took a personal interest and wished me the best. As soon as the new passport arrived I sent it along with a letter faxed from the hospital in China to the Chinese consulates office in Chicago. An agency acted as a go between for obtaining my visa. In the mean time my husband ordered my airline tickets and they showed up in the mail while we were waiting for the visa.

With a ticket in hand it was all starting to become more than a dream and reality was slowly seeping in.

It seemed like the days flew as I made my list of things to pack and tried to accomplish everything in the weeks before I was to leave. It seemed that everyone wanted to get together one last time before I left. There was so much to do in preparing the house, packing, getting medical records, packing, and medication for 3 months, and did I mention packing. One week before I was to leave I found out that the hospital offered dialup Internet but I had to bring my own computer. Well that sounded great but I didn't have a laptop computer to bring. Well, I learned a long time ago that if you don't ask - the answer is no, so why not ask? I've bought several computers from iTech in Cedar Falls, Iowa and decided to see if they would be interested in providing me with a computer. It would allow me to maintain contact with friends and family and provide a way to keep a record of my treatment.

At the same time I spoke with iTech I contacted our local newspaper and television station. Yup! Good things happen in threes; they did a story in the paper, the TV station planned a broadcast, and iTech gave me a computer! It was a busy last week before the flight, in addition to getting me ready to leave we put JinWei on a plane to China and I helped Yiwei move into an apartment and register for classes at the University of Iowa.

Steve took JinWei to meet her plane as I headed with Yiwei to Iowa City. We spent several days cleaning her apartment and buying all those little "on your own" things that are apartment "musts". JinWei called me on my cell phone from Washington enroute to China and assured me that she would have someone meet me in Beijing.

I got Yiwei settled and headed back home in time to finish packing and meet the news reporter from TV 7 KWWL that showed for an interview. Her name was Megan and after our first talk on the phone I knew she understood what a big venture this would be. She graciously spoke to and met the entire family and chatted with me at length about my stroke and upcoming plans to seek treatment in China. It was amazing to flip on the TV and see a report about the upcoming trip to China. Reality slapped me in the face when my passport and visa showed up with a day to spare before I was to board my flight. I guess there was no denying it now I was going to China!

7

Heading to China

Wednesday June 9, 2004

The day never ended or seemed to start but I spent the entire night awake, packing and rechecking my bags to make certain that everything that was supposed to be included was. Elizabeth curled up in a chair and David took over the couch in the front room. Roy was the smart one and slept in his bed. It seemed that by midnight everyone was fast asleep. Knowing that there is a big time difference I thought

I'd stay up and try to sleep on the plane. Steve crawled out of bed at around 4 a.m. and we started rousing the troops at 4:30. They sleepily they came to wish me goodbye and offer hugs and kisses and then posted themselves at the front door. It all seemed a bit surreal as I climbed into the car and waved goodbye. Steve and I used the hour long early morning trip to go over last minute plans and confer about travel strategies. He had arranged a wheelchair at each of the airports to expedite my transfer between flights and guarantee my arrival at each gate. The trip to the airport went all too fast and before I knew it I had said my goodbyes to Steve and was heading to security

I really didn't know what to expect so I made a point to show up early and give myself plenty of time to get through all the new security. It was obvious that I was nervous because I could feel my right side tighten up as I fumbled to put things on the x-ray machine. They were very patient with me and helped me with my jacket, shoes, and bags as I was escorted through the barrage of baracades. I walked down to my gate using the wall for support as I went. As I arrived at the gate I introduced myself to the woman behind the counter and explained my needs. She was extremely helpful and sat me in a chair opposite the door and informed me she would be back to get me to board first. About 30 minutes passed and she showed up and assisted me as I walked down the ramp to the plane. I took my seat and had a very uneventful flight to Chicago. I was met there with the wheelchair that was requested and wheeled on the long trek to my next gate to meet my flight to Denver, after watching how far we had traveled I was glad I was seated and someone else was pushing. I had quite a wait before I was wheeled backwards down the ramp to the plane. I boarded only to find my seat toward the back of the plane. Using the tops of the seats to help I proceeded to walk to my seat. I stopped several times to wait as people put things in overhead bins and while other people seemed lost checking their tickets and the seat numbers frequently. I finally made it to my seat and settled in. The trip to Denver was a familiar one and the flight as usual was full. I closed my eyes and attempted to rest knowing that I had a long day ahead of me. When I arrived in Denver I was escorted to the ramp where I sat and waited for a wheelchair, 5 minutes passed, then 10. They called again for a chair. Finally after waiting 30 minutes and watching the next set of passenger's board the plane I exited, the wheelchair arrived. I got in and we flew up the ramp and down several gates. The plane was already full and I was one of the last to board. I sat down in my seat which was situated in between a woman and what appeared to be a Buddhist monk dressed in an orange robe, he quietly smiled and nodded and I smiled back. The woman seated next to me on the aisle was kind enough to help me put my bag under the seat in front of me. We found ourselves striking up a friendly conversation and chatted during a good part of the flight.

It was quiet a long flight and I was able to doze a bit and spent the rest of my time flipping through the in flight magazine. Before I knew it we were descending into L.A. and I contacted the flight attendant to confirm that a wheelchair would be on standby for me. I didn't want to endure waiting and rushing for my international flight. I exited the plane and just as they promised a chair was waiting.

The attendant wheeled me through the terminal for what seemed like an eternity. We continued on until we came to the front doors and outside we went. She appeared to know the area far better than I so I was not about to question her.

As soon as we exited the terminal we crossed the street and entered the international terminal. As she pushed us to the front of the line I could hear the girl behind the counter addressing another individual in Chinese. As soon as she finished she looked down at me in the chair and asked. "Ticket and passport please."

I handed them both to the attendant who passed them to the agent. She typed something on her computer screen and then spoke to the attendant as she handed back the passport and ticket providing her with both the flight and gate information. With this in hand we headed off to another security section.

We pulled up and several security personnel were kind enough to help me pass through the security-screening machine and usher me to a chair so I could wait for the attendant and wheelchair. In a matter of minutes she reappeared and we headed toward the gate. As we approached I was reminded of something JinWei had said about culture shock and coming to America. When she boarded her flight to Des Moines, Iowa she was the only one on the flight who was Chinese. Now as I glanced around at all the Asian faces awaiting the flight, I understood her feelings. Here I was still in America and yet I felt like I was already in China. We waited for almost 30 minutes before boarding began. I was allowed to pre-board and with my seat being at the back of the plane I was thrilled with the extra time. I thanked my attendant and proceeded down the long aisle to my seat.

I was positioned 3/4 of the way back in the plan on the left outside aisle. I ended up seated next to a man who had immigrated from China long ago, he was retired and heading to China to meet his wife and travel. He was pleasant and a wonderful help to me on the flight opening all those fun things that come sealed in plastic. I was onboard an Air China flight so all the food served was Chinese and the movies were dubbed in Chinese as well. I tried to rest during most of the flight and was amazed to discover how nimble me seat companion was. Not once did he ask me to move he just leapt over me and into the aisle, I was impressed. I slept most of the flight and was thrilled when I looked at the overhead map that followed our progress and saw we were approaching Shanghai. My travel mate offered to fill out the customs card for me as soon as they were passed out. With the completed card and passport in hand I was ready to exit the plane. We landed and almost everyone around me flipped open and turned on a cell phone and placed a call. We sat at the gate for only a short while before the doors of the aircraft opened and people began heading out. I followed the mass of bodies as we slowly made our way up the ramp.

I was very happy for the slow pace it allowed my leg a chance to wake up after sitting for so long. The mass of people split just passed me and I heard an attendant say Shanghai and point to the left. I turned and followed her arm as I saw a number of people ahead of me doing the same thing. We zigzagged through the terminal and arrived at what appeared to be a security station. The people that staffed it were donned in white uniforms with a white surgical mask over their face. As each person approached their temperature was checked and they were allowed to continue on after presenting their customs form for inspection. A short way further was another more impressive area that had glass faced cubicles with uniformed people staffing them, this was the "entry" point. I presented my passport and visa and they were examined and stamped. I followed the now dwindling crowd as they turned a corner on the right and lined up by a desk situated in front of a door. Here, I gathered by watching, you present your ticket and are issued a boarding pass for the final leg to Beijing.

Just as I thought I was presented with my pass after displaying my ticket and then gingerly made my way down a number of stairs to the gate to await boarding. As I glanced back I saw my seatmate from the previous flight immediately behind me, he followed me down the stairs and found a row of empty seats and gestured to them. I was thrilled to have a native speaker nearby. The reality of my arrival in China did not seem to bother anyone else; I was obviously a foreigner in China. The language they spoke wasn't even close to my own and I listened intently to the intercom with the hope of understanding when my flight was called. As I glanced about everyone looked quite at ease, or so it felt. I sat patiently and waited some 40 minutes before our flight was called. Amazingly enough after the flight was called in Chinese it was called again in British English, WHEW! What a relief! I walked toward the gate and watched as a tram pulled up outside. The doors opened and there was a surge for the door as all the passengers jockeyed for position. I made my way forward as aggressively as I dared making certain that I did not fall in the process. As I boarded the tram a young woman gestured in my direction, offering me her seat. The stroke has made me quick to accept help when offered and a seat was a pleasant surprise. When the tram filled, the doors closed and we headed out on the tarmac to the waiting plane. It had been some time since I walked up stairs to a waiting plane, but that's exactly what I did. My seatmate was right behind me and patiently waited as I climbed the stairs. He ended up seated next to me on the flight to Beijing and I appreciated the ability to speak with him in English.

It was a short flight and as soon as the plane reached a cruising altitude it felt as if we began descending. This would be my ultimate test, I'd finally made it to my destination and hopefully the English speaker that JinWei had promised would be there to meet me. As the aircraft pulled into its gate there seemed to be a rush of people in a hurry to leave. I gingerly got up and made my way out and up the ramp. I was impressed as I took note of signs in both Chinese and English pointing the way toward the baggage area. I prayed fervently that my bag had arrived in one piece and that I could get it lifted off the carousel. As I looked ahead I saw it, if I kept up at my current pace I would reach it in time and now the question loomed before me: "could I lift it?" I reached down and braced my good left leg against the side as I pulled up with my left hand. "Got it!" I thought to myself as I swung it onto the floor beside me. Again with my left hand I sat it up and pulled the handle out until it locked in position and I could roll the bag. I looked around it was obvious that I was tired because the signs in the distance were blurry. It was after 11 p.m. as I headed toward what looked like customs and the exit and I was motioned to continue. I passed through a large opening and then became aware of people standing and waiting. I looked forward as I walked and observed a young woman looking at me. She smiled and as I got closer I noticed she was carrying a sign with my name on it. I approached her cautiously.

"Are you Ruth?" she asked.

"Yes I am" I replied.

"Huang JinWei's father asked us to meet you." She continued, "one minute." With that she quickly dial a cell phone and spoke some Chinese. I turned in time to see her outstretched hand holding the phone towards me.

"It's JinWei for you." She said smiling.

I placed my bags down and brought the phone to my ear. "JinWei?" I said cautiously.

"Hi Mom!" She uttered, "Did you arrive okay?"

"Yes, fine" I replied, "boy, you don't know how good it is to hear your voice."

"They will take you to a motel tonight and back to a plane tomorrow that will bring you here, I'm in Changsha." She continued, "Do you have any questions? If not I'll see you tomorrow okay?"

"Okay" I replied, "I'll see you tomorrow."

With that I gave back the phone and there was another smattering of Chinese before we headed toward the car. It was now that I noticed we were not alone and I was introduced to Mr. Z, his wife, and daughter. He was our driver and they all came to meet me. It was getting very late so we dropped Mr. Z's wife and daughter and then proceeded to a restaurant to get a bite to eat. This was my first introduction to Chinese night-life and real Chinese food. We went to a place inside of the lower level of a shopping mall and passed a lively dance spot. The old me would have loved to take it in but I was content to have a quick bite to eat before they checked me into my motel for the night.

The food was great and having an English-speaking escort was wonderful. After we ate I was taken to a 5 star hotel and checked in. They both graciously saw me to my room and said their good-bye. I was exhausted, the entire day was whirling in my head and the last thought I remember having before closing my eyes for the night was… I'm not in Iowa anymore!

8

A Visit to Changsha

Thursday June 10ᵗʰ 2004

Yesterday was a whirlwind of activity that ended when I collapsed on my bed. Today would be a day I could actually remember. I was picked up by 9:00 by Mr. Z who paid the hotel bill and escorted me to the car for the trip to the Beijing airport. He was listening to Chinese music when I got in the car but I noticed he changed it to American music shortly thereafter. The trip to the airport was uneventful if you consider Chinese traffic uneventful. He drove and I sat. I could tell he spoke little if any English. For those who have not traveled to Beijing, China it is a very busy and growing city. Traffic was the first noticeable difference. Not that they didn't have it, No... they do! But driving in it appears to require a course in offensive and defensive driving skills. They bob and weave with the very best and can get a car into spaces that I thought only a bike would fit in. And speaking of bikes... they are everywhere. You see them on every road along with hand drawn carts and pedestrians. I think the people who travel this way must have a death wish but they act as if they rule the road and I must confess I think they do. The drivers take care in avoiding them and what appears at first to be chaos takes on a carefully balanced flow.

All I can say is if they are a fraction as good at restoring balance to the body through acupuncture as they are at maintaining traffic flow, I should bounce back quite nicely.

We arrived at the airport in good fashion and Mr. Z quickly retrieved my luggage from the trunk. We proceeded to the terminal and that's when I was impressed with how busy it was. As I listened to the intercom flights were announced in Chinese. I was not in Kansas anymore or any place else in the U.S. I continued to listen and heard a distinct English voice calling out the flights as well. I was impressed! Here in the land of the rising sun they were courteous enough to add English. All of the people behind the counters were kind and patient and spoke English remarkably well. We quickly proceeded through the airport tax station to the ticketing area. My bag was checked and found to be slightly over weight so Mr. Z quickly took the papers and ran off to pay the fee while I waited in line. Once he returned I was issued my boarding pass and off we went to the security area. Mr. Z waited as my tickets were checked and we parted with a smile, a handshake, and the mutually understood word: "bye".

My passage through security was uneventful and then off I was to the gates. Fortunately for me it wasn't far. I had decided early on to attempt this part of the trip without the use of a wheel chair. I made my way to the gate using moving walks when available and hadn't even gotten a chance to sit down when I noticed a line forming in front of my gate. Sure enough, the intercom came to life and my flight was called to board. As I rambled down the ramp I couldn't help but notice I was a very apparent minority. It again brought to mind the "culture shock" that JinWei spoke of when she came to the US. At least here the people who worked in the airline industry spoke my language!

I hobbled back to my seat and spent the rest of the time (2 hours in all) reflecting on how far I had come and how relatively easy the trip had been. The inner concerns that I had, focused mainly on my inability to speak Chinese. I had found that a smile and the greeting "ni hao" went a long way and I was faithful to utter "xie xie" whenever I meant thank you.

I was the last to leave the plane and was very thankful for the words "ARRIVAL" that appeared on the Chinese signs leading to the baggage area. It was a long and tedious walk that ended with a ride down an escalator. I was so happy to see arms waving behind the glass partition and upon closer inspection it was indeed JinWei and her family. I ushered a smile and a quick wave while I headed towards the baggage claim area. I arrived just in time to see my bag as it headed back into the unloading area and out of sight. A matter of minutes later I saw it emerge on the conveyor in front of me. No sooner had it appeared than I noticed JinWei beside me with a cart and a baggage handler who reached out and retrieved the bag. She gave me a quick hug and we headed to the cars as she made introductions on the way. Everyone was there to greet me, and when I say everyone I mean both JinWei and Yiwei's parents were there. After quick introductions I was placed into the car that JinWei was riding in. It made sense because she was the only one that spoke English. I was fascinated by the way she effortlessly transitioned between speaking English to me and Chinese to her father it was really quite impressive. It was remarkably different seeing her in familiar surroundings in China. She was definitely not the timid young girl who got off the plane 2 years ago in Iowa. Now as I watched a beautiful, self-assured, young woman had emerged that was taking command of this potentially awkward situation. I got a warm feeling deep inside as I realized that none of this could have taken place two years earlier. God, I thought to myself, is so good! He knew what had to be prepared before I made the trip to China.

We continued to the hotel where they checked me in and then JinWei and her mom together with Yiwei's mom piled back in the car to take me to a supermarket. We arrived and I was given the job of pushing the cart as we went up and down the aisles looking for food I recognized. The cart was very different from the ones I was familiar with, the wheels were attached so it rolled in every direction. And unlike the carts I was used to getting this one rolled freely. We had the most fun as we looked over the fruits and vegetables. Many things were easy to recognize but many things were different. We purchased several items and headed back to the hotel.

After unloading our haul I pulled out my laptop and began showing the digital pictures that we had taken of the girls over the past two years. We all had fun as we looked intently at how they had changed since their arrival in the states. Time seemed to pass too quickly and before I realized it, it was time for dinner. JinWei, her mom, and Yiwei's mom climbed into the backseat of the car with Yiwei's dad driving and I was placed in the front seat to allow ample space for my legs. We headed to a restaurant where we were quickly escorted to a room upstairs. The meal was ordered and the food was placed on a turntable in the center. Dish after dish came and I lost track of names as JinWei proceeded to place food on the plate before me. It was all so good and I ate until I could eat no more! We sat and chatted as JinWei faithfully translated and did her best to juggle the many questions that came my way. Most of the questions dealt with my initial perception of China and then we started talking about Yiwei and JinWei. I asked JinWei several times if she was telling me all that they were asking. "Sure Mom!" She would say with a smile. We finished the meal and I could feel the time change catching up with me. They graciously escorted me back to my motel room where JinWei assured me she would call for me early the next morning.

The bed was comfortable and I really don't remember even hitting the pillow, I was that tired.

Friday June 11, 2004

Morning came early and I felt as if I was beginning to shift time zones and felt much better today. Pushing myself yesterday really helped. The phone rang last night at 11 and the person on the other end said, "wei, wei ni hao ma " Obviously I was not who the wanted to talk to! Note to self: priority Chinese words to learn for today… wrong number!

At about 6:30 a.m. my time the phone rang and it was Steve and the kids! They were a joy to hear from. It took some time for the kids to collect their thoughts but they did okay. Steve said he was going to give Carolyn a call and Invite her for a meal so she can talk too! Pleasantries were exchanged along with the day's plan of events and a time was set up to talk tomorrow. I decided that we will try visit daily on the phone while I'm in Changsha and before I have Internet access. JinWei was due at 8:00 for breakfast we will see how good she is at waking up! I found that I need to get a small alarm clock; it is one of the few things I've forgotten. I also need to exchange money today so I have Chinese Yuan instead of dollars.

JinWei came about 8:45, which is good for a college student on vacation. After her arrival we went downstairs for breakfast and were ushered into the restaurant by two beautiful young girls who quickly seated us and poured tea. We hadn't been but a minute and JinWei's phone rang, it was Yiwei's mother and she informed us that if we wanted to have an English speaking tour of a local museum we had better hurry and be at the museum by 9:15. We quickly ate and met Yiwei's mother downstairs with her driver. I must confess that I enjoyed the fact that someone else dealt with the interesting aspects of commuting. We drove to the museum and were allowed access to drive, not walk, up the steep hill and to the entrance. Most people walk up the many stairs and through the beautiful greenery.

A short time later were led inside where we were greeted by a very well dressed young lady who began with a polite "Hello". She introduced herself and the museum and I was immediately intrigued by a secondary conversation that ensued what ended with JinWei asking me in English if I would prefer using a wheelchair. I have learned through past experiences that most displays are just taller than the wheelchair and it is difficult to see. I assured them that as we walked I would sit down as necessary and call for the chair if I needed it. We began our tour with little fanfare as I listened intently to our newfound friend and guide. She carefully explained each of the display cases and I was fascinated with the three tombs and how they were originally discovered. I continued in wonderment with the story and marveled at the detailed and well-preserved objects that had been unearthed. In all my travels around the world I had not seen such treasures as these. Little did I know what lay in store at the end of the exhibit? We rode up in the elevator only to be greeted by a much cooler environment. Upon turning a corner she led us by enclosed chilled cases top a great display in the center of the room. Looking down through glass at an object some 6 feet below lay a corpse of an older woman that was partially covered with her head, shoulders, arms, legs and feet exposed. She was completely undamaged, and unlike mummies she was discovered sealed in a liquid bath and her skin was found to be soft and supple and her organs were intact. We were then led to the tomb that was built to encase the body. It was as large as a house and built from the wood of fir trees. There were several compartments surrounding the one that held the coffin, or should I say coffins. There were a total of 4, each fit inside the other and all but the last one were intricately decorated. The last and final coffin was black lacquer without any designs. This ended my tour, but I was in awe of what else this historic and ancient land held for those who looked.

The day continued with a stop for lunch and I must say there are no shortages of places to eat. The food was exotic, spicy and abundant. Girls pushed carts by us that were filled with different dishes, you need simply to pick them and they were placed on your table. It definitely gave new meaning to fast food and forget buffets, here the food comes to you hot and delicious. Today I mastered the words "hen hao" (very good). It seemed a bit redundant uttering the same thing after trying each dish but they were all truly very good and I would be hard pressed to pick a favorite. I found out during the meal that all of these dishes were Yiwei's favorites so I asked her mom to make certain to mention what we ate the next time she spoke with her. It was then that I realized that my children would have starved because nothing on the menu resembled anything close to a burger and fries!

Lunch ended and we headed back to the hotel so I could take a rest before continuing the day. Although I do not customarily take naps it was a welcome respite. JinWei accompanied me to my room and while I rested she attempted to keep up with friends who were sending her text messages on her cell phone. I listened with my smile tucked carefully under the covers as she worked to get one message out for every two that came in. I would have had a hard time just seeing the keys on the phone, let alone type a message – and in pin yin (Chinese)!

I rested for an hour before JinWei's mom was at the door. She entered and we spent the next hour or so looking at pictures and talking. We then went downstairs and met JinWei's father. After hopping in his car we headed off to retrieve her grandfather. We drove only a few minutes before we entered a secured housing area. There he met us and off we headed for dinner. I answered questions through JinWei and it seemed like only minutes passed when we pulled up to a huge complex of buildings. They were magnificent to look at, a high wall encircled them and they were old in style and decorated ornately with dragons and symbols.

JinWei informed me that this restaurant was not here when she left and had been opened only in the last year. It was enormous and looked like it could seat thousands in separate rooms. We were lead to one on the second floor and seated again at a large round table with a turntable in the middle. This was becoming second nature to me as I sipped my tea and waited as the food began to arrive. Changsha is in the Hunan province of China and noted for its spicy food. There was no lack of it tonight. JinWei got her favorite dish, spicy snake along with a spicy fish. There were 4 different kinds of vegetable dishes, noodles, two soups, several more platters of meat, tofu, and fruits. Tonight was JinWei's families turn and the questions were too many to count. We talked and ate until late into the night and then we headed out toward the hotel. We took the scenic route as they showed me a bit of the lights of Changsha. It's a bustling city of over 5.7 million people, small by Chinese standards but huge considering there are only about 2.9 million people in the entire state of Iowa.

We dropped JinWei's grandfather off and then JinWei got out with me at the hotel. It was within walking distance to her home so she saw me to my room. We chatted briefly, it was fun to see her in her "native" environment and it was obvious she was enjoying being back in China. She helped me get ready for bed and as I walked her to the door of my room she reached out and gave me a hug. This was definitely a learned behavior that she picked up from our family. I smiled, hugged her back and said I would look forward to seeing her in the morning.

Saturday June 12, 2004

The morning began with the customary visit to the bathroom, cold water applied to the face and the early a.m. shuffle for the obligatory 15 minutes. I started plunking on the computer while still in my pajamas. It seems that typing one handed has slowed me down a bit and I have found that if I don't get the previous days events entered, they tend to get a bit foggy. Memory or lapses in it are one of the joys left from the stroke. I tell people that I have an outstanding memory but my recall stinks!

Steve and the kids called at 7:30 my time and we were able to chat about the previous days events. Carolyn came over for supper so she too got a chance to chat. I am blessed to be able to have friends that care for both my kids and me. Carolyn shared that she and my daughter went shopping and were forced to visit several garage sales that bit their bumper as they passed by! I updated Steve regarding the day's upcoming events and shared with him that tomorrow would be the last day we could talk for a while because I will be in transit to Tianjin via train after 5 p.m. We finished our conversation in time for me to relax and catch CNN Headline News before JinWei Arrived.

JinWei showed up at 9:00 and the trek to Shao Shan began. It was close to an hours ride in the car and before I knew it we pulled over to the side of the road and were greeted by two cars with friends, family and water bottles. We proceeded to a hotel close to our destination and were able to take a brief bathroom break prior to heading to the museum of Chairman Mao. We climbed back into the cars and

headed just a few more minutes down the road. The parking area was packed as cars, buses, and people were all descending on the museum and a huge statue in a garden area off to one side.

Families and travel groups all wanting a picture posed beneath the great man's likeness surrounded the statue of Mao Ze Dong. This was like visiting the Lincoln memorial in the United States. It appeared it would be some time before we could approach so we opted to take a family photo seated on a garden wall prior to reaching the statue. From here we proceeded to the museum that displayed his life's work and climb from humble beginnings to a position of power. JinWei's cousin Lao Hung spoke English and between the two of them they translated much of the museums content. It was obvious that I was the only foreigner there at that time but everyone bent over backwards to see to it that I had a memorable experience. We got back in the cars after the museum stop and headed the short drive down the road to his birthplace. After a brief walk up a small hill and down a paved walk we arrived at a small house. Here I was ushered to a chair to rest, everyone was concerned with my health and took pains to provide me with periods of respite. It was here that I became aware that the town minister or mayor, as we would call him, was accompanying us.

JinWei and her cousin had fun taking a few photos and after a brief rest I followed them inside the small structure. It was a very plain and simple house with dirt floors. We meandered through the 6 small rooms taking note of the meager furnishings and surroundings. We finished our tour and headed back to the hotel for lunch. Upon our arrival we were led to a large room with a huge circular table in the middle. I was seated and JinWei took the seat to my left

and Lao Hung the seat to my right. Next to JinWei; her uncle, the Minister, her father, and then the driver. Next to Lao Hung; JinWei's mother followed by his mother, JinWei's aunt. In the center of the table sat the now familiar large glass turntable that was filled and rotated with all the delicious dishes. The meal started with a toast in my honor. The Minister then came to my seat and provided me with a second toast, which I have learned is customary.

Lunch was exceptional, all the food was superb and the company surrounding it was equally pleasurable. Although we shared a language barrier, JinWei and Leo Hung were gracious enough to translate for all and we were able to share in humorous stories. I have learned that family in China is treasured and honored and because of my relationship with JinWei I am considered part of the family. I felt that there was a tremendous amount that we could learn from their example.

After the meal they were all anxious that I feel rested to begin the trip back to Changsha. I assured them I felt fine and we began the long drive back. I was amazed at the beauty of the countryside as we drove. It was lush and fertile and although it provided subsistence to the farmers in this region, I was impressed with the simplicity of their small farms. Having come from a farming state I could see their farms and fields obviously lacked the size and commercialism that surrounds the Midwest farming community today. I must say, however, having tasted of the fruits of their labors I was indeed grateful for their plentiful and delicious produce.

Upon arriving back at my hotel I took a customary rest while JinWei and her cousin took a walk around Changsha. I guess I should know better, when I have no interaction with others I fall fast asleep! I awoke to the phone ringing with JinWei on the other end asking if I was ready for supper, she had tried knocking at the door an I didn't reply. Oh well, it felt as if all I did was eat and sleep! We were greeted by JinWei's mother in the dining room on the second floor of the hotel. We found our way to a table and JinWei and her mother examined the menu carefully and ordered for the table. By this time I had become fairly good with using chopsticks and my left hand. They were always faithful to ask for a fork but I found that Chinese food is made for and best eaten with chopsticks. As the food came I noticed that my plate was never empty, JinWei and her mother faithfully filled it with samplings from each dish if they saw it getting low.

Halfway through the meal we were joined by Yiwei's mother and her cousin, Rosalie. Rosalie is majoring in English at University and agreed to join us on the train trip to Beijing and drive to Tianjin. Introductions were made and it was an honor having Rosalie consider taking time away from classes to act as an interpreter. I have been so amazed at the outpouring and graciousness that has been shown to me by JinWei and Yiwei's parents. They have spared nothing to make my trip both easy and pleasurable. I am again reminded that without their help this trip and subsequent treatments could not be possible. I am indeed forever grateful for their help and this opportunity.

Night came much too quickly, they all accompanied me back to my room where JinWei asked for my laundry so they could wash it and return it prior to my departure on the train tomorrow afternoon. It would have been much easier to put me back on a plane to Beijing and let the hospital collect me at the airport but I was family and they were determined to see me to my destination and oversee my arrival at the hospital personally.

Sunday, June 13, 2004

Morning came as I peered out from the covers at focused on my watch with one eye, only to discover it was already 6:30. The curtains in my room acted as a very good filter, keeping out all light. I was quick to get up, dress, and repack my suitcase for the train trip that was to begin around 4:00 p.m. JinWei was supposed to arrive at 9:30 this morning for the final days events in Changsha. She didn't arrive until 10:00, and I could tell she was a bit flustered that her friend was not there. She had been trying for the past 45 minutes to reach him on his cell phone but couldn't. Undaunted, she and I went on with the driver to the mountain close by to see Changsha in all its glory below. It was a relatively short trip and before I knew it we were at the base of the mountain. As we began our ascent in the car and saw people walking to the top I became extremely thankful to be riding, I would have never attempted it of foot in my present state. JinWei was upset and apologized that it was so foggy (like she could control the weather?), but I enjoyed what view I had and took pictures of the city below. We stopped for tea at the top and JinWei was finally able to contact her friend who said he would meet us for lunch. After a relaxing visit at the top we climbed back in the car and began the slow descent to the bottom with JinWei apologizing for the fog again as we made are way down.

We arrived for lunch at a Chinese / Western restaurant where JinWei was anxious to get my opinion of their idea of western food. We were escorted to a small room with sofas on either side of the rectangular table in the middle. Small TV's could be found in two of the corners and a computer was available for those who wanted to surf the Internet. I've since learned that Internet cafes are very popular and the private rooms (which were common in China) were a nice way to keep the conversations very personal. JinWei's friend arrived and we were introduced. She challenged me to speak as much English with him as possible because he had an English exam coming up. We had a nice quiet lunch as I gently tried to keep him focused on speaking English. He kept looking at JinWei and asking her questions in Chinese; she would get flustered and say, "Just ask her yourself in English". The entire event was rather humorous, I don't think JinWei realizes how much she has learned after spending 2 years in the U.S.

I ordered steak at JinWei's insistence to compare it with "real" western cooking. It was very good but very different, I found the cut of the meat very thin compared to an Iowa cut. It was served with plain macaroni and sauces that varied from mushroom (which I had) to a spicy selection (JinWei's choice). We finished the meal and headed back to the hotel to wait for Yiwei's mom and my immanent departure for the train.

After arriving at the hotel both JinWei and her friend seemed bored so I pulled out the computer with the digital pictures I had brought. Digital photography certainly has made life much easier, but now I'm afraid it got me in trouble. JinWei was vehemently opposed to any the idea of showing pictures of her. However, she soon gave in and we had a good time examining the photos from the last two years she had been in the U.S. The final hour was spent quizzing her friend in English and learning things about him.

Teenage energy gave way to sitting quietly and chatting so at 3:30 they both headed off to JinWei's house to retrieve my laundry. No sooner had they gone than Yiwei's mom and her niece, Rosalie appeared at my door. If I hadn't known any better I would have thought that they carefully choreographed the changing of the guard (I mean translator), but nothing could be further from the truth. Rosalie and I chatted and I thanked her again for coming along as a translator. JinWei returned after a short while with my clean laundry and I quickly packed it and made certain the bags were ready for the continuing journey. We shared small talk until it was time to leave and then JinWei gave me a brief hug goodbye and reassured me she would come visit me in the hospital in July. Wow! This was the first goodbye since Steve saw me off at the airport and it stung! I guess the reality and enormity of what had undertaken was beginning to hit.

After saying goodbye; Yiwei's parents, Rosalie, and I piled into the van and headed off to the train station. It was only a short 10-minute jaunt and we were able to pull directly onto the platform. It was only a matter of steps to the train and then Rosalie and I proceeded down the narrow hall. She glanced periodically at the tickets and then at the doors to find our cabin. At last we arrived and sat opposite each other in what was, I feel, a beautiful cabin. There were two lower sleeping benches that were to be used as seating during the day and two upper bunks for additional sleeping space at night. As I sat looking about the cabin Yiwei's father and a friend who accompanied him, hoisted my bag to the storage compartment above the top bunks. Each bunk appeared to come complete with a small reading light, and a separate TV screen with controls and headphones. Yiwei's mom, Rosalie and I sat in the cabin while Yiwei's father and his friend sat outside the cabin on two pull down chairs.

Rosalie acted as interpreter as Yiwei's mother asked question after question about Yiwei and her stay in the states. I answered them all to the best of my ability and then reached for the computer to share digital photos that we had taken over the past year. The pictures were a big hit and before I realized it, it was time to eat in the dining car.

We made our way forward as the train swayed and clicked along the track. The last time I remember riding on a train I was in Germany years before. The stroke had obviously taken its toll on my balance but with Rosalie's help I made it to the dining car. Yiwei's dad ordered the food, which showed up almost immediately. Rosalie served me and I was faithful to use my chopsticks, which seemed to amaze and humor everyone at the table. When the meal was finished we made the return trip back down the narrow corridor to our cabin. As we reentered the cabin Yiwei's mom (Wan yan ni) had a pair of slippers for everyone. I have learned that they wear slippers everywhere when they take off their shoes. A really good habit except my right foot can't seem to keep a slipper on. With foot attire in place we continued our conversation about Yiwei and my stroke. I was impressed by Rosalie's command of the English language and we spoke at length about her hopes for the future.

As night approached the lights outside grew in regularity and flew by as we clipped along. My eyes started to get heavy and Rosalie said she felt a bit ill so we all decided to call it a night and split up the bunks. Yiwei's parents took the top bunks leaving Rosalie and I to settle in to the bottom bunks. Everyone took turns heading to the bathroom down the corridor and one by one we were finally all tucked in for the night.

9

A Ray of Hope

Monday June 14, 2004

It was early in the morning (5 a.m.) and all around me were still sleeping. I made my way to the bathroom at about

4:00, and tried to do so quietly without rousing anyone. It had been some time since I last traveled overnight by rail, but it was a fun and pleasurable experience. As I peered out the window the sun was rising and we seemed to be in a more populated area. There were houses and buildings but we were far from the city. A small highway paralleled our train and the vehicles on it hurried to parts unknown. Rosalie went to bed last night feeling slightly ill and I only hoped she was feeling better this morning.

Considering my circumstances I guess if I were to feel any apprehension, today would be the day for it. I think the train trip was to last about 13 hours and that would put us in Beijing about 7:00 a.m. From there it is another 2 hours by car to Tianjin. I will check in at the hospital today, loose my current contact to the world of China and must re-establish new ones. I will have to remember to ask Yiwei's mom to call JinWei and give her my number at the hospital. All these transitions have brought about a whirlwind of emotions and post stroke that is saying a lot.

It was almost 7:00 now and every one in our compartment was awake and busy preparing for the day. I'm glad that I got up at 4:00 … I think I missed the rush. The train slowly pulled into the station and we waited for the rush of people to leave. As we exited the train we began the long journey through the terminal, all the while being diligent to look for a bathroom at my behest. We finally found a bathroom tucked in a corner just as we were about to leave the terminal. I don't think I've mentioned it until now… the toilets in the bathrooms are Asian and eastern European style, which means they are open at ground level and I must squat to use them. In my condition that requires a lot of concentration and patience, but I was determined to win at this challenge. We did discover that at most new locations there is a handicapped stall with an upright toilet available.

After my brief detour we climbed into a waiting car that took us into downtown Beijing. Wang Yan Ni wanted me to have the opportunity to see Tian an men Square. Skipping it would be like driving through Washington D.C. and not seeing the Capital or Whitehouse. The car parked and we headed across the busy 6-lane road to the square on the other side. This was my first opportunity to dodge Beijing traffic as a pedestrian and it was quite exciting. I found that there is strength as well as a great deal of comfort in numbers. We finally found ourselves on the opposite side of the road and I was taken back at the enormity

of the square. It looked big, but I felt dwarfed when I stood in the center. I was told that it could accommodate 1 million people and it's easy to see how that would be true. People visiting and standing in long lines surrounded us on every side. The buildings that encompassed this spot are, like Washington D.C., responsible for government. Ahead of us stood the beautiful Forbidden City and its gates. To say this was all very impressive is such an understatement, it was awe-inspiring to say the least. After taking several pictures we began the long hike back to the car, sidestepping traffic when needed and upon arriving at our 4 wheeled coach we piled in for the journey to Tianjin.

Once we managed to get out of Beijing the ride seemed quite uneventful. The expressway lay ahead and was surrounded on either side by plantings of trees that when fully mature would add a certain amount of grandeur to the trip. I could see billboards that dotted the landscape but because they were all in Chinese I could only guess at their meaning by observing the pictures displayed on each. We arrived in Tianjin after a little under 2 hours and I was amazed when our driver actually stopped and asked for directions. The city was big and sprawling and as we drove I was impressed with the newness and cleanliness that surrounded us. There were several beautiful parks located between the expressway and the housing areas and we seemed to drive forever when out of nowhere the hospital complex seemed to appear.

We pulled up to the international building of the hospital and headed inside to be greeted by throngs of people milling about in the lobby area. Rosalie (Luo Shu Yue) and I found a seat while Wang Yan Ni disappeared to find someone to take us to my room. Minutes later she reappeared with a pleasant looking, tall young man in tow. After some discussion between Wang Yan Ni and Luo Shu Yue, I was introduced to "Mr. Ma". He led us to the elevators, which were bustling with activity. It seemed everyone wanted to ride and there was a limited amount of room in each forcing a long line to develop. We patiently waited for our turn before we boarded the elevator and were headed to the 12th floor. Yiwei's parents were forced to wait with the luggage for the next car to call.

Upon my arrival I was shown into room 1202 where Wang Yan Ni began speaking intently to Mr. Ma. I was pleasantly surprised by both the size and décor of the room; it appeared to be more of a hotel room than a hospital room. There were chairs that flanked a small table complete with tea cups and thermos, a huge armoire for hanging clothes that was filled with extra linens, a large 4 drawer dresser

housing a color TV on top and telephone, and last but certainly not least a full size bed with two bedside tables. The only hint that this was a hospital room was the oxygen outlets and call light above the bed and an I.V. stand tucked beside the armoire.

No sooner had we arrived and begun to settle than we were inundated by nurses and doctors, who entered, were introduced, and departed. I then discovered that I could leave to have lunch and meet with the doctors at 2:00. The one individual who stuck out during this meet and greet was Yu Lan, the English interpreter. She was definitely going to be someone I looked to for a lot of understanding.

After leaving the luggage and locking the room we departed the hospital and drove around to find a good spot for lunch. I chuckled out loud when I spotted a TGIF Friday's restaurant. Asked if I wanted to eat there I quickly replied no, but I was surprised to see this American restaurant in Tianjin. We drove for a few more minutes and found what appeared to be a popular and busy Chinese restaurant. By now I had become quite proficient in the use of chopsticks and found that a fork does little good. This food was prepared to be eaten with chopsticks and as such is best eaten with

them. A fork is only useful to chase Chinese food in circles around the plate. Most Chinese that I am with are quite amazed that I can use chopsticks and even more impressed that I use them with my left hand.

We finished lunch and returned to my hospital room to await the doctor's visit. I was most impressed when at least 3 doctors entered my room and through Yu Lan began asking a series of questions regarding the stroke and my current state. I was more surprised that the director himself began treatments immediately. He inserted a number of needles in my right arm, hand, leg and then my left neck. When the needle was placed in my right arm on the inside aspect of my elbow it felt as if electricity was flowing directly into my right hand. It was the strangest feeling when for the last two years I had known nothing but numbness. When he placed a needle in my right knee it jerked and felt like lightning was shooting out of my toes. Again these were odd feelings and different than any that I had ever experienced. Even though I had had some acupuncture in The U.S. the reactions and feelings were nothing like this. The doctors continued to discuss several things amongst themselves and then Wang Yan Ni interrupted and spoke with the director. It was all in Chinese and I had no way of knowing what they were talking about. However I'm so honored that I have Chinese-speaking people looking out for me. I feel that they are doing more for me than I could ever ask.

The needles stayed in for about 20 minutes and when the nurse gently removed them she was careful to swab and massage each area. I was amazed to discover the feeling of normalcy that I had in my right little finger remained after the needles were removed. Wow how exciting! It's such a small change, but one that I had not expected so quickly. I was on the verge of tears and I didn't feel that anyone truly understood my sense of elation! My right side bounces between numbness and pain with a constant bloated and heavy feeling. It's hard to describe but most stroke survivors understand. To have any portion of your body feel normal is just amazing!

After the doctors were leaving and Wang Yen Ni spoke with the director, he relayed to her that my condition was treatable and that he felt my health and, even more, my body could be restored in three months of treatment. I couldn't believe it! This was the good news I was praying I would hear but preparing not to get. And to think I had surpassed every western doctors expectations only to reach a point where they encouraged me to be thankful and content for what I had regained, three months may seem like a long time to most but after spending years trying to maximize what little I had, three months is a blink of an eye. I will continue my daily treatments with guarded optimism and watch for any small but significant changes.

After the needles were removed a girl came in and gave my entire right side an aggressive and stimulating massage. It lasted a over 40 minutes and at times verged on being almost painful, but it was good and provided needed stimulation to the right side of my body. As the massage finished Rosalie informed me that her aunt would bring me something for supper and that they would leave now and return later. I bid her good-bye and after everyone had left contemplated just how far I had come, physically, emotionally and spiritually. This was a big step! Before I got any further in my contemplations a knock came at the door and a small young woman approached with a large wooden tub, uttering something in Chinese. It was obvious that this was the foot massage that the doctor spoke of, but the tub she carried looked bigger than her. She quietly left and then returned carrying a tub full of hot water that had something in it that colored the water brown. I placed my feet in the tub and soaked for at least 5 minutes. She then dried each of my feet carefully and placed them on the bed elevated by blankets.

She took care in wrapping my right foot in a towel that kept it warm and then she began the massage on the left foot with some salve. The massage was wonderful, invigorating while at the same time relaxing. After 15 minutes she carefully switched the wrap to the left foot and began massaging the right. I was concerned that it might be painful but surprised to find it quite stimulating. After another 15 minutes she had finished with the massage and I asked her to write down her name and what she did on my cards. I now know her name is Da Gui and she performs zu liao. She spoke very little English but I could now refer to her by name.

Evening seemed to come all too quickly as Rosalie knocked and entered the room. She was carrying two bags. One was filled with dumplings and the other a hard bread like roll. She explained that both were a gift from her aunt. She said that they had to go and check into a hotel for the night but that they would return to say goodbye in the morning. With that she headed out, and I was faced with silence again.

I decided to put a DVD in the computer and relax for the evening. It had been a very busy day filled with change and challenges. No sooner did I start the DVD than the phone rang It was JinWei. She was calling to make certain the phone number she had worked and to see if I was settling in okay. We chatted briefly and she assured me she would call back in a few days to see how I'm doing. With that we both said good night and I returned to my DVD.

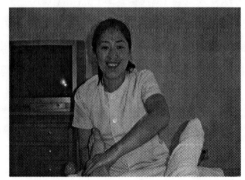

Tuesday June 15, 2004

Today started slow but picked up steam all day long. It began simply enough, rising at 4:30 with morning duties and washing my hair. I am still amazed that my right little finger feels fine and there has only been one treatment. The nurse asked me not to visit the bathroom before the ultrasound so I am diligently obeying. The girl with the portable Ultrasound showed up at 6:20 and took pictures of the liver, duodenum, stomach, pancreas and bladder. She was pleasant, but spoke little English. Through a number of gestures I gathered that she wanted me to flip and lay with my head were my feet were. All in all the experience was a pleasant one even with the language gap.

After she left I visited the bathroom and gathered the final sample they needed for their tests, I'm just glad the technician came promptly and I didn't have to wait any longer. At about 7:00 breakfast came, I asked for just one scrambled egg in the morning, between that and water I should do just fine. Before I ate I had to wait about 15 minutes until they came and drew blood. She took about 6 or 7 tubes worth so I know they were doing a thorough series to establish a good baseline.

No sooner did I finish my breakfast than a nurse stuck her head in and informed me I was headed off for another test. She helped me on with my shoes and off we went. We proceeded down the elevator across an enclosed walkway to another building. It was apparent that outpatients were treated here because the halls were lined with people. My nurse learned quickly to walk to my left and I would follow with my left hand on her right shoulder. It was the only way I could navigate these busy halls without falling or colliding into someone. At last we came to a door, as we entered I noticed a man who was seated just outside a doorway listening intently to a man speaking inside. I was ushered to a chair to sit and as I passed the doorway I could see the room was filled with people dressed in white coats listening carefully. I sat quietly and listened as I heard the man speaking in what was quite obviously Chinese pause and then begin speaking again. It was at this time that I noticed my nurse, now accompanied by Yu Lan the translator, motioning me to follow them. I rose and carefully made my way back past the doorway and exited with the women. Yu Lan informed me that they were having a meeting so I would continue with another test. I was led to an elevator where we ascended two floors and the down a series of halls to a very busy Ultrasound room. The hall was lined with people and a conversation ensued between my nurse and one of the family members of someone waiting. I was escorted into the room where a man was just departing having completed his Ultrasound. I lay down on the table where my translator told me I would have an ultrasound of the heart. The test proceeded without incident and we headed back to our first destination. We found ourselves waiting for what seemed like an eternity by the elevator and I assured my nurse I could walk the two flights down as long as I had a railing to cling to. Seeing that the elevator was nowhere in sight she cautiously allowed me to go down the stairs and it a short while we were back at what I now learned was the MRI facility. I was brought to a row of chairs where I first became aware that Yu Lan had been replaced by another translator. She was reading a form and translating it to me. It appeared to be a standard patient consent form and after we finished reading it I was asked to sign. I had not noticed before but the area for signatures on a Chinese form is very small, expecting two or three characters for the name. It was quite a challenge trying to fit my left-handed scrawl into the small area.

From here it was back to my room. We made a shortcut outside and took in some air as we went from building to building. No sooner had I sat on the edge of my bed than the doctors arrived. I must confess I was beginning to feel a bit like a celebrity, there were always at least 3-4 doctors in attendance. I took my place on the bed as Dr Shi asked my translator to inquire as to how I was feeling. "Very good" was my rapid reply and I continued saying how amazed I was that the small finger on my right hand felt remarkably normal. He smiled and with his large hands began to compare my right and left forearms while talking with the other doctors. They began the treatment and Dr Shi carefully inserted needles in my right arm and head, while another doctor tended to my leg. The same feeling of current surging through my body was felt when he placed the needles in my arm. The needles in my neck and scalp were much different. A heavier feeling almost a headache accompanied their insertion but it did not appear to last. While the needles where being placed I became aware that Rosalie and Yiwei's parents had come. Rosalie smiled and remarked, "Are we having fun yet?" A saying that I had been trying to teach her, along with helping her to understand my odd sense of humor. I looked back at her and smiled and remarked, "Oh yea"

Wang Yan Ni was busy speaking to the doctor, while another female doctor leaned over me, smiled and said, "30 minutes." All the doctors departed and it was just Luo Shu Yue, Yiwei's parents, and me. I was a captive audience and wasn't going anywhere as long as the needles were in place. Luo Shu Yue took this opportunity to take pictures of me in my confined state and I could do little to stop her. We all shared a good laugh, and then Luo Shu Yue shared what the doctor had told Wang Yan Ni. He felt my condition was treatable and that with TCM treatments I could be completely restored in three months. I asked her twice to elaborate to make certain that I understood what he said correctly... completely restored? I know he felt good after seeing me yesterday but this was his second visit and I thought he might change his mind. Luo Shu Yue reassured me and repeated herself, "Completely restored," she said, "healthy, feeling and moving." This was more than my mind could handle, it would take quite a bit of time for reality to set in. The doubter in me remained cautious while the optimist was exploding inside.

With this reassurance Luo Shu Yue explained that they would be leaving Tianjin now and returning to Changsha. I smiled while holding back tears. Tears of joy for all that they had done and tears of sorrow that it would be some time before I would see them again. I waved as they exited the room and shared a "bye bye" that we all understood.

Now the reality of being alone in a foreign country could really set in. My last connection had just parted and I was faced with communicating and making progress on my own. It was too much to handle so I decided to bury the feelings and deal with them later. No sooner had they gone than the nurse returned to remove the needles. This seeming ordeal was rapidly becoming second nature, needles in, needles out and evaluating any changes that might occur.

Lunch was supposed to be spicy chicken but I guess the girls have me trained to Changsha food, it didn't seem very spicy but it was very tasty. I was a bit tired and closed my eyes for about an hour. Shortly after I awoke, 4 people and the translator came to my room determined to set up the dialup connection to the Internet. They all seemed very determined to see to it that my time here was most pleasant and worked diligently to try to establish a connection. No luck! They all left with nothing quite decided, except that they were determined to get me connected later.

I thought after the busy morning I would have a quiet afternoon. Nothing could be further from the truth. The massage therapist came next and I was in for another intense session. She used a cloth that covers the part of the body she is working on. I say work because the massage she gives is deep and borders on being painful. Another doctor who came to do an EKG interrupted us. Well so much for a quiet afternoon, the EKG was finished and the massage continued. I must admit I have only experienced two of these deep muscle massages but I have already developed a love/hate relationship with them. They are a challenge to endure but the results seem to be worth it. Between the treatments and the massage the right side appears to be responding. What was a numb half of the body that only felt extreme hot and cold and fluctuated with constant discomfort and pain was now experiencing moments of a somewhat normal feeling. I know it is difficult to understand, but there is a constant heaviness that appeared to be lifting. The massage ended and I rolled over to rest only to be greeted by a smiling nurse.

In her hand she held what is now becoming a familiar sight, the metal pan that holds the acupuncture needles. I began to move to the right side of the bed when the nurse stopped me. She moved the chair in front of the bed and gestured toward it.

"Sit please." She beckoned.

With that I moved toward the chair and took a seat, anxious to see what else lay in store. Two doctors entered the room and smiled as they faced me in the chair.

"How you feeling?" asked the senior of the two.

"Fine," I replied, "I have a more normal feeling in some fingers in my right hand and my lip feels good."

They both smiled. "You'll feel much better." she said.

With that she began inserting needles in my right forearm with the help of the other doctor. The nurse grabbed a pillow and placed it on the arm of the chair to provide support for my now needle laden arm. "Great" I thought. This is a new experience   treatment sitting up! Little did I know what lay in store. She finished with the arm and began placing several in my scull around the hairline and then she began on the face and under my chin and the back of my neck. Now it began to become clear why I was sitting up. When all of the needles were in place the other doctor smiled and said, "20 minutes."

I sat quietly not moving a muscle for fear I would disturb the placement of any one of the needles. When you are sitting in a chair with no one else in the room 20 minutes can feel like a lifetime. The time pasted slowly but soon the nurse came in and carefully removed each of the needles. I actually had a few minutes before there was another knock at the door. This time it was Yu Lan, she wanted to know if the dial up Internet in my room worked yet and if I wanted the phone moved closer to my bed. I informed her that the Internet was not connecting and that I thought it was a phone-dialing problem. She made a quick call and we hooked up the phone line to the computer and tried again. Success! We finally made contact with the outside world! And none too soon. The door opened again and it was the phone technician to add a longer phone line for my computer to reach from the bed.

As he began to install the new line, there came another knock at the door. Talk about a busy day! This time it was my foot massage therapist. She quickly filled the tub and I began, what I learned from Da Gui (the therapists name) was a 10 minute soak before the massage. During my massage Yu Lan said the phone technician wanted to know if I had any American coins. She said he would be happy to pay for them. I scrounged around in my bag and came up with 2 dimes and three pennies. I insisted he take them for free, I was just sorry I didn't have anything else. He thanked me and left and Yu Lan excused herself for the day.

It was almost 6 p.m. before Da Gui had finished my foot massage and parted as well. Finally, I could lie on the bed quietly, or so I thought. One last knock, it was supper. The young girl quickly placed my dinner plate on my table and excused herself. Quiet at last!

I finished my supper and then thought I'd try out my new phone by trying to call JinWei. I reached her on her cell phone at her Grandfathers house. I let her know I now had online access and had sent an email to Steve at work with the number to the hospital. She was about to eat supper, so we talked briefly and I said goodbye.

I curled up around the computer and put in a DVD. This, after I had searched the TV for English speaking programs, only to be convinced that the DVD offered a better choice. I sat quietly and reflected on the day and the emotions it brought. I had parted with all the people familiar to me only to replace them with a new group that did not share a common language with me. They were, however, just as committed to my well being as those with whom I was familiar. I had come thousands of miles in search of an answer to my question of finding a cure for my disabilities after the stroke. I have found not only a pleasant answer but also people who share common goals, interests, and likes. We just don't happen to share the same language. Well, I have three months of treatments ahead and I am determined to be a good ambassador for the U.S. I will also work hard at adding a Chinese phrase to my vocabulary each day.

Wednesday June 16, 2004

Morning again at 4;30, it gives me ample time to get bathroom and grooming duties out of the way before I attempt to log on for the morning. Internet access is such a great privilege and the high-speed access I enjoy at home has spoiled me. I am content, however, with just having access no matter the kind. I spent the time online retrieving mail and sending a couple of quick messages. I think in order to save time I will compose messages in advance and paste them in and send them. Having email access is invaluable and I have a lot to catch up on! I thought I would be bored but things have kept me more than busy. I hope to catch up on my writing today. It seems that I've been destined to being a day behind. The last hour has been spent catching up and at this rate if the day is uneventful maybe I can catch up at noon!

Breakfast showed up at 7 this morning, my customary egg and water. It's nice having a water dispenser in the room but I'm afraid I might get a bit spoiled. Breakfast went fast and the nurse showed up shortly thereafter to get a blood pressure. It's back to 100/70 it had been a bit higher at 120/80 the past two days but with all that has been happening it makes sense.

Today is moving much slower and much to my liking, yesterday was a bit too hectic and I'm glad its over. The nurse came in around 8:30 to make up my bed and I've decided that the room lacks only one thing to be truly western and that is a recliner!

Liang Hui stopped in briefly to ask how I was doing; she is the other translator that I have met. She is currently translating a book that professor Shi wrote and has asked me for my help in it. I said I would be happy to help; after all he is doing so much for me. We chatted a bit more and then she had to head off to a meeting. She said she would return this afternoon.

A short while later housekeeping came to sweep the room and clean the bathroom. I'm seeing today just how much I missed when I was running about having tests done. I was just settling in for a writing spree when the knock on the door came. Two doctors and a nurse entered and the one doctor introduced the other doctor as professor Bian. I was told her English is limited but it seemed very good when she used it. She asked how I was feeling and I am trying to learn to reply in both Chinese and English. They began by inserting needles in the right arm and asking how I felt. It was obvious from my response that she hadn't found the spot she was looking for. Seconds later my arm exploded with the feeling of electricity and a smile crept across her face. That was what she was looking for! They continued down the arm and hand and with each needle came a flash of electricity. You have to understand that coming from numbness this feeling is not only foreign but also totally unexpected. She next moved to my head and face I closed my eyes only to open them and discover 3 needles around my nose and lips. I could feel as she inserted another under my chin. From here they began by lifting my right leg. "Very strong." She said as she smiled in my direction. I felt my leg jerk, as a surge of current appeared to travel down my leg and out my toes. I could tell by the repeated flashes of energy that she was continuing to place needles in my leg and foot. They pulled a blanket over the unaffected areas and then the younger doctor smiled and said, "20 minutes."

This time I was prepared! I had my camera at my left hand and reached to take several pictures of my current state. I then grabbed one of the earphones to my MP3 player and listened to music as the twenty minutes passed. Sure enough like clockwork a nurse entered to remove the needles. She smiled and gave a brief laugh as she looked at the needles coming from my face. I had to laugh too, they didn't hurt and I knew I had to look funny. She carefully removed them and then gently felt my scalp for any she might have missed. Taking them out of my arm, hands, leg and foot were easy and provided much less humor. I am definitely different in that they have never had an American patient, let alone one who is seeking treatment for a stroke.

Finished with the morning treatment I rested a bit before lunch, which arrived shortly after noon. I must confess that the food has been outstanding and I am enjoying trying each new dish. I'm going to find it difficult to repeat these meals but I'll certainly give it a try. I forgot to mention that three times a day for 40 minutes I place an herb filled fabric headband on that was developed by Professor Shi Xuemin. It is especially developed for those who are post-stroke to promote increased brain function and good health.

It has been approximately 4 hours since my last treatment and I have found dramatically increased feeling in the fingers especially the right thumb. The thumb and fingers, with the exception of the little one, feel stiff when bent. My right leg still feels very stiff but the foot, which had no feeling, now has some sensation on the pad of the foot and heel.

The doctor has come for my "body massage" or so it is called. I don't quite understand the technique but it is very effective at stimulating the muscles and increasing circulation.

Thursday June 17, 2004

After spending last night on line and anticipating a call this morning, I was quick to bathe and dress. I say "quick" but you must understand reality couldn't be further from the truth. It actually takes me close to 1 hour to sit in a tub, lather up, rise off and wash my hair. Quick is something I did pre-stroke when I was able to shower, wash my hair and dress in 10minutes! When I came out of the bathroom a brief rest was in order, it takes a lot of energy to prepare for the day.

I sat in a chair propping my feet up on the bed and set the computer in my lap. iTech was more than generous when they donated this laptop, I don't know what I would have done without it. It provides access to the English speaking world, music to relax by, DVD's and audio books to fill my time, and the ability to journal what I feel is an historic leap forward in the treatment of strokes.

I've begun my day by adding email addresses to a word document. I found that the mail servers' I used in the states now time out when I am trying to send a message from China. Now I can't use my mail lists that I so diligently created before I left. Instead all the email addresses are in a document that I copy and paste on the web page for composing mail. It is slow and tedious but it works! While I am typing the itching of my right hand continually interrupts me. I know it sounds trivial but when you have only experienced numbness and discomfort for years it's really exciting, annoying but exciting.

Steve said he would call this morning. It never ceases to amaze me than when you are anticipating a call the clock on the wall seems to slow down. It feels like an eternity has passed between 6:00 and 6:05, but I will wait patiently… NOT!

I was intrigued to discover that although students have come from the U.S. to study acupuncture or visit the hospital, patients had not. I guess many feel that the treatment they receive in the states is second to none and that seeking treatment anywhere else is redundant if not foolish. In my short time here I've discovered nothing could be further from the truth. The doctors are just that, doctors! Schooled in western medicine but also having a mastery of traditional Chinese medicine that surpasses my level of comprehension. Having been taught as a paramedic, nurse and surgical specialist I well know and understand the workings of the body, but the focus here is so much on working _with_ the body and providing the best circumstances and environment for health and healing to occur. Their goal is to stimulate the body to heal itself and I have been totally astounded at the progress that I have personally experienced in such a short time.

Prior to leaving home I spoke with my personal physician and although she wished me well in my journey I'm certain that her expectations were, as mine, low. She will be one of my first stops back in the states so she can see first hand what they can do. I don't quite know how my recovery will impact those who suffer with strokes or other disorders in the states. I would imagine that something that seems so miraculous would be greeted with a lot of skepticism. After all they can't quite put this treatment in a test tube or under a microscope. It reminds me of the man who discovered germs. He was confined to and died in a mental hospital because his ideas and concepts were unacceptable at the time.

I believe people today are far more discriminating about their medical care and personal health. We are more interested in the maintenance of health utilizing natural methods rather than bombarding the body with drugs. For that reason I guess I feel my situation is not totally unique. Yes, I dodged a bullet and survived a stroke that kills most of its victims, but I survived only to be faced with the daily hassle of dealing with the disabilities that it left me with. Prior to my treatment here in China I had learned to live with hemiparathesia (half of my body being numb), walking difficulties as a result, little control of my right hand (I used to be right-handed prior to the stroke), problems with balance, urinary incontinence, and vision disturbances. All of these problems combined made me 100% disabled and I was not happy or content. On top of all of this I was battling weight gain because I could no longer maintain an exercise program. Although I knew I was taking a risk coming here I could not pass up the opportunity and everything was falling into place, including having a person in China who could make all of the contacts and connections.

The phone just rang and a very pleasant voice greeted me, it was Jiang Yiwei. Evidently Steve had been trying to call and kept getting someone who only spoke Chinese, so Steve had Yiwei call to discover how he does it! We'll see if he can get through or not, it's already 8:15. Well the phone rang again and this time it was Steve! It was good to hear his voice even if we are 10,000 miles apart. He had the MRI and wanted to know where to send it. I gave him the address and reiterated what the doctors had said about my condition and prognosis.

"That's great." came his reply.

Although I knew he was happy, 10,000 miles still didn't change his demeanor on the phone; he was as dry as ever. I thought maybe seeing me bound down the walkway in the airport might do it… but we'll have to wait and see. Elizabeth was next on the phone she was excited and bubbly and it seemed the miles apart had not dampened her spirits at all. She was quick to share about her day and then jumped into a thousand questions. How was the treatment? How many have you had? Did they hurt? How many needles do they use? Do you feel them? How do you talk to the nurses? They went on and on. I tried my best to answer all of her questions but I knew the big one was, will you be okay?

"100%" I told her. "The doctors here feel they can send me back in great shape." I continued sensing the joy and relief in her voice.

"Really?" She exclaimed. I detected a slight bounce of excitement in her remark.

"Really, 100% A Okay." I reassured her.

For the first time since I had been planning the trip I felt a sense of calm and resolute joy in her voice. After all she was the youngest and the only girl in the house. The stroke had hit all of the kids hard but she took it personally making it her duty to care and look out for me. She wasn't particularly excited about my going all the way to China for treatment, but she more than anyone understood my determination to give it my all and recover all that I could. It gave me a great sense of relief knowing I could share with her the trip had not been made in vain. Once her fears had been relieved she quickly passed the phone to David.

"Hello, mom is that you?" David said slowly, testing the line.

"Hi," I replied quickly "Are you staying out of trouble and doing your chores?"

"Sure!" came the pat response.

Both he and I knew that trouble was his middle name. I don't know how but it always seemed to find him. He was probably my second biggest concern. Having Dad at work while he was home all day could prove to make for an interesting summer. I could tell from his obvious deviations from our conversation that Pepper, or minpin, must be entertaining him or sitting on his lap. After listening carefully to his whispered comments I could tell that the latter was true. David said he was busy getting our above ground pool ready for use and questioned me on the specifics of how to burn a CD on the computer.

With the apparent important issues dealt with it was time to turn the phone over to Roy, our oldest. This is the one who was the least of my concerns. He likes to reason things out and had come to the obvious conclusion that my going and seeking treatment was by far the best thing to do.

"Hi Mom." he answered the phone matter-of-factly.

"Hi." I replied. "Did dad tell you what the doctors think?"

"Yea, I think that's great!" His demeanor was just like his dad's. I could tell through our brief conversation that he approved of my staying the required three months.

Just then the doctor peered for the second time in my doorway.

"I've gotta go but ask dad to call me tomorrow morning before work." I asked as I quickly hung up the phone and none too soon, Liang Hui entered followed by three nurses.

"We will take pictures of you with the doctor and the TV crew is coming" Liang Hui informed me as they began to straighten up the room.

Housekeeping had just left while I was on the phone but the nurses were quick to look over everything and pickup any remaining items that looked out of place. I guess this was not a total surprise, I mean Americans just were not in the habit of seeking treatment in China. The story, it appeared had launched the doctor and university hospital into a somewhat celebrity status. Professor Shi Xuemin, followed by another man, entered and I rose to shake his hand. This is the first time I was standing next to him. He was a tall, well-structured man that stood at least 6' 2" and his smile was remarkably disarming. He gently but firmly shook my hand and ushered me to the right side of the bed for my treatment. All the while speaking to the nurses and translator who spoke with him at length and gestured several times in my direction. I could tell that she was relaying the information that I had given her about my condition and how I was feeling after the treatments. Following their conversations became much like a tennis match going back and forth. He smiled again in my direction and began inserting needles. I responded with a smile each time he placed one, electricity seeming to surge with each one.

He rapidly and precisely placed each needle moving from the shoulder, to the arm, hand and finally the face and neck. While he was busy two others were busy placing needles in the leg and foot. It was hard to keep up with all the activity and it was a bit before I noticed a TV camera and

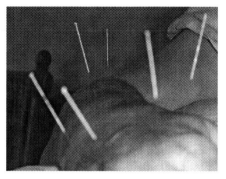

lights pointed at the doctor as he tapped and spun needles that were inserted on my neck and face. I just smiled! Not exactly making a fashion statement, but we were making progress on restoring me to health. Professor Shi Xuemin rose and stood in the middle of the room answering questions from what appeared to be a reporter.

The activity subsided and I rested quietly the prescribed 20 minutes and like clockwork my nurse returned to remove the needles.

"Finished." she said with a smile.

"Thank you" I replied.

The morning, which I thought would be so quiet, had come alive with activity and now for the moment appeared to be settling down. Minutes later came a gentle rap on the door, it was Liang Hui. She entered and informed me she had a special treat... Americans! Wow, the day just kept getting better. A young man and woman entered, she was obviously Chinese and when she spoke to Liang Hui it confirmed it. They were both students at the University Hospital and interested in my case. I remarked at how good their English was and got a chuckle. They too have only just arrived. Greg is going to study deep muscle massage while his wife Zhong Yanqun (Kathleen), studies acupuncture.

"Learn all you can," I said, "they're very good here."

She explained that she felt that understanding Chinese was a very important key to being able to practice TCM and acupuncture. She herself was from China and spoke

Mandarin fluently. We continued to talk in great detail about the future of acupuncture in the US. One thing I noted was that those who practice acupuncture at the hospital were all doctors. I felt that gave the doctors here added knowledge that they could draw on. I had experienced first hand the skill and mastery with which the needles are placed, turned and manipulated and there seems to be as much art as there is science behind the practice. We continued to chat and before leaving they assured me they would return to talk again.

As the two students parted, silence fell on the room as the sun shown through the window and started to heat the day. I guess I hadn't noticed that the sun had been shining until then and I was determined to say "sunny day" when Da Gui came late that afternoon for my foot massage. I began to look in my book for the appropriate words and then resigned myself to asking my translator next time I saw her.

Lunch passed without much fanfare and I spent the early afternoon hunched over the computer. Not having a desk forces me to change positions frequently. Sitting in the chair with my feet on the bed, sitting on the bed with my back against the wall, or just sitting on the bed bent over the screen. It really didn't matter because I changed my position every 15 minutes. It was 3 in the afternoon before I realized it and as I stood to stretch, my right hand hit the wall. The feeling that I was used to was a pressure at the shoulder that told me I was too close to the wall and should back away, I was not prepared for the sensation that I did get. I actually felt the wall! Not a pressure in the shoulder but my hand touched the wall! It was faint, kind of a shadow of a feeling but it was definitely there. I reached out and put my right hand on the wall, it was cool to the touch and smooth... no a slight texture, it definitely had a slight texture. I reached out with my left hand to touch the wall and compare the feelings. Anyone who would have stuck his or her head in at that moment would have thought I was crazy. I was like a kid with a new toy; I couldn't get enough of feeling that wall. The excitement tempered as I realized this was just the first of many sensations that I would feel over the next three months. I'd have to get used to re-establishing connections that I thought had been lost forever.

I sat on the bed trying to take it all in when a knock on the door came, followed by a petite young girl who motioned that she was here to do the body massage. We found the cloth that had been neatly folded and placed inside a drawer during the morning fiasco. Her technique was a pleasant surprise and although not quite as rough, extremely effective. She had rolled me onto my side when one of the doctors stuck their head in and said something to her. She finished her massage quickly as the doctor positioned a chair for me to sit in.

I moved to the chair and then noticed an older doctor had entered the room. I later learned he is one of the top doctors at the hospital. I sat quietly as he placed a series of needles at the base of my hairline and then began inserting a series in my arm and hand. This was becoming quite familiar as a pillow was placed to support my right hand. I closed my eyes as he inserted a number of needles in my lip, cheek, and nose. I sat quietly in the chair for the prescribed 20 minutes, when as expected the nurse arrived to remove the needles. I am continually amazed at the accuracy of their placement of the needles they appear to position them without effort and yet the desired effect is achieved.

I sat anxiously awaiting Da Gui's entrance and although we can speak very little she is a joy. The foot massages that she gives are bringing about slow and steady change in the feeling that I have. I had prepared for my visit with Da Gui by learning to say, "xing tian" or sunny day. I hoped she would both be able to understand and be impressed that I leaned words for her. She came in just as doctor Bian and Yu Lan entered. The doctor had a number of questions regarding the feelings that were beginning to return. Through Yu Lan we had quite a conversation and began having a bit of fun with Da Gui. The doctor was asking how I liked my foot massage and I told her that Da Gui was taking good care of me. When she explained that nothing like this existed in the US, I told her I would take Da Gui home with me. Upon translation that comment sparked hurls of laughter from all present. Da Gui continued with my foot massage after the doctor and Yu Lan left. She quietly finished and spoke her, "bye, bye" as she headed out the door.

Finally, a room to myself and I was absolutely exhausted. I vowed to eat, surf and sleep in that order.

Friday June 18, 2004

I think I'm finally getting used to the schedule here. I rise early in the morning with the sun and begin my day. The first hour, of course, is dedicated to personal grooming but the next few hours are given to learning Chinese. After all it is the number 1 language spoken in the world and it only makes sense to learn it.

The staff here at the hospital is wonderful. Every time I have a treatment the translator is available for the doctor. It's amazing though how much we communicate without words. Gestures cross all language barriers and the staff is having fun with my attempts at Chinese. They are faithful to attempt to understand my feeble attempts and speaking the right words and using the right tones. They usually end up correcting me and repeating the words several times for my benefit. I am determined, however, to hold a meaningful conversation in Chinese before I leave.

Last night Luo Shu Yue (Rosalie) offered to come stay with me for a few days during her summer break. What a blessing! I am cared for so much by so many people it boggles the mind. JinWei called last night. She was at a place that gave foot massages and couldn't go anywhere while they worked on her feet so she called me. It was a great diversion for both of us. She got to practice her English and I got someone to talk to! She informed me that she would go to Beijing in July to get her visa renewed, I'm a bit nervous for her; the US Embassy is very choosy about issuing visas. I told her if she had any difficulty to let me know and I would speak with them. Certainly you would think that they would allow her to return and finish her college education and travel home during breaks… but they can and are very finicky.

I sent Steve an email last night so I hope he calls this morning before everything gets hectic. I always think that things will go slow and easy in a methodical pattern… but something always interrupts and adds excitement! They are supposed to add an herb hand soak and massage so we will see where in the day that fits. There is rehab equipment on the second floor but I don't dare leave the room until I know we have a routine established. I got several emails last night responding to the 40 or so emails I sent updating people on my current status and prognosis. Most just wished me well and were happy that I found something that worked for me. I am intent on speaking in more detail with the doctors because both my research and the initial impression that they gave me was that strokes do not have to be the debilitating disease that they are. Leave it to me to shake up the medical establishment! If true, this could set the stroke rehab methodology on its ear. Not exactly an easy pill for the established medical establishment to take, but for the stroke survivor… what an opportunity.

I am continually interrupted in my writing by itching on my right side. Now my inner thigh is beginning to itch! It's really amazing to be feeling my body awake slowly after being asleep for so many years. Words cannot express the emotions that are churning inside; I have had so many disappointments over the years that doubt still reigns. Slowly I am seeing and believing that what they say is true.

The nurse came in to take my blood pressure and temperature, 120/70 and normal. I guess on that front there are no bells and whistles going off. I have noticed that she always asks how I slept so I will ad the word "shuijiao" to my vocabulary today, pronounced shoeejow, I can now use the phrase "wo shuijiao hen hao", which means I slept very good! Wow! She was impressed! Of course I had to point to the word in my book and ask her to pronounce it, but I've added it to my brain trust. Now if I can only get that recall thing to work when I want to use my new word!

Like clockwork 7:00 came and my breakfast of one egg scrambbled was delivered and my lunch and supper choices taken. I guess it's going to be hard to cook again when I return but I have a feeling that hungry stomachs and my desire to use a once limited limb will prevail. Out come my chopsticks and I don't like to sound proud but I'm getting pretty good at this left-handed thing! I have a dear friend,

Joe who has always been left handed and he tells me I am finally in my right mind.

I don't know what I was thinking! Oh that a day would be calm and uneventful. Steve called at about 7:30 local time, it seems the computer that the server at home runs on was acting up, just like it to wait until I'm gone to have fits. He is going to work on it and call in three hours if he still has problems. Elizabeth was online waiting for me this morning but I had to wait on a download that took forever. We chatted and will try again tonight at 8 my time. David wanted to chat too. It appears he found his old baseball card collection and he wants to check out card values online. He also got a 3 man inflatable raft that he has been enjoying in the pool. He said he'd really like to take it out and try it. I suggested that he talk with dad and look into taking it to the lake sometime. I let Steve go under the proviso that he would call if the server was still not up at 10 p.m. his time.

It seemed I no sooner hung up than a knock came at the door and my massage therapist walked in. She pulled her cloth from the drawer and immediately began thrusting her fingers deep into the muscles on my upper arm. The doctors had told me that the massage would be intense and that was the only way it would be effective. I must admit that as uncomfortable as the massage is, it is very effective and I always feel invigorated afterwards. The massage therapist finished as Dr Bian came in for my morning acupuncture treatment. It was different today. She had me start by lying on my left side as she worked on my hip. I'm not certain what she was doing but in short order my leg came alive, jerked and contracted. With that she asked me to roll onto my back.

"What do you feel? She asked.

Not quite knowing how to respond I finally settled on an answer. "Do you understand cramp?" I looked at her questioningly.

"Cramp… good." She replied with a smile.

She then continued to insert needles in my arm, hand, leg and foot. It's hard to believe in such a short time but I'd gotten used to the electric surge that accompanied each placement. I still smiled and uttered the proverbial, "oh" but the surprise was gone and replaced by a somewhat moral justification, a confidence that this was leading to an exciting end. I still grimaced and closed my eyes when it came to the needles on my neck and face. Today she seemed a bit more intent and by the time she was done I had some 50 needles protruding from my body. I thought we were done and I'd wait the customary 20 minutes when she left, but to my surprise the other doctor remained. She pulled a small black and white box from the back of the counter and until now I hadn't even noticed it. It was difficult to see it but it appeared to be about 5x7 inches in size and about 2 1/2 inches thick. There was a meter on the top and wires with clips coiled around it. It appeared that there were 4 knobs surrounding the meter and all I could envision was electro-shock therapy. Were they actually going to hook that up to the needles?

She leaned forward with the box, smiled and said, "electricity."

I ushered a weak smile and answered, "okay."

She connected the wires to the needles by the knee and the one in between the right thumb and first finger. The machine made a clicking sound and with each click I could feel my knee and hand jerk softly.

"20 minutes." She said with a smile, and then she left the room.

Before, 20 minutes was easy to make pass by closing my eyes and taking a shot nap, but this box and the clicking sound were keeping me wide awake and alert. The idea of 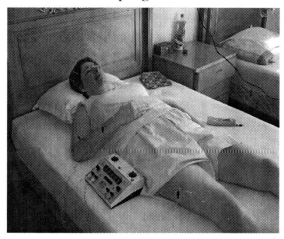 being connected up to any voltage no matter how small was somewhat unnerving and 20 minutes will pass... eventually

When a knock came at the door I glanced at the clock. "That's funny," I thought "there's still 5 minutes left." With that the door opened and Liang Hui walked in.

"Oh," she exclaimed "you're having a treatment."

She seemed to look past the needles an ignored the constant clicking and struck up a conversation. "How much longer?" she asked.

"Only about 5 minutes." I muttered, watching needles bounce on my lip as I talked.

She continued to speak and I listened as the next five minutes passed. I felt I dared not even nod for fear I might dislodge one of the carefully placed needles. I was ever so happy to see the nurse as she gently removed each of the needles after first shutting off and removing the box.

Liang Hui, the translator, and I continued our conversation and as I stretched and yawned the doctor reentered the room carrying a tray of what appeared to be small round glass cups. I began to get up and Liang Hui informed me that my treatment was to continue. I was asked to lie on my left side and the doctor leaned forward, smiled and said, "You've had cupping before?"

"No." I replied innocently enough.

At least I had heard of it. Heat is applied to the inside of the glass cup and it is immediately inverted and placed strategically on the skin. Suction in the cup is formed and blood is brought to the surface of the skin. Sounded great in theory, but I wasn't too sure I was ready to succumb to the treatment. Too late, the doctor asked me to roll on my left side, and then she propped my right hand up on a pillow and began. She took one cup at a time quickly inserted a burning ball of cotton held by a hemostat, removed it, inverted the cup and placed them on my arms and legs. As each cup came into contact with the skin it formed a vacuum drawing a raised portion of flesh into the inverted cup. The entire process of placing the cups took her less than a minute and was completely painless.

She leaned forward and this time uttered. "5 minutes."

It was obvious that I wasn't going anywhere and sure enough in 5 minutes she returned and removed each of the cups. I was no worse for wear, with the apparent rings that my body displayed where the cups had once been. It appeared that the activity for the morning had finally subsided and I could get some uninterrupted time writing.

Lunch was fairly uneventful, I am trying to use the right hand again, this time to hold and eat a dumpling. It's shaky, but I feel it… so we'll keep up the attempts. Steve didn't call so I'm assuming He got the server fixed. Just like a machine to wait until I'm 10,000 miles away before it glitches! I'm enjoying the free time so I can catch up on some emails. It is so good to get notes of encouragement. I pray each day that someone will write and each day so far there is at least one new message that isn't junk mail. I compose my messages slowly so I save them in word and paste them into the web mail page when I go online. I use a dialup and I'm finding out just how spoiled I've been over the years with a high-speed connection that is always on.

The nurse just stuck her head in to let me know the doctor is on the floor for the next treatment. Sure enough Dr. Bian Jinling came in and I took my seat in the chair.

"Same?" She asked as she gestured between my two arms.

"Almost" I replied. It felt like I had made so much progress in just a matter of days but she seemed to take it all in stride and matter of fact. She placed a number of needles on my arm and hand and the switched to the head, neck and face. I don't know if I will ever get used to the treatments but I'm happy to have them. If anyone had told me I'd have feeling on the right side by this time I would have laughed out loud in their face. I sat quietly for the next 15 minutes when Luing Hui entered. She had a booklet with her that introduced the hospital that she offered me to read. It should be interesting there is both Chinese and English translation in the booklet. We talked as the nurse entered to remove the needles. As she took out all the needles on my face I asked if I could take a picture.

"With the needles in? came Liang Hui's reply.

"Yes!" I resoundingly said. "People back home want to see."

She snapped the photo using the digital camera that I brought along. (It makes sharing pictures so easy over the internet.) We discussed the fact that she would take me around the hospital to see the out patients and other in patients. She felt it was very important that I see and understand what they were doing and how they combine both western and traditional Chinese medicine. She explained that during the acute phases of many diseases western medicine, even surgery was indicated but in many cases especially chronic cases, Chinese traditional medicine was very effective. I am excited to see all that they are doing and speak with as many patients as possible. Now I understand why God gave me a medical education. So I can see and effectively communicate with others in the medical profession. They all left and I was again surrounded by what I was beginning to enjoy… silence!

A short time later a nurse entered carrying a bucket, she disappeared and I could hear the sound of running water coming from the bathroom. She reappeared, bucket in hand and placed it on one of the chairs. She reached into her pocket and produced a small white bottle that looked much like a bottle of cough syrup. She carefully removed the cap and poured the entire amount of dark liquid into the bucket of water. She carefully re-submerged the bottle, filling it with water and dumping out the contents several times to make certain that she had gotten it all. She then looked at me and smiled.

"Sit please," as she motioned to the chair immediately to the left of the one holding the bucket. I followed her lead and sat down cautiously, peering into the bucket to see first hand the swirling dark water. From this vantage point I could now see the steam rising off of the water in the bucket. I wasn't sure what she had in mind but I had a good idea. She gently took my right arm and placed it carefully into the water. "Hot?" She looked at me intently.

"No" I replied. The water was remarkably soothing on my hand and arm, and although the water was hot, it wasn't too hot. She gently placed what appeared to be a piece of gauze or cheese cloth over my lower forearm and then, using a cup began to slowly pour the liquid in the bucket over my lower arm. The hot liquid trickled down my forearm to the hand resting in the bottom of the bucket. It was all rather soothing, the warm water and her gentle touch. This continued for at least five minutes and then she gently squeezed out the cloth and used it to massage and somewhat dry my forearm and hand. I thought we were done when she placed the bucket on the floor but to my amazement she poured steaming hot water into the bucket from a thermos that until now had escaped my notice. She continued by placing my right foot into the bucket and stretching the cloth over my lower leg. She began to pour hot liquid over me knee and it flowed down the cloth over my lower leg. She only stopped once to carefully fill the cup with steaming hot water and gently add it to the bucket, making certain to not scald me in the process. She finished with much the same technique of wringing out the cloth and massaging and drying off my leg and foot. She helped me back to my bed where I could rest.

It wasn't long before Da Gui popped her head in and began to fill her tub with hot water. I could really get used to this. People seemed to wait on me hand and foot... literally! Not only was this treatment extremely successful it was pleasurable as well. I harkened to think of a nurse in the states who would have, let alone taken, the time for some of these treatments and therapies. But each of the nurses and therapists seemed genuinely concerned for my well-being and diligent about practicing their job with expertise and kindness.

Da Gui returned with her bucket of hot water treated with herbs and placed my feet in it for my 10-minute soak. I pulled out my Chinese language book and she anxiously sat looking at what I was about to do. For a 24 year old Da Gui has the energy of a 16 year old. She could hardly contain her excitement as I pointed to a page and began to read the Chinese words written there. She gasped with excitement and uttered, "Hao, hen hao!" Which translated means good, very good! I continued to read and she followed along correcting me when I had difficulty with a word. When my time to soak had finished she dried my feet and placed them gently on a clean cloth for my massage. As she worked on my feet I continued to read the words. Her excitement at my meager attempts to learn Chinese was encouraging. When I finished reading she broadly smiled and exclaimed, "Hen hao!" I gasped letting her know it was tough work and she chuckled.

The foot massage takes about an hour so when I finished the Chinese lesson I picked up the booklet that Liang Hui had left earlier. There were small paragraphs of Chinese characters followed by several paragraphs of English. As I read I could see that much of this was an exact translation and many extra words and statements were included. The booklet showed an extensive use of the latest technology for both diagnosis and treatment. It appeared from reading this booklet that they have tried, very successfully I might add, to incorporate both new technology and old proven treatments. I am more anxious than ever to go on a tour of the hospital.

Da Gui was busy rubbing the right foot when I began to feel increased sensations in the heel and outside bottom. She smiled as I put down the booklet and began to try and focus on the sensations and where they emanated from. They seemed to be limited to the foot. The leg, it appeared, was still sleeping. Da Gui finished and said her cheerful bye bye and the room returned to a quiet state.

With the exception of dinner the night remained quiet. Only the sound of traffic could be heard as it rose from the city below, quite a change of pace for this country girl. I marveled at how far I'd come on this journey for answers. I'd left the farm life in Iowa far behind as I boarded the first of many planes that brought me here. It seems like a dream to be in a foreign land with a people who don't speak my language seeking not just a treatment, but a cure for a stroke that left me disabled some 2 years ago. That dream was now a reality and speaking of reality, looking at the clock reminded me that I had promised my daughter I'd be online at 8 to chat with her. Technology has more than made this trip possible. It also allows me the ability to keep in touch real time.

I logged online just in time as the computer sprang to life with a customary "brrr...ing" letting me know a message was waiting. I began the chat with Elizabeth, being concerned that my one handed typing would slow me down. I was more than able to keep up and at the same time launched another program that would allow me to rebuild my website. We chatted at length, me answering questions and Elizabeth trying to think of what to ask. It is a bit difficult for a 12 year old to hold an online conversation. Elizabeth and I finished our chat as I began to get tired. It was past 10 p.m. my time when we called it a night.

Saturday June 19, 2004

It's hard to believe I've been here five days and this is my first Saturday. It seems like so much has happened in such a short time. The sun is up and I slept in until 6:30 and almost feel guilty. Last night I bathed and Liang Hui is very worried that I might fall so she asked that I only get in and out of the tub with a nurse. It's okay even though I've been doing it by myself for over a year. Bathing the night before has made the morning go faster and fills the evening when there is not much to do. Breakfast came and I am having fun eating eggs with chopsticks. It's like a game seeing if I can pick up all the little pieces. Enough already, I must be really bored to make mealtime a game, I guess I just haven't grown up yet.

They have me taking 4 green capsules of a Chinese medication after each meal. I know they could tell me what it is but I probably wouldn't understand them. They also have me drinking a liquid (50 cc's) after supper and after breakfast. Tastes suspiciously like Prune juice, my mother would be so proud! Yuck! But this is all an adventure and what doesn't kill me will make me better, right? I really can't complain, I feel great and the results I'm having are nothing short of miraculous.

One of the doctors and several of the nurses stuck their heads in at about 8:30. They all smiled, said something in Chinese and left again. I guess I was alive and well and that's what mattered. At 9 the door opened and it was housekeeping. She took my clothes to be laundered and began cleaning the room. Moments later Dr Bian entered to start the morning's treatment.

"How are you feeling? She asked with a smile.

"Very good!" and with that I gestured to my two arms, "same," I said. denoting that the feeling had completely been restored to the upper right arm.

She reached down and stroked my left leg and the right, "same?" She asked.

"Not yet," I replied "close."

She nodded and spoke with the other doctor and then felt my legs comparing every aspect, one to the other. She then motioned and the tray of needles was brought to her. She began again with my right arm. The electricity shot through my hand and I responded with, "ooh". She chuckled and continued to the face and neck. She placed at least 15 needles before moving to my leg. I've learned to try and relax even when I see my leg being raised in the air and I know the sensations that will follow. She finished and the other doctor placed a blanket over the non-needled portion of my body to keep me warm. Then that dreaded box came out and this time I paid attention as she connected the needles by my knee and ankle to one set of wires and my hand and elbow to another. The current was turned on and I could hear the steady clicking that the box made and feel the gentle jerking as the muscles contracted. I lay still as the treatment continued knowing that in 20 minutes the nurse would return and the needles would come out. Sure enough at the end of 20 minutes the nurse was back. I think she realized that I had extra needles around my neck and face because she smiled and chuckled when she saw me.

With the needles out I thought I'd stretch out to watch a DVD... no such luck. No sooner had I stretched out than a knock came at the door and the doctor entered carrying a familiar tray. It was time for cupping! No rest for the weary! I rolled onto my left side and she applied the cups not only to the arm and leg but to my back too! Five minutes passed quickly and before I knew it the cups were being removed. Finally a break and I decided to turn on the TV. There are a number of channels but only two that have English. I didn't want to watch Japanese TV news translated and the other choice was fashion TV, so I settled on a Chinese program about animals. I was just settling in when a rap on the door gave way to my body massage doctor. So much for relaxing! I've tried diligently to pay attention to each area and how it feels. When we began this process 5 days ago all I felt was numbness followed by pain. Now the upper torso feels sensations and my lower body still verges between numbness and pain. Although I feel as if I endure torture for an hour each day I know that it is slowly having its desired effect and the portion of my body that has been "asleep" is slowly waking up.

After lunch was a quiet and relaxing day, I was able to kick back and watch a DVD without interruption. Spoke too soon! A group of 10+ students from the University of Michigan just came in with Liang Hui; they're a fun bunch. Lots of questions about the treatment here and why I came and what treatments I had sought in the U.S.. I got the idea that they are as surprised as I am at the results I have gotten so far. They were most concerned at how I communicate with the staff and both, how attentive and the amount of time the nurses spend with me. It was fun speaking with them. I enjoyed their energy and enthusiasm. Time seemed to get away from us and before I knew it time had come for my soaks. The students graciously said their good byes and I took my position in the chair.

It had only been my second of these treatments but I was impressed by the care and dedication shown to me by this nurse. I realize as the only American patient to come for treatment I was a bit of an anomaly but their concern and efforts on my behalf were real. For them there was no line in the sand or big note on my forehead that said I was different in any way or an "American". To them I was simply Ruth, a stroke patient seeking treatment and recovery. How refreshing! My soaking treatment finished and I hopped up on my bed and began to write when Liang Hui entered the room without her white lab coat, something I'd not seen before. I was impressed Ms Liang was a striking woman all of 5' 3 with short black hair. She was smartly dressed in beige slacks and a beautiful light cable knit short sleeve gold blouse. She smiled and asked if I would like to see a piece of Tianjin. How could I pass up such an opportunity? I quickly agreed, and off she went to find a wheelchair while I changed into "real" clothes, leaving the hospital garments aside.

They were very careful about my walking. You wouldn't have known that I'd gotten along for the past several years (tipsy as I was) on my own. She wheeled me down the hall and to the elevator, commenting only once about my weight. We both chuckled and knew that weight was something that I desperately wanted to loose. That had been one of the most frustrating side effects of the stroke, the decrease in mobility brought on unwanted pounds and I had to practically starve to take weight off. Prior to my coming I had lost 20 pounds and was intent on continuing the process. We rode down the elevator from my 12th floor room and headed outside. The fresh air was invigorating and the sun, although hidden by haziness, warmed the air. It was quite comfortable and you could see by the puddles of standing water where it had rained earlier in the day. Liang Hui informed me that if there had not been any cloud cover it would have been unbearably hot. Instead it was very pleasant and that brought people out into the streets. As Liang Hui pushed me out of the hospital we were passed by a girl and her mother, the little girl obviously intrigued by my condition asked why I was there and not my own home for treatment. Liang Hui replied to her in Chinese and she seemed to accept the explanation, however she kept looking back at me and smiling.

"I guess we'll not only educate the American medical establishment but little girls in China too!" I said as we headed across the parking lot.

"It's just hard for her to understand that you don't have this same treatment in the United States." Replied Liang Hui.

We cut across one street, dodging traffic as Liang Hui pushed the chair. I marveled at her skill to know just when to go to avoid the oncoming bikes, scooters and cars. We entered a residential area where the street was gated and people ruled, walking about chatting and paying us very little attention. We were periodically passed by bikes with people young and old riding casually by. The entire scene was very serene, no one appeared hurried or hassled or late. Parents were walking hand in hand with their children and I just enjoyed the trip as Liang Hui continued pushing me along. As we came to the end of the residential area we approached a busy street, complete with cars, bikes, people, taxis and buses. Liang Hui made her way skillfully across, stopping to dodge traffic and then moving rapidly forward. It was all a bit surreal I didn't even feel like I was in any danger as she pushed me out into the middle of the busy street. I can't even imagine this scene in downtown New York; I'd be one with the pavement in no time. We approached a building bustling with people and Liang Hui carefully guided me inside. We were immediately greeted with smells of fish and fruits and yes, the scent of fresh baked goods, all intertwined with the aroma of perfumes and soaps. We had entered into a large grocery super store. People milling about and looking at the different wares and chatting surrounded us in all directions.

I was suddenly confronted with the fact that all of these people around me were talking and I had no idea what they were saying. I smiled and almost chuckled out loud, this is what JinWei had been referring to, culture shock at its finest! I decided to take it in and greet each inquisitive look with a smile.

Instead of escalators with stairs, they have moving sidewalks that angle between floors. This allows you to easily push a cart on and ride to the next level. Liang Hui looked at me and at the moving sidewalk and asked. "Can you do it?"

I knew she was dreading having me in a wheelchair on the way up. "No problem." I said reassuring her.

I slowly climbed out of the wheelchair and pushed Liang Hui ahead of me and she reluctantly went forward. I approached the moving sidewalk slowly and reached forward with my good left hand and grasped the moving railing tightly, I then stepped forward with my good leg and felt the upward movement of the sidewalk and quickly pulled my right leg beside it. "Not bad," I thought to myself, "different but not bad at all." I was rather pleased with myself for conquering another "unknown". Not many people look at these things in life as challenges unless you are either very young, very old, or disabled. The walkway continued its slow steady movement to the second floor and I quickly realized it took all my energy and balance to hold on and maintain my position without falling into the crowd of people behind me. I was just happy that unlike the moving sidewalks in airports, there did not appear to be a correct side to stand on and no one was trying to pass me and hurry on their way. I made it to the top were I gingerly exited noticing Liang Hui to my left. She motioned for me to get back in the chair and

I willingly obliged. We proceeded to check out all that the second floor had to offer, there were clothes of every sort, grills, sports equipment, toys, kitchen cookware, and almost anything you could imagine.

"You know"" I said, "We joke that almost everything that is sold in the stores in America is made in China."

"That's because it costs less." She replied.

"I guess that makes everything here local and cheap." I retorted.

"You're right." She said bearing a big grin.

We made our way through the goods on the second floor and to the walkway that headed down. We repeated our performance, this time in reverse. I found it much more difficult to maintain my balance with the walkway pitched down, and this was from somebody who prided herself on balance and athleticism just a few years ago. As I exited the walkway at the bottom I was more than pleased to take a seat. Before we left the hospital I felt that the wheelchair was a bit of an over kill and unnecessary. Now I was happy it was there!

Liang Hui pushed me through aisle after aisle of food, many things I recognized, and even more things I didn't. We passed fresh fish and meats, vegetables, fruit, and canned goods. I recognized labels such as Pringles, and Nestles, and several other brands all sporting Chinese wording too. As we came to the end of an aisle Liang Hui paused. "You like coffee?" She asked.

"Sure" was my reply.

"It's on sale, a very good price." She continued "You can use it in the hospital."

I reflected on the fact that the water cooler in my room had a spigot for hot water that I never used. "Sure" I said,

"I'll get some." Upon closer inspection I even recognized the brand, Maxwell House! She gathered a box and we continued on past the soap and make-up aisle where I recognized names such as Maybelline, Revlon, and Head and Shoulders. We proceeded to the checkout line where I was surprised to not see a line, even though the store seemed packed. Come to think of it I saw people with yellow vests throughout the store, always available to help. I placed my item on the counter and the girl quickly scanned it and gave me a total. I only had 100-Yuan bills so I handed her one. She said something to me in Chinese and Liang Hui leaned forward and asked me if I had any change. "No" was my reply, and she said something to the clerk who nodded and gave me back a receipt and change. I grabbed my new purchase and we headed out toward the busy street again. I cannot stress enough how impressed I was at Liang Hui's ability to maneuver the wheelchair, with me in it, through traffic. We again headed through the residential area, this time taking a quite different route. We passed a small open market were Liang Hui remarked, "The food is even cheaper here."

"Farmers selling directly?" I asked.

"Yes" She replied.

We continued down the busy street filled with people and farmers displaying their produce on white sheets laid on the pavement. People on bikes continued to pass us and only stopped if they spotted something that caught their eye. When we came to the end of the street we turned and preceded down a separated part of a major street. There were shops and businesses that lined our path and shopkeepers spoke intently to potential buyers on the street, it seemed that no one who passed by was ignored. We stopped briefly outside a bakery where Liang Hui informed me she wanted to stop inside and get some breakfast bread. Content to take in the scenery, I waited patiently parked outside the shop as Liang Hui entered. She returned shortly holding a bag of breads. I offered to carry it while we headed back to the hospital and she graciously accepted. It was the least I could do considering the outing she had taken me on during her free time.

We made the short trip back to the hospital and headed up to my room in the elevator. It had been quite an excursion but I was happy to be back. I handed Liang Hui her bag of breads and she headed off to return the wheelchair as I sat on the edge of my bed. She returned shortly only to issue a quick good bye and tell me she would see me on Monday. I sat relaxing on my bed when the phone rang. It's too early in the morning for Steve to be calling, or anyone from the states. Maybe it was JinWei I thought, to my amazement it was Da Gui! In an interesting and difficult conversation on my part, she manage to get across to me on the phone that she would be there soon to do my foot massage, she was just calling to make certain I was there. All this and I speak little, if any Chinese. I thought it was gutsy on Da Gui's part to call me and trust I would understand. Will miracles never cease? After I looked at the clock I realized that I was not there at 5 when she usually comes.

A short while later Da Gui entered, filled her tub and I began my traditional 10 minute soak. As I sat she grabbed my left hand and began to massage it. This was definitely above and beyond the call of duty, but she smiled and continued to message my hand and arm. Then after several minutes she switched and began on my right hand. This was wonderful, I was almost sorry that it had to end and my foot massage had to begin. I know, you're thinking how tough to choose between a foot or hand massage! Really this is treatment and rehab, it's just so darned enjoyable at times.

Da Gui continued with the foot massage as I exercised my right hand, opening and closing the fist and stretching the fingers while trying to hold them still and straight. Although the feeling in my right hand was beginning to return to normal, it was apparent that I had a lot of work ahead of me to return the control and coordination. I had spent the better part of the last two years working on control and coordination with poor results. It would be interesting to see how the treatments and massage helped. After all the doctors said a complete recovery, this will determine their definition of complete. Da Gui finished her massage and if I understood her Chinese she would not be back until Monday.

I hadn't realized how late it was until I glanced at the clock. It was after 7 and I hadn't eaten my supper yet. Found it waiting on the table, still sealed in plastic wrap and amazingly enough, still warm. I slowly ate and when the nurse entered to take my BP and temperature I told her, "No bath tonight, too tired." After a bit of playing the word match game (she didn't understand the word tired) she understood and left me for the night.

Sunday June 20, 2004

Today is a day of rest and the doctor told me to rest and not write, so I am being diligent and listening for a change and won't write much. Treatments are only given once today so I do get to rest! I will spend the day in thanks that I got here and here seems to be the perfect place!

Monday June 21, 2004

Well it's difficult to believe but today is my one-week anniversary. I slept in until 5:00 and it was so refreshing! After the morning rituals I logged on fast to check emails and send a couple quick messages. Typing with one hand never makes anything quick. I'll be excited when function is completely restored to the right hand, I really do miss it! I feel I can't spend much time on line because I'm tying up the only phone line.

Today as did last week, will mark several first in my life but the most important is the opportunity I have to grade the medical treatment I've received thus far. The students who visited on Friday were particularly interested in the type and quality of care given to me and while I'm not privy to their charts and daily writings (a lot of good that would do they're all in Chinese), I have been impressed with both the quality and type of care I have received. The doctors and staff have all been extremely professional and yet not distant or aloof. There seems to be a genuine concern for my well being, I'm not simply the stroke in 1202. I am a person to them; an individual with needs and concerns not simply a case study. At first I thought it was my "celebrity" status here, being the first American to seek treatment. But it is more than an act put on to impress me. You can see in their eyes and the way they speak to each other. I know I don't understand the language yet but I've always been a good judge of character (just look at the friends I keep, Ha Ha!)

As for what the treatments have done, speechless comes to mind and for those who know me I am never left without words to say. I have been astounded at the results they have accomplished in one week! I have now replaced the ever-present numbness with feeling in my right arm, hand and upper leg. And this persistent itching in my right ankle is such a joy, annoying as all get out, but a joy to realize that the portion of the body that has been asleep is now awakening!

The nurse just knocked and I was thrilled to say "qing jinlai," or please come in. I then marveled her by continuing with, "wo shujiao hen hao" which means I slept very well. She smiled but inside I know she was laughing out loud at my feeble attempts to speak their language. It's all in the pronunciation, which I massacre every time I utter a word. They are gracious, I will give them that. Oh well, so much for the exciting interlude now back to my boring body!

I've been trying very diligently to feel and sense any and all changes that occur but sometimes they just do. My vision, for example, I spend a good portion of my morning (at least 2 hours) getting everything to focus. I have a tendency to wake up and see 1-1/2 to 2 of everything until I wake the brain up totally and begin to focus correctly. I've been to the best eye doctors and upon exam they all say my right eye sees perfectly and my left eye sees perfectly, the two just don't always play well together. This morning I awoke and much to my amazement I didn't need time to practice focusing. They just did! I'm still troubled by a slight tremor or bounce in my eyes but it appears to be getting better. So much for the glasses I'd been wearing to read by. My cousin is going to have a fit, she said that after 40 my eyes would start to go and it took a stroke to affect them. Guess now she'll have to eat those words. Something deep inside tells me that's not going to be a problem. I even changed my setting on the computer to a smaller size. Now that says a lot!

The feeling seems to be completely restored in my arm and upper leg. There is still a shadow of extra weight in the arm but I'm attributing that to a lack of coordination that has not quite returned. There is complete feeling in my hand as I touch it but the joints all feel tight and stiff. Although there is now feeling there still appears to be a disconnect in the wiring of my brain. It's hard to describe but I'm looking forward to having that disappear too. It's going to be extremely difficult to explain to the doctors but through my translator I will try.

My back and chest are all "feeling" now but tight and stiff, like I need to stretch them out. My inner thigh feels normal and my outer thigh itches and is kind of there! My lower leg has feeling but everything feels distant still. The foot is very sensitive but feels wrapped or portions feel yet uncovered. The arch of the foot is extremely sensitive and seems to be leading in the race for normalcy.

I hope the doctor can make sense of all of this, I mean its only been a week right? It seems I had gotten quite accustomed to numbness. These new aches and pains are welcome but a bother.

Ling Hui came by after breakfast to see how I was feeling. I was so glad to see her! I wanted to tell the doctors what I had been feeling and where we were with treatments. I have learned very well that what I say figures into what they do, so I wanted to give them accurate information. We spoke at length and she was happy that we did. She left and returned a short time later with Dr. Zhang. She seemed pleased with the progress so far, but concerned about the outer right thigh region. They chatted a bit in Chinese and then Liang Hui showed me a document in Chinese. "This is the letter from the doctor about your treatment and the hospital stay." She said. "I will translate it and bring it to you." She smiled and they both left.

Steve had asked for a letter stating that the hospitalization was required for ongoing treatment of the stroke. He was to present it to our insurance company in hopes that they would pay for the stay and part if not all of the treatments. We knew when I went that we were in virgin territory. If only the insurance company realized that the treatment here was as close to a cure as I had ever seen. The doctors here were convinced of a complete recovery and from their progress thus far I had to agree! The progress they have made in one week more than equals the progress I feel I've made since suffering the stroke.

This morning the nurses put new linens on my bed and housekeeping diligently cleaned the floor. I swear it's clean enough to eat off of. They finished their chores in rapid fashion giving me time to begin the process of going over my writings. I wanted to get them done so I could post them on the web for my kids to read. I write for my kid's sake. It allows them to feel they are apart of the therapy even though we're a great distance apart.

Today I was honored to be seen and treated by Dr. Shi, Dr. Han, Dr. Bian, and Dr Zhang. They were accompanied by several nurses and after some brief discussions, led by Dr Zhang reporting my earlier comments, the treatment began in earnest. They seemed to be using more needles on my face an outer thigh. When they were done all left but Dr. Zhang who pulled out, you guessed it, the box. We both had a good chuckle and then she leaned forward and started to hook me up.

"You are very kind." She said as she uncoiled the wires.

"You've done so much in such a short period of time." I replied, "I'm very excited and surprised"

All I could think of is the difference in just 1 short week. Besides she had the box! I smiled and chuckled as she connected the wires and I felt the now familiar pulsing of muscles as they contracted and relaxed. "20 minutes" she smiled and winked. "It is good if you sleep."

I think if she had suggested that 1 week ago I would have laughed in her face but the truth of the matter was that after the needles were inserted it was easy to forget they were even there. Sleep, I thought, is just what the doctor ordered and it sounds like a good idea. The nurse returned in 20 minutes and I was startled when I heard the knock on the door. I had gotten 20 minutes rest and it felt remarkably refreshing. Through gestures and words I managed to convey to the nurse that I wanted her to take a picture before she took the needles out. I think she thought it an odd request but she happily obliged. I must confess that the yellow and orange hospital garments are not exactly flattering. In fact they are not my color and make me look sick if not dead. I guess they'll do for now!

I expected Dr. Zhang would come and do my cupping treatment but I got almost an hour's reprieve before she came. The cupping was a chance for me to speak with Dr. Zhang, her English is really quite good. I think she was a bit hesitant to speak with me thinking her English was not that good. I commented on how good I thought it was and she has opened up and speaks to me more freely. She finished with the cupping treatment and told me that a man would come later today and bring a holter heart monitor. I must confess they are thorough and will make certain that they miss nothing.

I began writing again only to be interrupted by a knock at the door. It was Dr. Zhang. She was back and the man she spoke of accompanied her. I hadn't expected them until this afternoon, but no matter, now was as good a time as any. He pulled out the small monitor which was about 3x5 size and plugged in a cable that consisted of 7 wires each having a different color assigned to it that plugged into the 3x5 pack. On the other end of each cable was a corresponding colored snap. He attached an adhesive square to each of these wires and handed the pack to Dr. Zhang. She carefully located each of these squares to a spot surrounding my heart so that it could provide the correct feed to map out the electrical pattern of my heart. I would wear the monitor for 24 hours to provide them with a picture of a full day. With all the wires attached Dr Zhang stretched out the belt so I could sling the pack over my neck and right shoulder. "Done "she exclaimed as the pack was placed around my neck and arms, "24 hours, then we'll take it off."

"Okay" I replied having little choice in the matter, but I must say they hadn't taken a wrong step yet in my eyes. I retuned to writing as they departed. I only got three more sentences typed before my massage doctor walked in.

I must say I wasn't thrilled at the prospect of an hour of torture but I vowed to make the best of it. I suddenly realized that for the first time since the stroke I had an ease of turning my head that I hadn't felt before. I was determined to use this new mobility to my advantage and began watching in earnest as she held my arm and began to massage it briskly. I don't know quite how to describe it, almost like an out of body experience. Although I could now feel the movement of her hands it didn't quite connect in my head. It was at this moment that I began to sense something else, the pain or I should say the lack of it was hard to believe. Before this had been an exercise of wills, will I scream or will I keep silent.

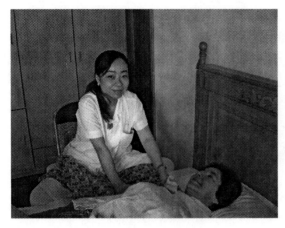

I could feel her and don't get me wrong the massage was intense and deep. But it didn't hurt.

I continued to watch in amazement as she continued down the arm and hand to the leg. No pain! This was wonderful, then I realized I spoke too soon. As soon as she reached the lower leg I thought I would go into orbit. The entire lower leg throbbed and felt as if it were being attacked by massive amounts of pins and needles. I don't think I have ever had a feeling so intense. She continued to massage the lower leg and I continued to writhe in pain silently. I knew that this was all part of the process but it seemed a high price to pay. Then again it is a little price to pay for having half your body back. When I was able to focus again I realized that the portions of the body to which feeling had been restored didn't have the level of "discomfort" that the lower leg, which was lacking almost all feeling still, had. I know it doesn't sound like much but it gave me a reason to endure the "discomfort" knowing that in time this too will improve.

She finished and for the first time really, I was thankful for the massage. I guess it is a small price to pay, but I would have preferred to skip this lesson in life. I got an hours worth of reprieve from people knocking but it ended too soon. This time the rap on the door was from Yu Lan, a very pleasant surprise. She had a copy of the expenses up to now. This was something that Steve was very interested in because we were stepping out in faith and venturing into non-insured territory. We had written a letter to a few asking for financial help from close friends, but most just wished us well and said I'd be in their thoughts and prayers. I guess that is the most important place to be... where God wants you.. looking to Him. Just then Dr Bian and Dr Zhang came for my afternoon treatment. Dr. Bian was particularly interested in how I was feeling and any changes that might have occurred since the morning session. Evidently the doctors had gotten together and come up with a plan for treatment. I would meet with another doctor this afternoon and begin rehab therapy tomorrow. We continued with the afternoon session and I felt that there was a greater number in my head, neck and face, than usual, but they had a plan and it seemed to be working very effectively. We finished with the needle placement and Yu Lan stayed to wait for the other doctor. We chatted through the entire 20 minutes, me talking through needles that bounced with every word and Yu Lan looking this whole time as if nothing out of the ordinary were starring her in the face. Actually I guess I was to one side! The nurse entered to remove the needles and chuckled as I smiled and needles in my face seemed to bounce in agreement. Yu Lan continued our conversation as the needles were removed only to pause when I used a word she didn't understand and she was forced to look it up. I felt her English was remarkable considering she had never stepped foot in the U.S.. Dr Zhang returned shortly with a short and intense doctor of some 35 years I thought. He immediately launched into a discussion with Dr Zhang and I soon determined that according to the gestures being made in my direction they must be discussing me. Yu Lan entered into the discussion and finally the Dr that I later learned was called Dr Yu grabbed my hands and said something to Yu Lan.

"He wants you to grab his fingers with your fists and keep him from moving your hands." She looked at me hoping I understood.

I grasped his two fingers that he extended with my right hand, then he extended his other hand and I obliged by grasping it too. He then began to twist his hands hoping to rotate mine or loose my grip. I held fast, this was a game and I have a very competitive nature, I don't like to lose! He smiled and I got a nod of approval. He spoke more with Yu Lan and she explained that he wanted to see me walk in a straight line. I laughed out loud.

"Do you understand the word drunk" I asked Yu Lan, "I look like one if I walk any distance."

She smiled, obviously not dissuaded by my comment. I proceeded to walk back and forth across the room. As I walked Dr Yu got excited we moved from the room to the hall where through Yu Lan he pointed out a path he wanted me to practice at least 30 minutes each day. He and Dr Zhang talked some more and he smiled and shook my hand. "He'll see you in therapy tomorrow at 2:00" she stated, "the nurse will take you to the second floor and I'll meet you there with Dr Yu."

"Great! I'm all for it." I replied. A change of scenery would be good I thought, if only for an hour each afternoon. As the doctors departed I headed into my room as Yu Lan made way for a nurse in the doorway.

"Looks like you're busy! I'll see you tomorrow" She said as she headed toward the elevator.

My hopes for a quiet afternoon were dashed again. They faithfully kept me busy each and every waking moment. The nurse was there to soak my hand and foot in herbs and it started out quietly enough. I figured I had a captive audience so I asked her to pronounce some Chinese words. Well one thing led to another and before you knew it we were both laughing. I was making my attempts at speaking Chinese and she was being diligent to teach me. She didn't speak much during the first few days but I have a feeling she won't be shy in the future. As she was drying my foot Da Gui arrived in the doorway a smile on her face and enthusiasm in her step. This had to be one of my favorite parts to the day, I was only sorry we had such a communication gap. It has forced me to add several statements to my vocabulary: "dong bu dong" - do you understand? , "dong le" – I understand, and "bu dong" – I don't understand, small, but very important phrases. She has gotten accustomed to massaging my hands while I soak for 10 minutes and I have found that I can tolerate it. I know that there are some things in life that we must bear, but someone has to do it and I'm glad it's me. She watched intently as I began a new "game" during massage time. I gingerly attempted to pick up AAA batteries and drop them into an ashtray using each of my fingers and thumb. It's a bit monotonous but good therapy. For fun I mix in a round of "pick up the business cards off the bed," after I scatter about a half dozen of them around. It keeps us both busy for the hour it takes for the foot massage and all the while we attempt to share simple phrases and ideas. The hour passes and before I know it Da Gui is exclaiming "finished".

I waved goodbye and lay quietly for the next 15 minutes just reflecting on the day. It had been a busy day but I felt like we had been accomplishing so much. I felt as if I had come so far, not only in distance but also in response to the treatments. The stroke, when it happened, took everything away in a matter of minutes. This treatment has reversed in a matter of days, what I had spent years trying to get. Amazing! Simply amazing! Dinner came and while eating I downloaded my mail hoping to get something to respond to. 42 pieces of junk mail and 3 real letters! I eagerly read my "real" mail after discarding the "last chances to buy Viagra" letters. Don't get me started when it comes to junk email... I'll never stop!

I logged on again to send responses to my mail and a weekly update. It's hard to believe its already been a week, so much has happened but with feeling returning and rehab beginning I guess I had better call it a day.

Tuesday June 22, 2004

Well it's a beautiful day a "xing tian" (sunny day) outside and I've got a sunny outlook on life! I cornered the nurses on their rounds today and was able to get a picture. I'll ask later for names. I know they have told me a dozen times but now I will have faces to go with the names! I got an unexpected call this morning from Steve and the kids; it was good to hear their voices. He moved a file onto the server for me to access. It's still unbelievable that I can access the computer in my home from here and update the information daily providing photos and movie files to my family on a daily basis. Elizabeth is going to set up another hotmail account, her old one has problems and Steve has agreed to help her. David is on his way to scout camp beginning this weekend and lasting for at least 7 days. He seems to be looking forward to it. Roy spent today cleaning. I guess it was raining out and he decided to clean the attic. He ran across the old roll of bills that my father had collected during WWII. I told him to ask dad about it and I was confident that Steve could provide him with an ample explanation. Steve said they would see Yiwei this weekend and all in all, everyone seemed to be getting along quite well. We completed our phone conversation and I finished my breakfast.

Liang Hui stopped in with the letter to the insurance company explaining my treatment and care. She was going to fax it back to Steve who would then in turn submit the bills as they came. We were definitely treading on new ground with them, seeking treatment in China. While we talked the nurse brought in a detailed bill for my first week. I looked at the paper and smiled, of course it was all in Chinese! Liang Hui went through it item by item so that I would understand; it listed medications, acupuncture treatments, lab tests, Ultrasound, MRI, massage and the room costs. We discussed it all to make certain that I understood. As we spoke Dr Bian entered the room. Both she and Liang spoke gesturing periodically in my direction. I was ushered back to my bed and the treatment session began. She started today by inserting a needle into my right hip. My leg came alive and she smiled confidently. " She's very good at that." I said to Liang Hui, who gave me a perplexed look. "I mean hitting what she looking for at the first try." I continued.

With that Dr Bian gave a chuckle, she obviously understood my comment, and continued with placing the needles. I closed my eyes as she approached my face and only opened them when I felt her at my foot. I looked up at the ceiling, peering as it were through an abundance of needles, resembling a small forest from my perspective, and then lowered my gaze to observe Yang Dong Mei, the head nurse, giving me an understanding look. (I made a point of asking for all the nurses names after I took their picture this morning. It helped to have a guide to learn by!) Dr Bian finished the insertions and I was left to rest for the prescribed 20 minutes. I was surprised not to see Dr Zhang or to have the "box" attached but I enjoyed the rest. A short while passed and I heard the door open and saw that it was Zhang Quan. She tried to hide her feelings but we both laughed out loud as soon as I saw her gaze at my face. "Many needles." She said, as she began the process of removing them. She ran her fingers gently through my hair to make certain that she hadn't missed any. I smiled as she quickly pulled the needles from my arm and hand and moved to my leg. When she finished I couldn't resist the urge I had to stretch. I extended my arm and stretched my toes. It felt remarkably strange to "feel" something as the muscled stretched out with my slow and very intentional movement. My entire lower leg was beginning to itch and the heel of my foot felt decidedly strange. I wish I could come up with a better explanation but strange will have to do for now. Just when I felt I could snuggle up to my computer, Dr Zhang came in smiling with the tray of glass cups.

"Fun?" I asked sarcastically.

"Fun!" She replied, with a smile glowing brightly on her face.

She applied the cups and the 5 minutes they remained in place seemed to go rather quickly. The nurse returned to remove the cups and as she entered she pushed a small metal cart in front of her. From my vantage point I couldn't see quite what was on it. She quickly removed the cups and as I rolled onto my back I could clearly see a small EKG machine perched on top of the cart. I looked at her and then motioned to the "holter" monitor that I still had attached to me, did she really intend to hook me up and get a reading with the other wires in place? She smiled and nodded, I guess that means yes. It was a little tricky getting all the wires in position but she did it. I motioned to her that I wanted to see the strip of tape before she added it to my chart. She kindly obliged and I peered at the tape, p wave… qrs complex… t wave… yup! I look okay on paper! Having been a paramedic one of the things I got good at was reading EKG's, looking at my own was something of a treat. She left me in utter silence as she wheeled the cart and its contents out.

I got to enjoy 30 minutes of writing before the next knock came. It was time for massage therapy and something that I regretted just days before I now looked forward to with a great deal of admiration. As she began my shoulder seemed a bit tender. I closed my eyes as I tried to map out the location of her fingertips in my brain. Her hands moved quickly, up and down my arm, thrusting her fingers into each muscle as I kept trying to place the location in my head. It became kind of a game to see if I could mentally map it before she moved on. Her hands never touched my skin; she kept a cloth in between us at all times. Her rhythm was constant and the speed with which she kept one hand moving and the cloth in place was astounding. I could continually hear the cloth snap into place as she held it steady, keeping my arm and hand covered at all times. She rapidly rotated my arm, first the inside aspect then the outside, all without missing a beat. The massage almost became hypnotic as she continued, 10 minutes, then 20, and finally 30 minutes passed when at last she quickly moved the cloth to my leg. This had been the part of the massage I dreaded, I knew my leg was still somewhat numb and the massage here would be more painful. The feelings that I had were not as bad as I had anticipated. This meant the leg was beginning to respond to treatments. The massage, however, was not pain free. As she worked on the lower leg the battle to keep silent raged in my head. Finally it was time for me to roll on my side, at last the worst was over. It was only a few minutes more and she flicked the cloth on the bed. "Finished" She said.

"Xia, xia (thank you)" I replied.

The morning ended with a short lunch and I lay down to take a short nap. I got to rest today until 2:00 then everything got busy. I went with to the second floor rehab unit with Chu Jia Qi. We met Dr Yu there, whom I had seen the previous day. He introduced me to the nurse and took me to a table to literally try my hand at several of their games. After seeing me at work he began to outline a regimene of therapy. I was to be there a total of 1-hour, 20 minutes at the first station and 10 minutes at each of 4 other stations. The rehab unit was not air-conditioned and I was getting hot, the doctors insisted that my pulse and BP be taken and I assured them that other than being hot I felt fine. They seemed convinced and I was allowed to proceed to the other stations to learn

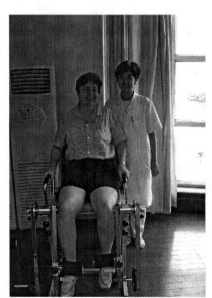

each therapy. We continued on with the stationary bike, weights, and hand exercises.

They were all very similar to the rehab treatments I had received in the U.S but this time my extremities had feeling. I felt like a fish out of water, with each task my brain had to account for feelings that I hadn't experienced in years! I had learned to do many of these same tasks but using sight and not touch to accomplish the job. I thought it would be easy to jump right in were I had left off almost 3 years ago. Boy, did I have some learning ahead of me. I have often been quoted as saying, "It's not what you know that matters, but what you are willing to learn!" I was being forced to learn all over again things that I thought I knew. These feelings of sensations that used to be commonplace were now as foreign to me as I was an American in China. We finished with my tour of rehab only to have it decided that I would come at 8:00 a.m. to make better use of the cool of the morning. With that, Yu Lan, who joined me as my translator in rehab, escorted me back to my room. We chatted on the way and I mentioned that today was the first day I had been out of my room walking and that I was a bit dizzy but that was normal for me.

"Did you tell the doctors?" She asked, her concern showed on her face.

"No, I haven't seen them yet this afternoon." I said.

I could tell she was rather concerned and sure enough as soon as we got back to my room she headed down the hall to find one of the doctors. It wasn't long before I felt like I had a medical convention in my room. Dr Bian, and Dr Zhang accompanied by Yang Dong Mei ,Zhing Quan, Yu Lan and a female Dr whom I hadn't yet met. I moved from the bed to the chair where I always receive my afternoon treatment. Dr Bian smiled and uttered a gentle " Ni Hao" and then began intently talking to the group. Yang Dong Mei held the small metal tray of needles and passed several to Dr Bian as she placed them carefully about my head and neck. Just then Yu Lan leaned forward, "The doctor wants to know how you have been feeling after the needles are taken out."

"Fine, really good, I mean almost normal.' I replied, " It seems to wear off a bit but the feeling lasts longer each time." I looked at them as they all continued to speak around me. Finally I looked at Yu Lan who had glanced in my direction and asked, who is the doctor next to you. Yu Lan grinned, realizing I had no idea who this person was. "Professor Han" She replied.

"Han Lasuhi?" I restated in my best Chinese. With this Professor Han smiled broadly and Dr Bian chuckled and said something to her. They all seemed to be impressed that at least I was making an attempt to learn a little of their language. The treatment ended and the procession of people left with the exception of Yu Lan. She stayed and talked for a bit and only left when Zhing Quan came in to do my soaks. Zhing Quan was petite and quiet and I was certain that the bucket filled with water for my soaks weighed more than she did. We chatted in broken English and my feeble attempts at Chinese. I found out that she is 24, married a year in May, and has a friend studying in New York. Not bad considering it took the full 30 minutes to find that all out! As we were conversing a knock came at the door, it was Da Gui. Seems I was just finishing one soak to start another! Da Gui filled her tub and I moved from the chair and placed my feet into the hot solution. Boy it felt good, almost too good. Da Gui reached forward, as was now her custom, and grabbed my right hand. She began to massage it, cupping it and rolling it in her palm, applying a steady but firm pressure. I felt her grasp my forearm and pull it towards her releasing it slowly as she worked her fingers down my arm. First the left and then the right. Soon it was time for the foot massage and she dried off each of my feet as she rotated them, placing them on the clean towel. I remember telling her I had a busy day, "wo hen mang", and she said "ni hen lai". That's the last thing I remember! I woke up with a start as I heard the phone ringing. Who could that be I thought. I looked at the clock, it was passed 6:00 and I had been neatly tucked under a blanket my foot massage most evidently complete. I reached for the phone and uttered and unsure, "hello?"

"Mom, is that you?" came the reply. It was JinWei. This was a pleasant surprise.

"How are you?" I asked.

"Oh mom, I had my surgery today" she moaned, "and I can't use my eyes for a week." I could tell she was not pleased about the wait time before she could be out and about. As a teenager with energy to burn I could tell this was not on her top 10 lists of fun things to do. I commiserated with her and shared my progress and reassured I wasn't going anywhere and she could feel free to call while she was recuperating. She had to go eat dinner and mine was waiting too.

I finished supper and used the evening time to write and go online for emails. The last thing I did was update the web before hitting the hay. I have a feeling that tomorrow will be a busy day too!

10

Light Ahead

Wednesday June 23, 2004

Another sunny day, and the first using my new schedule. I got up and bathed, being careful to keep my right ear dry. Oh yeah, I forgot to mention that on top of everything else that happened yesterday after-

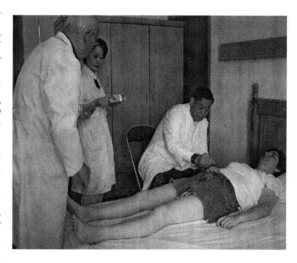

noon, Dr Zhang placed a series of small needles with seeds on the inside aspect of my right outer ear. It was really quite fascinating, I will ask today to make certain but after all the treatments yesterday my balance seems much improved and the dizziness that I seem to always have has diminished

Zhang Quan was in early this morning to bring my morning medicines and check my blood pressure.

"Normal" She said smiling. "You always smile, happy? She asked.

"Happy!" I replied. I would have loved to have shared with her the feelings of frustration and doubt that I had experienced prior to making this trip but she couldn't understand me on that level. I did chuckle inside to myself. You learned early on after a severe stroke to laugh at yourself and your circumstances or you would spend countless hours each day crying. The loss that you experience is immediate and devastating and you are taught to be happy with anything that returns. I have been so conditioned to set my expectations low that the results I have experienced here make me positively giddy. There is no way that I can express the joy and happiness that I feel welling up inside me every day. I don't think even my husband could understand it; only another stroke survivor who had experienced the loss could begin to comprehend the gift I feel I have been given.

I am, as I write, sitting on my bed and tucking my right leg beside me. Sounds simple, huh? It's something I wouldn't have ever dreamed I could do again, and what's more, I feel the muscle burn as it stretches. Listen to me, "I feel", that's so foreign to me; I've spent the past 3 years trapped in numbness and pain. I'm like a kid in a candy shop, I don't know where to start. Each morning when I wake up I want to pinch myself, and on my right side no less, to make certain this isn't a dream.

Breakfast came and I thought I'd play a little game: how much egg can we get in the mouth. I positioned the fork in my right hand and attempted to stab the scrambled eggs on the plate before they escaped off the side. This game is one I have played countless times over the past several years, only to have no success and finally revert to using the left hand. To my surprise and apparent indignation I caught it! I have egg on my fork! Now for the tough part, raising the hand to the mouth. You must understand that since the stroke my hand is… spastic, meaning… I lack a lot of the fine motor control and as a result I experience tremors. When raising a sharp object, such as a fork, towards the face I am putting myself in mortal danger and jeopardy. I mean I could poke an eye out. I took a deep breath and began, slowly, slowly, just a little bit further… Yes! Success at last, and on the first try! Too bad there was no one to take a picture, I mean I could have been there with literal egg on my face. Well I did it once but could I repeat the feat?

Not only did I repeat it, I ate the whole meal with my right hand. Okay, so it was only one scrambled egg, at least I did it. To the average Joe citizen this isn't something to get excited about, but to a stroke survivor this is headline news. I looked at the clock and it was almost 8:00. Soon my nurse would show up to escort me to rehab.

Rehab was a lot cooler in the morning; I started out seated at a small inclined table. In front of me on the table was a square board with circular holes cut onto it. Into each hole was a 1" piece of wooden dowel that was approximately 4" long. One end of the peg was painted red. My task was to remove the pegs with my right hand, place them on the table and then place them back into the holes. No problem! I had mastered this game with 1/4" dowels at home. Little did I know that having feeling in my hands would cause such a dramatic and undesired reaction? Upon trying to touch the pegs I found my hand returning to its spastic and uncontrollable state. It seemed the harder I tried the more difficult it became to grasp the pegs. The nurse with me kept saying slower, slower, of course she was also the one with the watch who was timing me. I was determined to get hold of just one peg, so I took a deep breath and concentrated. I could feel the sweat building on my brow as I focused on the peg. Thumb, middle finger, pointer finger... that's it... slowly now squeeze... got it! I gently lifted the peg out of the hole and... oops... dropped it on the floor. At least I held it for a couple of seconds anyway! The peg had felt strange in my hand, another out of body experience where the brain was obviously on a 10 second delay. After a bit of practice I slowly adapted to "feeling" the peg. It wasn't all there yet but I felt like I as making progress. It's hard to be patient when you see such dramatic results, I wanted it all back as quickly as I had lost it, but they told me it would take 3 months to return to normal. Now I was beginning to comprehend all that would have to take place in that time. It meant a lot of hard work ahead on my part. I mastered the peg game and quickly moved on to what has got to be the most boring type of rehab there is. I got to push a 6" x 6" block of wood 1"thick with a dowel handle stuck in the middle, up and down and up and down and up and down and up and down and...monotonous huh... get the picture. This went on for 10 minutes. I could feel the muscles in my right shoulder starting to burn. There I go again talking about feeling again, and it was a strange sensation. Although I knew I kept busy since the stroke and still tried to do much of what I'd done before the stroke, it was becoming strikingly obvious that there were a great number of muscles I hadn't used in the same way. I was experiencing aches and pains I never dreamed were possible.

I finally graduated to the leg lift machine where I sat with my ankles behind foam guards. As I extended my legs I lifted a weight. I'd seen similar machines in our YMCA prior to the stroke. I sat and was told to alternate between the two legs making certain that I held the leg in an extended position for 2-5 seconds. This seemed easy at first but my right leg soon tired and it became more difficult. I did sets of ten with rests in between. Before I knew it I was finished with that exercise and led to yet another weight training machine. Here I was to sit and grasp the handlebars and pull the rope down beside me while rotating each wrist as I pulled , maintaining balance and pulling with the left and right hands equally. Seemed easy enough, but in practice it was difficult to maintain a good grip with the right hand and extremely hard to keep both hands pulling at the same rate. I was intent on doing the exercise right and before I knew it Chu Jia Qi was waiting to take me back. I thanked the rehab staff and began the trek back to my room. As we entered the waiting room I saw a large crowd gathered and starring intently at something on the floor. As we approached a saw that it was an old man who was being attended to by a nurse. Normally I would have been wary of passing through such a crowd, fearing I would stumble or fall into the crowd, but today I felt remarkably steady and passed through the group without incident, even while being pushed from people behind me. We got back to the room and I immediately went to the bed to remove my shoes, I've only been here a week and already I'm adopting their customs. I arose to go into the bathroom and managed to get all the way to the door when I was greeted by Hong Wen Mei and a blood pressure cuff. I spun around and headed to the bed where she checked my pressure. Normal! No sooner had she finished then Dr Bian walked through the doorway (I really need to look into a revolving door). She was followed closely by Yang Dong Mei who immediately began to prepare me for treatment.

"Hello" said Dr Bian in her best English tone. "How do you feel today?"

"Great" I replied, ""Rehab went good and I don't have any dizziness."

I looked at her carefully making certain she had understood me. She smiled and repeated' "No dizziness?"

"No, ma yao." I responded.

It was obvious she had understood me and was happy for how well rehab had gone. I was pleased, I knew that Yang Dong Mei understood only a little English, and it was apparent from Dr Bian's conversation with her that she was telling her what I said. The treatment continued and I dozed off while waiting before the needles came out. I awoke when Hong Wen Mai tapped me gently on the shoulder. She removed the needles and suggested I rest. I took her advice, stretched out and observed the construction of the school across the road.

I had only been watching for a short while when Dr Zhang entered carrying her now familiar tray of cups. "I missed you." I said as I rolled onto my left side and pulled a pillow up under my right arm. "

"Missed me?" She queried.

"Yes you weren't with Dr Bian for my treatment." I informed her.

"Busy." She said with a smile. She spoke much more openly with me and I think I passed her communication test. Meaning even if her English lacked a bit, I seemed to understand and welcome it. She applied the cups and left for the standard 5 minutes. After she returned and began to remove the cups from the lower leg it started to itch intensely. She stopped and looked at it and the smiled. "Good" She said, "Dr Bian and I should be back at 2:00."

With that she left and I sat up and began jotting down the events of the day.

I got an unexpected break in the routine until 3:15 this afternoon so I used the time to catch up on a few emails and write a bit. I even tried my right hand on typing. It was slow and tedious but I was able to hit individual keys. I can hardly wait to be a two handed typist again.

At 3:15 we started with the afternoon session of acupuncture followed by a 30 minute wait before the nurse returned. I've actually gotten to the point of cat napping while the needles are in. Dr Bian said they work best if I am relaxed, I don't know if I can get much more relaxed than sleeping. Hong Wen Mei returned shortly after removing the needles this time with the bucket of water filled with the herb solution. We spoke in broken English and Chinese, attempting to communicate. I learned a bit more about her and she was able to learn more about my family. We finished up the treatment just in time as Dr Zhang entered the room she was there to provide the "torture" treatment as I jokingly call it. A small hike device that is all black is used, the handle is thin metal making it flexible and one side of the "hammer" is covered with fine needles. It is moved very rapidly back and forth across the skin bouncing as it were and making small pinpricks in the skin. Dr Zhang informed me that to an individual who has feeling this would be excruciating, but to someone such as myself who feels only numbness there is no pain. I could sense that she was doing something but I didn't know exactly what. It wasn't until she finished that I got a look at her handiwork on my leg.

"I looked like a piece of tenderized meat." I proclaimed

"It stimulates blood flow and feeling." She said, as she cleaned the metal hammer with alcohol. Just then Da Gui entered the room and spoke with Dr Zhang; I could tell they were talking about me. I understood the word sleep in Chinese and decided they were talking about yesterday and my falling asleep during the foot massage. Sure enough Dr Zhang smiled and said it was good to rest during and after the treatments.

Da Gui then asked, "Ni hen lai?" (Are you very tired?)

"No, Mei yoa." I replied. I felt terrible about falling asleep yesterday, but according to the Dr that was a good thing to do. We continued with the foot soak as Dr Zhang left. As was now her habit Da Gui removed the watch from my left wrist and placed salve on her hands. She grasped my left hand in her hands and it amazed me watched as they slid over my knuckles and she pulled my hand forcefully towards her. If I wasn't secure in my seat on the bed I think she would have pulled me off. I was taken back with how much power this little 5' petite-framed woman could wield. She continued up the forearm working the muscles deeply. As she came back to the wrist she flipped my hand back and forth like a rag doll, before proceeding on to the hand. She carefully worked to muscles and tendons, I could feel her as she followed the path of each bone, stopping and applying pressure at various points on my hand. She vigorously pulled each finger and I heard a pop as her fingers released mine. It wasn't my joint as I originally expected but her own fingers as they snapped together. The massage was rough and ret relaxing, she gently placed my left hand on my left thigh and began the process all over again. It was hard to stay awake, the process, while

168

rough, was methodical and relaxing. I found myself drifting and had to catch myself as I nearly fell asleep.

With the hand massage completed and the foot soak finished it was time for the foot massage. She applied the same care and skill as first she dried off each foot and placed them on the clean cloth before her. I guess I hadn't paid attention before but she was continually adding salve to her hands to provide lubrication between them and my feet. I settled back and put in a DVD, not paying attention to what it was. I was surprised when the Disney logo appeared and it announced that it was "Freaky Friday". Oh well, I thought a bit of humor to end the day! I could handle the antics of Jamie Lee Curtis and Lindsay Lohan, if fact they were a good diversion from reality. Da Gui remarked DVD as the movie began to play. She continued the massage without interruption and before I realized it she was done. I paused the DVD as she pulled a blanket over my feet and tucked it up gently under my arms.

"Rest" She said.

I thanked her as she smiled turned and uttered her bye bye. Alone at last I snuggled up under my blanket and finished the movie. When it was over I decided to call JinWei to see how she was doing after her surgery. After only two rings she answered her cell phone,

Way" She tentatively replied.

"Hi" I said. Hoping she would recognize the voice.

"Oh it's you mom," she exclaimed, "I couldn't see the number, well I'm not supposed to look."

I could tell by the sound of her voice that she was not enjoying her recuperative phase. "I'm so bored mom." She said, a downcast tone in her usual energetic demeanor.

"I'm sorry!" I replied, "I wish I could make it all better."
I don't quite know why but we, as moms always want to
make things better. There she was at home with her real
mother and I still wanted to reach out and help. JinWei and
I had become very close over the past 2 years and I felt as if
she felt free to confide in me.

"You're bored too, aren't you?" came her inquisitive
response.

"That's why I called, to fill the time and check on you."
I replied.

We continued talking for at least 30 minutes, she paused
and uttered something in Chinese and I knew she was
talking with her mother. I gave up long ago trying to hear
words that I recognized when she spoke to her mother, they
used a Changsha dialect that didn't even seem to resemble
Mandarin Chinese. I was content to pause my conversation
long enough for her to respond to the question. We finished
our conversation and I promised to call back in a few days
to make certain she was surviving.

I stretched back after my call to JinWei and pulled the
computer close. I began to hammer out more of the day's
activities when the phone came to life. Now who could that
be, I thought, its after 10 in China and only 9 a.m. in the
states. "Hello?" I said as I cautiously answered the phone.

"Well how are you missy?" came the reply. It could only
be one person, Carolyn, and what an unexpected joy to hear
her voice.

"I just got off the phone with JinWei." I continued.

"Well you were talking to somebody, it took me over 15
minutes to get through!" she chastened. It was good to talk
with her, she had a dozen questions and her number one was
"how are you I doing?"

"I'm great" I related, "they're taking real good care of me and fixing me to boot. It's downright miraculous!"

"It is!" she exclaimed, "you and that angel I sent with you are going to be pretty busy sharing all that has happened when you get back."

Not wanting to add weight to my luggage, Carolyn had given me a small pewter angel before I had left on my journey. "God will be looking out for you!" she had said. I had tucked it in my fanny pack during the trip and now it resided on my bedside table. It served as an ever-present reminder of God's daily faithfulness. I got in the habit of placing it in my pocket when I went to rehab, a reminder that I never go anywhere alone.

"People will either believe or make excuses," I continued, "I can already hear them, 'you didn't have a real stroke', 'your right side wasn't really numb for 3 years' or 'you were always going to get better, this just made it happen sooner.' People who want to doubt will doubt."

"But its well documented" she stated.

"I know, but I'm prepared for the nay sayer" I concluded.

We continued our chat and then Carolyn said she had to go so she could call back another time. We parted over the phone but I know I am in her thoughts and prayers daily. Knowing that people care is the one thing that makes each day possible. Hearing from them even if it is a simple, 'Hi thinking of you!' email brings tremendous comfort. It's like having a cheering section at a ball game. When you are on the court you block out all the negative input and feedback but you can hear even one voice if it's cheering you on!

I typed a bit more and as I look at the clock I'd better call it a night, it's getting late and I'm certain that tomorrow will be a busy day.

Thursday June 24, 2004

Today began quietly enough, the subtle sounds of traffic that grew as the sun began to rise. I've learned to enjoy this solitude before the day officially begins. Yang Dong Mei brought my medications and checked my blood pressure today. "Good!" was all she said as she took off the cuff.

I've learned to play another little game of 'pick up the pills' with my right hand, it takes a while to catch them, but it is good therapy. Before I would often resign myself to placing a pill in my right hand and putting it in my mouth. It always felt like an artificial limb, something that didn't belong, that was shoving a pill at me. Now I can begin to close my eyes and feel the pill. I also no longer have that artificial limb thing going on.

Rehab was exhilarating to say the least! I started out at the table with the pegs and spent time practicing slowly grabbing and moving the pegs in and out of the holes. I then progressed to the lower leg lift machine where I got to learn how to count to ten in Chinese. I did 10 repetitions of 10 lifts each. I was able to convince the student that helped me to stop and let me take her picture, she agreed but only if I would take a picture with the two of us. I agreed and those are the pictures I've included on today's update. I moved on to the upper arm strength machine, She wanted me to do 25 repetitions. I was only lifting 1 pound so this was quite easy. Then we progressed to the stationary bike, "20 minutes she said!"

"20?" I repeated.

"20!" She affirmed.

This was going to take some doing. 20 minutes is a lot of time and she had upped the resistance on the bike so it was more challenging. I began slowly and got into a rhythm, this wouldn't be so bad I thought. About halfway into my routine the two American students I had met earlier in the week appeared. They stopped by and chatted. It was nice to have people that spoke English. I hadn't realized how little I had actually said during the past week until I had a chance to be fully understood. It definitely gave me a deep appreciation for what the exchange students feel. We talked about what they were learning and my progress thus far. We parted vowing to see each other again as the days went by.

The student I had gotten to know asked how she could get a copy of the picture. I suggested I email it to her and when she had difficulty remembering her email address, I gave her mine.

"Just send a message and I'll reply with the picture." I told her.

Email certainly has made life easy! I finished my workout on the bike and was starting to drip at the forehead. Pulse was only 130 and BP only 145/85. Not bad for an out of shape, overweight, female over 40! I could lie and say I'm in shape, trim and only 29 but who am I trying to fool? My goal is to drop 30+ pounds and get back in shape here; it helps to only have healthy food and a forced exercise program! I took a well-earned rest and saw Chu Jia Qi come through the door. I grabbed my water bottle and we headed back to my room.

With sweat dripping from my brow I thought I'd go in the bathroom and splash some cold water on my face. I made it as far as the door when the nurse entered and said acupuncture. I hurried and grabbed a towel, as I turned I was greeted by a man bearing a striking resemblance to one I'd seen on the hospitals website. He led quite an entourage of doctors and nurses. I said "ni hao" and he smiled and said "hello". I was ushered to my bed to begin the treatment and he began speaking to the doctors surrounding the bed.

Dr Bian leaned forward and said, "How do you feel?"

"A bit tired after my exercise but good" I replied

"Dizzy?" she asked.

"No" I affirmed.

"How do you feel?" The man who was now seated beside me repeated the question, trying out the words, "how do you feel?" He smiled as he repeated the words and then said something to Dr Bian as he inserted a needle into my wrist. He then rotated my arm out at 90 degrees to my body and the nurse held it as he placed a second needle.

"Ooo" I said as I felt a jolt run down my arm.

"Electricity!" Dr Bian said as she looked at the doctor seated beside me.

"Electricity?" He repeated the word several times "Electricity!" he nodded and preceded to my face. He was very fast and very good, I felt very little as each needle found its mark. It wasn't until he tapped and spun each of them that I could feel their combined affect. As he was busy placing needles in my face I could feel Dr Bian placing needles on my leg and foot. It was hard to keep up with it all. They finished and he smiled and turned to leave.

"Okay?" I heard Dr Bian ask.

"Okay!" I replied.

Dr Zhang stayed and began to connect the "box" and as she worked I asked, "Who was that doctor?"

"Professor Han Jingxan," she answered, "the president of the First Teaching Hospital of Tianjin University of Traditional Chinese Medicine."

"Ohh!" I replied, as it became clear who it was that gave me my day's treatment. I must confess that at a teaching hospital in the U.S. you usually expect to get residents and interns not the president himself! I had been seen by every leading physician they had and they all had come to the same conclusion, they could restore me to normal. Of course my husband, relatives, and close friends will tell you I've never been normal, but you get the idea.

I laid there quietly reflecting on the doctor's consensus and diagnosis. Unbelievable was my only thought; I kept waiting for someone to disagree but they had apparently gone all the way to the top and were still in agreement, I could be fixed. As I continued in this thought I slowly drifted off to sleep. I awoke as the nurse was removing the needles and immediately behind her was Dr Zhang with the familiar cups. She applied them and then asked if she could take my lunch order because I was gone when the girl stopped by to get them. This was far and above the call of duty, but most appreciated nonetheless. She went to phone the order in when she discovered the cord was broken.

"Oh," I replied, "I forgot. They need to fix that."

"It's okay.," she said as she headed down the hall to the nurses station.

She had no sooner left than a rap came at the door and a man entered to put a new end on the phone cable. He clipped off the old broken connecter and crimped on a new one. By the time Dr Zhang returned to remove the cups, he had left and the phone was fixed.

I was not to get a break today. As Dr Zhang left a new girl entered to give me my body massage. Her technique was much gentler and I had a hard time staying awake during what was a very relaxing massage. I later learned her name was Wang Rui when she wrote it down before she headed out. I seriously thought I was done for the morning when Hong Wen Mei appeared in the door smiling. Why did I get the feeling that I'd been had! She asked if I was ready for the hand and foot soaks, "mei wen ti," or "no problem" translated of course! She prepared the bucket containing the hot water and herbs and I thrust my hand into it.

"Hot?" she inquired.

"Just right" I replied, quickly realizing I used words she might not understand. "Okay!" I said as I corrected myself.

We chatted in broken Chinese and English as was becoming our habit. I pulled out my translator, which helped us over a great number of verbal hurdles. I learned she had a seven-y ear old son who was learning English in school and when she was helping him she was learning at the same time. I encouraged her to bring him by and I would speak to him in English and give him some first hand experience. The soaks seemed to finish too quickly; I was enjoying our conversation, or at least the attempt.

Lunch came and for the first time in days I was actually hungry, I devoured it quickly and then debated writing for a bit. A nap won out in the mental battle for supremacy and for the first time sine I arrived I felt, if uninterrupted, I might catch a few zzz's.

It was almost 2:30 when I awoke with a start. I could have sworn I heard a knock at the door; sure enough it was Dr Zhang.

"Sleeping?" she asked.

"Just a little nap." I replied.

"Good!" she said smiling.

Dr Bian was close on Dr Zhang's heels and smiled broadly as she entered the room.

"How are you feeling? You had sleep?" she asked.

"I'm feeling great, energetic." I answered.

"Energetic?" she asked.

"Strong, clear. Lots of energy." I stated.

"Good!" was her reply.

She began at the back of my neck and seemed to place a number of needles in my head, face and neck before moving on to my right arm and hand. I had gotten very accustomed to the afternoon treatments that were always done with me seated in a chair, my right hand and arm resting on a pillow propped up on the arm of the chair. After the needles were placed I waited for Dr Bian's final questions for the day before she departed. I was not quite prepared for what she asked.

"I want to learn more English," she said, "would you teach me?"

Without hesitation I replied, "Yes! Certainly."

"30 minutes each day?" she inquired.

"That's fine. Yes!" I answered.

Both she and Dr Zhang seemed pleased. I felt it was the least I could do. After all she is giving me my life back! I thought that was enough excitement for one day, but no, she had one more question. She struggled with the words; then Dr Zhang said, "Go out". It appeared that Dr Bian wanted me to accompany herself and Dr Zhang out on Sunday, food and shopping as Dr Zhang put it. I'd be a fool to say no, so I heartily agreed. Then they chatted again in Chinese and seemed to be struggling to find a word. By the gestures that Dr Zhang was making I came to the conclusion it was wheelchair. They were concerned that I would need a wheel chair. I assured them that for this day I would be okay. With that they were both pleased and headed on their way.

It never ceases to amaze me how God works it mysterious ways. I guess I shouldn't be surprised... just enjoy it! 3o minutes passed and Hong Wen Mei returned to remove the needles.

"You are going out Sunday," she asked "with Dr Bian?"

"Yes." I replied.

Well, it seemed the nurses were informed that I'd be skipping out of the hospital on Sunday. I was looking forward to it. What had me concerned was what English Dr Bian wanted to learn, conversational or professional or both? I called JinWei on her cell phone to ask her if she had any tips to what I had taught her. She vowed to think on it and let me know.

I had only an hour before Da Gui showed up so I used it effectively to write. It always seems my mind thinks so much faster than one hand can type,,, I'll be thankful when I can use two handsagain. Da Gui showed up on time just as I was having a prolonged and fruitless discussion with the nurses about bath time. They want me to bath when a nurse is available to get me in and out of the tub – 6:00 p.m. I want to bathe at 5:00 a.m. and don't feel I need the nurse...I've been bathing by myself for over 2 years now. After a call from the translator on duty I assured him that I would bathe at 6:00 with the nurses and speak with the doctors tomorrow.

What are the Chinese words for "pain in the butt," because in these matters I know I am. Da Gui waited patiently as I spoke with the nurses and resolved the situation for tonight.

I soaked and Da Gui massaged. We began our conversation with me repeating words I was trying to learn, she either corrected me or uttered, "hen hao." We then developed a new game where each of the toes on my right foot assume a Chinese number 1 through 5, I would close my eyes and see if I could accurately identify the toe that Da Gui was working on. It made the time go quickly and taught me my numbers while helping me to focus on the awakening part of my body. The time passed quickly and before I knew it Da Gui was saying goodbye and I was headed to a bath.

Bathing was, as I expected, without incident. Dinner was fast and all I could think of was finishing my writing and going to bed. One final login and I call it a night.

Friday June 25, 2004

This morning I woke up at 4:30. It's so quiet, it's hard to believe a city of 10 million people can be so silent one minute and bustling with activity the next. I am perched watching a job site below, it looks so immaculate from this height, with everything neatly in it's place. It is almost 5 now and people are beginning to mill about the job site. I can hear the sounds of traffic in the distance and now a bus moves steadily down the street. It seems as if someone turned on a spigot somewhere in the distance and the people are slowly flowing in. I sit way up here above it watching as it all lays out below. The city is remarkably short, considering its size. Most of the buildings are only 6 stories (6 lo) tall. As I sit in the 12th floor surveying the city I am in one of the tallest buildings in sight.

It should be interesting to see what the day brings. I have been evaluating my body this morning and the arm and face feel remarkably normal, its not until I get to my hand that I really detect a definite difference. Although feeling has been restored it still feels awkwardly heavy and clumsy. Considering the number of nerve endings and sensors in the hand it should be more than interesting as they "wake up" after years of inactivity. My upper leg, with the exception of a narrow strip up the back feels remarkably "normal." The lower leg is still resisting the process of coming alive. It seems to move okay, it just lacks fine feeling and a definite heaviness still seems to encase it. The bottom of my foot seems alive with activity the sensations run rampant, from seemingly normal in the arch to almost total numbness on the right outside aspect. I imagine I'm a physicians dream or nightmare when it comes to my nervous system.

It's almost 5:30 and the work sites as well as the street below are buzzing with activity. The day is beginning here as well; I can hear the sounds of people milling about. Unlike American hospitals, relatives here are encouraged to stay. Beds are brought in and they provide the patient both with an advocate and a support mechanism all in one. You can see beds and wheelchairs being taken from floor to floor, pushed by family members. The elevators are a bit congested at times but everyone seems to work well together. This would probably be a lawyer's dream of a potential for lawsuits… but there aren't any and people take a remarkable sense of responsibility upon themselves. It's all rather refreshing. I feel bad for having to use a nurse's time to escort me to rehab. Maybe when Rosalie or JinWei visit, they will allow them to act as escorts and guides. Everyone here has been so kind and are overly cautious when it comes to my stability. I've tried to explain the concept of "Weebles" to the… you know, "Weebles" wobble but they don't fall down. I am much the same. As unsteady as I might seem, in three years since the stroke I have only fallen once, and that was after I was home 3 days and tripped over my own shoelaces. I now wear Velcro thank you.

I am trying something a bit different before rehab. I am trying to tire out the shoulder muscle by extending it and holding it for a period of several minutes and repeating this several times. We'll see if that affects the peg game. The nurse has come and gone all ready and I'm just waiting for breakfast before heading off to rehab. I have to remember to find out if they have a scale so I can keep track of my weight. It would be a wonderful benefit if I could drop a few pounds while I'm here!

You know, I just finished "the pill game" and drank my morning medicine and I think I can honestly say that it tastes like really bad prune juice. As a kid I would have gagged, as an adult I've come to the conclusion it must be good for me because it tastes so bad! It definitely motivates me to brush my teeth; Dr Urbanoski & Foster (my dentists) take note, that's one way to get people to brush! I don't suggest it though.

I was just reading my morning email: 24 pieces of junk and 2 count them 2 actual letters. I'll compose my letters off line and paste and send them later when I go online. I do try and reply to each email within a day. When I can type two handed I'll reply on the spot!

Rehab started out on the bike today, 20 minutes is a long time I think I'll bring my mp3 player along next time to keep me company. I rapidly progressed to the leg lift machine and then the arm pulleys. I focused on duplicating what the left hand was doing. After all, it looked easy! I rediscovered that looks are indeed deceiving and what appears to be very simple is… but simple and easy are two different concepts.

It was simple enough, there were only a few motions: down, slowly rotate, pull, hold, rotate and return. My left hand had no problem following and completing these steps. The right hand, however, was a different matter. I could pull and return but slowly rotating was not in my vocabulary. I jerked the hand and turned it rapidly, it seemed it would take time to make the hand glide again. We finished up and went to my favorite, the pegs! I had hoped that by placing them last on the schedule for the day, my arm muscles would be tired and therefore more receptive to the paces that awaited it.

I began by removing the pegs in record time! It still was clumsy and thinking of returning to normal seemed like a joke, but I persisted. I focused on getting the pegs into the hole in record time no matter how it looked. This was good and I carved minutes off of my time with practice. Then I decided to focus on technique and pushed time aside. I was more concerned that I involve d the middle finger in the process, not just the thumb and fore finger. Getting the two to coordinate had been difficult when no feeling was involved now with feeling it seemed almost impossible. Now whenever one finger felt the other seemed to spasm. Over time I seemed to start to get the hang of things but it would take time.

I returned with Yand Dong Mei to my room and saw the doctors in the hall as I entered the floor. I made it a point to not get involved in anything because I could be interrupted any minute. Moments later Zhang Quan entered my room and through the use of my handheld translator and a number of gestures I managed to convey my current evaluation of myself to her. She spoke with Dr Zhang who returned to my room to confirm my feelings before Dr Bian came. It was obvious to me that feeling was beginning to return to the lower leg because rather than a numb feeling it felt more like my lower leg was covered by a blanket. All the feelings seemed to be there but at a diminished level.

Dr Bian entered and began speaking with Dr Zhang, who conveyed my feelings to her.

"Covering?" She asked.

I grabbed my blanket and placed it over my leg and gestured toward just the lower leg. "Covering, like a blanket I said.

"You have feeling now and it was numb before?" Dr Zhang pointed at the leg.

"Yes" I replied, "but the feeling is 'distant.'"

It was the only way I could describe it. Dr Bian asked me to roll on my side and began placing a number of needles in my lower leg. For the first time I felt her as she worked on the leg, it was a funny sensation and still one that defies description. She finished with my leg and went on to my arm, hand and face. As she placed a needle she asked, "Where do you feel?"

I paused and thought, just then she spun the needle and a pulse surged through my right middle finger. "ooh'" I exclaimed.

"That needle'" she said' "goes to that finger."

It was obvious that she knew what she was doing! I was amazed at the power that something so small could wield in the hands of someone so skilled. When all the needles were placed Dr Bian began to leave."

"Xaa, xia (pronounced shea shea)" I called after her.

"Do not to mention it." She said in her best English.

Dr Zhang stayed and hooked up the "box" to the arm and foot this time.

"She's very kind." Dr Zhang remarked.

"Yes" I said, "very kind!"

I was reflecting on all the fears and concerns that I had before leaving the states. There were so many unknowns, the least of which was the language barrier. I was going 10,000 miles to be treated by... I didn't know who, and I was going to be treated with... I don't know what for I don't know how long. Just a few minor holes to be filled.

Dr Zhang left and I closed my eyes to catch a little catnap. I awoke to see Zhang Quan's smiling face as she removed the needles and began to prepare for the soaks.

"Cupping" I said, and she looked perplexed. Now I really wished I'd paid attention when it was said in Chinese. I tried to gesture toward my arm and leg. Just then Dr Zhang entered with her familiar tray. I pointed and smiled and the two of them held a brief discussion in Chinese. Zhang Quan continued to prepare the bucket while Dr Zhang applied the cups. Talk about feeling like you're in the middle of a traffic jam! I wanted to holler, 'hey! There's only one of me' but no one would have understood. The cupping only took about 5 minutes and when I was done Dr Zhang released me as it were to Zhang Quan's capable hands.

We had just started the soaks when there was a knock at the door; it was the body massage therapist! I had to laugh out loud; I guess I was popular this morning. The nurse and therapist had a brief talk and then the therapist sat down after turning on the TV. You had to strain to hear the TV so I pulled my translator out of my pocket. After typing in the word 'loud' I showed it to Zhang Quan.

"Ni yao (you want)," and I pointed to the words in Chinese on the translator screen. There was a lot of laughter as the therapist got up and adjusted the volume so she could hear. At least I got my point across! It didn't make sense that she had to wait her turn for me and couldn't hear the TV, besides it looked interesting. When the soaks were done I moved from the chair to the bed and she began the massage. No sooner had she begun when another knock came at the door, I couldn't imagine who this would be!

It was Liang Hui, she shared words with the therapist who obviously shared my hectic day's schedule with her. They both laughed and Liang Hui remarked that it sounded as if I had been a bit busy. She was there to add to it! It seems that the doctors had added a new steam treatment that would begin tomorrow, it would last 40 minutes, but would hopefully aid in restoring the feeling to my lower leg and foot. "Okay." I said. I mean who was I to argue they had been right up to now. Liang Hui said she would be back this afternoon and she parted. I don't know if I'd just gotten used to it or the feeling was starting to return, but the massage felt good and not painful. If it weren't for the TV keeping me engaged I would have zonked out. I thanked her as she left and realized I was free after lunch until my afternoon treatment.

I'll finish this Saturday afternoon!

Saturday June 26, 2004

I slept in today until 5:15 (Ha, Ha), and morning duties went as normal until I got around to brushing my hair. It was absolutely wonderful; I have a scalp, a feeling and itchy scalp. It actually tingles and itches and the brush feels wonderful! Then I realized while brushing my teeth they weren't numb or sensitive, depending on the day they would vary, my dentist always asked before touching them. I spent the rest of my early morning time touching various portions of my face and acting like a giddy schoolgirl.

I finished up breakfast and played a rousing hand of "the pill game" before the phone rang at 7:00. It was Steve; all was well on the home front and he said he'd been keeping up with me via the website but that I hadn't updated it yet today. I filled him on yesterday's schedule and vowed to put up what I had finished, updating it later in the day. It's so easy to get behind when they keep you hopping 15 hours a day. Yesterday I didn't finish until 8:30 p.m. And last time I checked a day only comes with 24 hours and I try and sleep at least 7! We chatted about my progress and eventual return home, and finished with Steve promising to call back with the kids on the phone tomorrow!

I hurried and got ready for rehab and none too soon, a knock came at the door and it was the nurse to take me downstairs. She asked me to walk in front of her. Now that I knew the way it seemed simple enough. I know that she wanted to have me in front just in case I fell I don't quite know what she would do I'm half again as tall as she is and we won't say how much I out weigh her, but it is a considerable amount.

We arrived at rehab and I was solo today except for one male nurse who spoke very little English. He motioned to a machine and I walked forward and took a seat. This one was new. It had what appeared to be foot rests that were attached to a bar that in turn extended on both sides, came up 90 degrees and formed handles on both sides. As I reached forward and pulled the handles back and it caused the feet to pitch back and bend at the ankles. When I moved the handles forward the ankles relaxed and the feet returned to a resting state. Simple I thought, but nothing could be further from the truth. Keeping my right foot positioned correctly was proving to be difficult. Every time I pulled the handle back I had to make certain that the ankle bent while the foot remained in position. This became more than a work out and I was thrilled when we shifted to the leg lift machine. This exercise was one I felt I had mastered but it was still a good workout and gave me a chance to practice my Chinese numbers.

I finished with that and moved to the dreaded stationary bike. Today I was prepared, I reached into my pocket and produced my MP3 player and headphones. I turned it on and placed the earphones in my ears. Finally a way to deal with some of the monotony that comes with pedaling to nowhere. I began the grueling ride looking frequently into the mirror only to be appalled at the figure that looked back. The stroke had definitely taken its toll, I was out of shape and at least 40+ pounds overweight. If you looked closely I dropped the right side and carried it differently. I always said that if I didn't walk and talk you wouldn't know I had a stroke! It was apparent in looking at the person starring back at me in the mirror, I had best take this opportunity to get back in shape and lose the pounds. I'd been given a unique opportunity to not only survive the stroke, but also fine a cure for the disabilities. I had better not blow this!

Only 10 minutes had passed when the nurse tapped me on the shoulder and motioned for me to quit. I used the opportunity to drink some water from the bottle that I had been given two day's ago by Liang Hui. He motioned to the padded exercise table and I sat down to take a break. While I was seated he motioned for me to watch him. I sat and looked intently as he demonstrated the next exercise that he wanted me to do. He got up on all fours and he extended his left leg out, suspending it in the air and keeping it straight. He then switched and extended his right leg. I watched, knowing that I was to repeat the task. I slowly got on all fours on the exercise table and attempted to extend my left leg. I could feel the wobble in the right leg as I stretched. I worked hard at maintaining balance as I repositioned the right hand to the left of where it originally sat. It took some more repositioning but I finally did it. He had me repeat the task several times before I was allowed to progress to the pegs.

Putting the pegs at the end of the session gave my arm muscles a chance to get 'tired' as it were and also give my body a chance to 'wake up'. I was able to remove the pegs in record time, but replacing them was a different matter. My fingers fumbled at the feeling of the wooden pegs and it was difficult to replace them in their holes. After several series of removing and replacing the pegs the nurse stopped me and massaged my hand. I returned to replacing the pegs and the time got better. I looked up and Yang Dong Mei was there to take me back.

We got back to the room and I had enough time to take off my shoes before the morning group of physicians descended on my room. This morning they were headed up by Professor Shi, Dr Bian was close behind followed by Dr Zhang. When they reached my bed Dr Bian spoke with Professor Shi, who in turned asked me, through Dr Bian, to grab his fingers with my right hand and squeeze. My grip had increased and he wanted me to put my thumb and little finer together and try and prevent him from pulling them apart. I obviously passed the test and he proceeded with the placement of needles in my arm, hand, face head and neck. While he was busy Dr Bian and Dr Zhang were busy putting needles in my leg and foot. It was difficult sorting out feelings with so much happening simultaneously. Dr

Zhang stayed after everyone had left and placed the "box" on. This time it was connected to the elbow and outer lower leg. I could feel the steady pulsing as the muscles contracted and relaxed. Dr Zhang encouraged me to 'take a rest' and I've gotten very good in a short period of time at sleeping with needles in.

I rested until Hong Wen Mei returned and removed the needles. I sat up and stretched and was about to get out of bed, when who should appear but Dr Zhang and her tray. I laughed out loud.

"We've got to stop meeting like this." I said as she grinned and headed toward me. I knew full well she didn't understand the humor in my statement, but I could tell by the look in her eyes she understood my meaning and laughter. Prior to placing the cups she took a small needle and gently pricked the back of my upper and lower legs.

"Ooh" I said with each poke. It was apparent that the treatments had been working. When I first arrived my entire right side was numb and now the remaining holdout was obviously beginning to wake.

With the cups applied I closed my eyes for the 5 minutes they needed to be on prior to Dr Zhang's return. I was just drifting off when a knock came at the door followed by the massage therapist, I pointed to the cups an after glancing at the clock said, "3 minutes." I pointed to the TV and she turned it on and the two of us watched a continuation of the show we had watched yesterday. Dr Zhang quickly returned and the two of them shared a brief conversation in Chinese while she removed the cups. She said her goodbye and added a, "see you tomorrow". The therapist wasted no time as she quickly began my 40+ minute session. The massage was as deep as normal but felt much more relaxing and less painful,

I was actually beginning to enjoy these sessions. When the 40 minutes were over she said her goodbyes and I actually just laid there hoping no one else would come. I was quite relaxed and just wanted to rest for a bit.

Lunch didn't come for another 30 minutes so I got my wish. After lunch Chu Jia Qi stuck her head in to let me know she would be by at 2:30 to take me to the new treatment the doctors had ordered. I thanked her and then settled in for an afternoon of writing and TV. It appeared "Bodyguard" was on and with Chinese voice overs' it was quite unique.

The movie hadn't yet ended when Chu Jia Qi returned to take me to my new treatment. We headed up in the elevators to the 13th floor, where she led me to a converted room. It was a double and extremely large. On either side were small beds that looked as if they had pieces cut out of them. They were cushioned and had sheets with the same cutout design so obviously they were designed for a use. My nurse ushered me to a chair while she left to let the nurse who manages that room, know we were there. A short time later they both arrived and began preparing one of the beds for my treatment. The bed I would use had two cutouts, one for the leg and one for the shoulder and arm. They each had a rubber bar that apparently supported the limb to be treated. I was prepared for the treatment by removing my regular hospital shirt and replacing it with one of those semi-private gowns with the back open. I was asked to hop up on the bed, remove my shoes and socks and lay down. I was then scooted into place with my hand and arm over one opening and my leg and foot over the other. The small bars acted well as supports, giving both my hand and foot something to rest on. As I was slid into place I could feel the warmth of the steam on my arm and hand as it was being generated below. I noticed a unique smell that permeated the room. I had detected it earlier but it wasn't as prevalent as it seemed now, come to think of it, it was coming from the source of the steam.

I lay comfortably on the bed as the nurse in attendance placed a blanket over me. The nurse who was there now 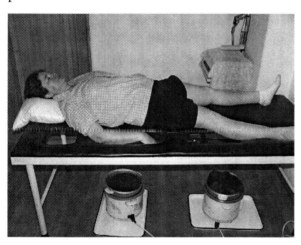 spoke no English and mine had returned to the floor and would retrieve me when I was done. I had been told to tell the nurse there if I was hot using "re" which is the Chinese word for hot. I remember laying there quietly thinking, I wonder it this is how steamed vegetables felt.

I must have drifted off because the next thing I remember was a phone ringing as I woke with a start. I lay still as the nurse put two boards on the bed beside me and a towel on each. She then disappeared out of my line of ight. She reappeared as she brought something up from under my bed. It was a dark sealed fabric bag that was piping hot. She rapidly placed it on the center of one of the towels and gingerly gabbed it from the corners and dropped it several times on the towel before neatly and tightly wrapping it up in the same towel. She set it on the other board as she grabbed the first and slid it under my arm, covering the opening below. She then stretched out my arm across the board and placed a clean white towel over it. I watched as she carefully placed the hot bundle on my hand. The warmth seeped through and the smell became stronger. Herbs! That's what filled the bag, herbs! I was slow but I was beginning to get it. The bag was used in the steaming process and them, when the desired time had passed the bag was wrapped and placed on my arm. I watched with anticipation this time as she repeated the steps and placed a towel and wrapped bag on my knee. She repositioned the bags every minute or so moving them up and down the arm and leg and at the end of about 10 minutes I noticed my nurse had reappeared at my bedside. They both removed the bags and I sat up and dressed.

Chu Ji Qi escorted me back to my room. "Take a rest." She said as she left me. Doesn't she realize that I just caught 30 minutes worth during the last treatment? I sat down and pulled the laptop close and started typing. It wasn't long before I began to feel tired, I guess that treatment took more out of me than I realized. As I pushed the laptop away a knock came at the door, it was Da Gui. What pleasant timing, I told her "Wo hen lai" which means I am very tired. To give you a glimpse into my twisted brain and how I remember so many little Chinese phrases, this one sounds like "what hens lay" – "wo hen lai", remember I've had a stroke… actually my spouse and close family and friends will tell you I was a bit twisted before the stroke. She smiled and repeated my words in a very concerned tone and then smiled again. It felt relaxing to soak my feet and I had to work at staying awake while she massaged my hands, arms, and shoulders, after all I was sitting and it would be a bit tacky to fall asleep now. With the soak over I rotated back and lay on the bed, I wouldn't mind falling asleep on Da Gui tonight and having been warned I think she expected it.

I woke up hearing the nurse come in to take my pressure. "Resting?" She asked.

"Yes." I replied, with obviously no energy expelled. She took my pressure and headed out. I looked up at the clock and it was already 7:00, all I could think of is the fact that if I didn't get up now I wouldn't finish the update to the site or get my email answered. I climbed out of bed and began to type.

11

Dawning of a New Day

July 26, 2004

Wow! It's Tuesday afternoon and Luo Shu Yu just returned from Beijing with my computer! You don't know how much I have missed it. I thought I had it working correctly several weeks ago but it died, now I have it back and I hope all is well.

So much has happened over the last month, I almost don't know where to begin. To bring you up to date I have feeling restored in 100% of my body. The hand and coordination are returning slowly. My foot is calming down and the hypersensitivity is decreasing and my walking is taking on a more normal look. Now for the good part: the photographic memory that I lost due to the stroke is returning and my eyes are slowly decreasing in registering constant movement. We have found a definite link to the outside pressure and my eye movements.

Two doctors from Britain stopped in today and inquired as to my recovery and ongoing progress. I really hope the medical establishment is willing to take a hard look at combining Chinese Traditional Medicine and western medicine, there is nothing to lose and a lot to be gained. The Europeans have been embracing it for some time but mostly for things other than strokes such as pain management. I have learned that this hospital is the best in China for treating strokes and I was fortunate to find it with the girls help. I might add that I am actually typing some of this using my right hand. It has never been coordinated enough to allow typing in the past. Shu Yu has crashed, she got very little sleep while she was in Beijing and she has her own bed in my room. Now that I have finished with just about everything except feet massage this afternoon: she can catch up on some shuteye while I type. We take so much for granted in the U.S., we use UPS and Fed Ex to ship anything but here I actually had to have someone hand deliver my computer and then pick it up. The repair only took a few days but the finding of trustworthy people going to Beijing took a little longer.

Wednesday July 28, 2004

Well, it's back on track for email updates and the computer appears to be working normally. I have finally convinced the staff that I will not fall in the bathtub and have been granted solo bathing rites. This means I am back to a bath in the morning at 5:00 when I get up. I know most are asking why 5:00 but the sun is up here and I am awake. Besides, it is such a waste to sit in bed and just lay there.

I used to teach that time once spent is gone and unlike money, you cannot get more. Although each of us would love to add days to our lives, it says in the Bible that each day has been ordained for us, you can't get any more so invest your time wisely. It seems foolish if I am wide-awake to use the time selfishly and crawl back into bed. I do not know how many days I have to invest but what time I have I will invest wisely. I have been given a unique opportunity to live when it was expected I would die. I feel that with this opportunity comes responsibility, not only have I been given life but a chance to experience healing. To keep this to myself and not share it would condemn others to a life of trials and disabilities that can in many cases be totally reversed.

I tried unsuccessfully to reach JinWei last night. I know that she wants to visit Tianjin before she returns to the U.S. but time is passing and her computer is still here. I have an opportunity to get it to her in Beijing saving her a trip, but I need to know what she wants me to do by Thursday morning which leaves today to get a hold of her! I know this is her last week in China for a while and she is very busy but I hope she calls.

Although I have the computer back getting online has been impossible. I hope to solve that dilemma this morning with the help of the hospitals computer technician.

The phone rang this morning and it was the family checking in. It is really difficult being so far away during the summer months but I suppose that there is never a good time to be gone from family. I guess I'll just have to be faithful with the time I have here and focus on improving. I finished my family chat and I'll check in tomorrow to see if anything has changed.

Breakfast came and I inhaled my egg and enjoyed a cup of hot tea. It is also prepared here and is used for its medicinal properties. I take it to cure the tickle I had in my throat after the rapid cure of the cold. I must confess that after coming here as a doubting Thomas they have definitely made a believer out of me. I want to finish breakfast and do a few warm up exercises on the bed prior to going to therapy for my daily workout.

12

Determined to Succeed

Sunday August 1, 2004

Well, it is high time that I begin to get back into a solo routine. After Monday all my visitors will be gone and I'll have my focus back again. The 5 am wake up has become my standard here, with the sun up so early it is hard to sleep in at all. It should be interesting to see if I change my pattern as fall arrives and the sun shifts.

JinWei and her mother came at about 11:30 and it was good to see them again. They are staying in the adjoining room to mine so we can open the door and share the rooms. I think JinWei is feeling a little better about this trip because she has already secured her visa and will be able to travel back to China and visit family over the Christmas break. It's been a joy seeing her in her "natural environment" I don't think she realizes it but she has learned so much in her time in the states. I've enjoyed the opportunity to get to know her mother more. We are both the same age and it is interesting to begin to understand the mother behind the young woman that we have considered as a daughter when she is in the states.

They both say they have seen change in the time that I've been here. Although that is encouraging I feel like I have so much further to go. I'm glad they came after acupuncture on a Sunday because I have the rest of the day that I can spend with them.

JinWei and I spent a great deal of time talking as both her mother and Luo Shu Yu took afternoon naps. We headed out as a group to Pizza Hut for dinner and I must confess it was a fun and yet different experience. This was the first time in 3 months that I had eaten pizza and although the atmosphere looked similar the toppings available on the pizza differed greatly. We ate our fill and then found that there was plenty to take back to the hospital and park in my little refrigerator.

The remainder of the night I sat on my bed and chatted with JinWei in between text messages on her cell phone. It would be her next to last night in China and she was busy burning up the text message airwaves. I was able to tell her how much her being in China and helping me during my stroke had meant to me. I have often shared that our first exchange student, Bundit taught me how to walk after the stroke, JinWei taught me how to run, and Yiwei helped me discover my wings. There were so many times during my recovery period when I was tempted to want to give up and then that quiet smile would appear on JinWei's face and I didn't have the heart to discourage her. As a result I would end up replaying lectures to myself in my head, get on my knees (figuratively of course!), and get back into the game!

I talked with JinWei until late into the night and when I curled up to sleep she was still sending messages on her phone. It was hard to believe that she would head to Beijing in the morning and see my family in the states in a matter of days.

Tuesday August 3, 2004

Today I woke up to rain and fog. Have discovered that pressure outside affects my vision or at least it has in the past. Today is the first day I am totally on my own JinWei was off to Beijing and Luo Shu Yu headed to Shanghi. No more friends to keep me company or to pass the time by speaking English. I must go in alone as a foreigner in a foreign land. Up to now I have been handled with care, although I know that will continue and they are very faithful to use English here in the hospital it is limited and the doctors have a very limited English vocabulary.

I sent an email off to NuStep company; they manufacture a rehab machine that I have found very useful with stroke patients. This morning I got a reply and will email them the additional info they need. I have discovered during this trip that I need to ask for things because if I don't the answer is "no" and when I ask, just maybe the answer is yes! I would very much like to see NuStep donate a machine to the hospital. We'll see!

I was a bit slow starting today, I got up and dressed and then took it easy by stretching out on the bed. I should have sensed it was going to be a busy day when the phone rang at the same time the nurse entered the room to take my BP. It is Steve's birthday back home and it is hard not being there but it sounds like the kids got gifts and made it fun. Being a patient in the hospital limits what I can do so he'll have to settle for a belated gift of me when I return. I chatted with the family and it sounds like all is going well and as soon as

I finished my conversation and hung up I was inundated by nurses.

I've gotten used to seeing all the nurses as they make their way into my room on their morning rounds, one acts as my escort to the rehab room. This morning they were all enamored with the Lego house I had built. They were all impressed with my work and examined it carefully. I think I'll be taking it apart and putting it together several times while I'm here. The nurse and I boarded the elevator and began the trip from the 12th floor to the second. As the only American patient here I stick out just a bit, even the women who staff the elevator look out for me. They will keep all others from boarding until I have a place at the back against the handrail. Now they have noticed my weight loss and are commenting to my nurse about how much I'm losing.

We arrived at the rehab room early and I went straight to work on one of the machines. I can't tell you how good it is to have feeling return on my right side. Muscles that I haven't felt for close to 3 years are all getting a work out. The acupuncture, medication and massage have all worked together to add control and stability. Something that with all the exercises I've done over the past several years has eluded me. I finished my repetitions after 5 minutes and switched to the squat machine. I've noticed that over the years I tend to drop my right shoulder slightly and this helps strengthen the back and leg muscles. From here I switch to pulling weight with my arms. I have always remained strong but coordination and stability are beginning to return. This is where the acupuncture is truly amazing, one day I can't do something and with the placement of needles the next day it feels as if I've had an overnight miracle. I have found that my right wrist is what needs quite a bit of work and they are focusing on that as well. I spend the next 15 minutes on the treadmill walking. My balance is beginning to return but I'll be happy when they totally correct the bounce in my vision. It's been 3 years since I've felt balanced when I walk and it is a good feeling to be able to hop on my left or right foot without the fear of falling. We finished up by playing the peg game and then a quick 10 minutes on the stationary bike. I'm becoming quite adept at placing the pegs and the "drop reaction" that having feeling return in the hand created is slowly being replaced by coordination and fine motor skill. As for the bike I stopped taking my baclofen 2 weeks ago and the muscle spacticity that I had in my legs is continuing to diminish without the drugs. My nurse returned to escort me back to my room and we ran into Dr. Bian along the way. She had been in Shanghai for the past week and it was good to see her.

"How are you feeling?" she asked smiling, noticing the sweat running down my neck after my workout in rehab.

"Very good...hen hao" I replied in my English followed quickly by my attempt at Chinese.

I was ushered into the elevator by the attendant and gave her a big smile when I exited. "Xia, Xia" I uttered, thanking her for looking out for me.

I made it back to my room and collapsed on the bed, being content to take whatever time I had to rest before the doctors entered. No sooner did I stretch out, when a rap came at the door and Yu Lan entered. She began to chat and I told her about the possibility of the hospital getting a machine and she passed on an email to use. She noticed that all my visitors had left and asked where they had all gone.

"Luo Shu Yu is headed to Shanghai for shopping" I replied, "and JinWei boards a plane at 4 this afternoon for America. That leaves me here alone to fend for myself."

With that another rap came at the door and Dr Bian, Dr Han and Dr. Zhang entered along with the head nurse. I took advantage of Yu Lan's presence and Dr Bian's return to ask how long she was going to ask me to extend my trip. It seems that all is on track except for the eyes, which are clearing up slowly. 2 months was the reply. It seems a small price to pay considering just weeks ago I had no hope of change. Dr Bian placed the needles on my head, neck, face, and arm; While Dr Han placed the needles on my leg and foot. Dr Zhang waited until they were both done and then connected "the box" to the appropriate needles and headed out. I continued to chat with Yu Lan until the nurse returned some 20 minutes later to remove the needles. After the needles were removed Yu Lan said her good bye and I settled in for a brief rest.

Brief is right, Dr Zhang returned within 10 minutes of the needle removal with her customary tray of glass cups for "ba huo guan". I'd gotten accustomed to having them placed on my back and the back of my legs. I rolled over on to my stomach and pulled a pillow up tightly under my chin. It allowed me a bit of comfort in this unusual position. Dr Zhang quickly applied the cups and then checked with me to make certain I was okay before heading out the door as I lay there for the customary 5 minutes. I had just gotten comfortable when she reappeared. It seemed the 5 minutes passed so quickly now that I was used to the procedure. As each of the cups was removed I could hear the air as it flowed back into the glass and the vacuum was released. I heard the clank on the tray as she placed each cup back after taking it off. Dr Zhang gently slapped the area where each cups were removed and once they were all off vigorously rubbed the back of my legs. It was a pleasant feeling and helped to relieve the itching sensation that always accompanied the removal of the cups.

It was close to 10:30 a.m. and I decided to call JinWei and wish her a pleasant flight and let her know that Elizabeth would be there to greet her. After saying goodbye for the last time in China and hanging up the phone, I felt the sting of her pending departure like never before. The tears welled up in my eyes as I fought them back. This is one part of the stroke, unleashed emotions, which I never learned to cope with. After all I was a grown woman and things like this should not affect me, or at least that is what I kept telling myself. The reality was that even though we didn't talk much, just knowing she was in the country was a great comfort. Now that was ending and at this time tomorrow she would be getting off the plane and seeing my family. The sting came again as I visualized my daughter giving JinWei a great big hug.

I was jealous and it showed. I'm just thankful that no one was here to witness my unglued demeanor. I lay down and closed my eyes to try and deal with the flood of emotions that I was feeling. I knew that it was just as difficult for JinWei to go to America, leaving family and friends behind but it was hard to see her go while I stayed. We joked and she had volunteered to switch with me on several occasions but we both knew as good as it sounded it wasn't possible. I was glad that no one entered the room for several hours, it gave me an uncommon break in the routine and watched a DVD while I lay on my bed.

Dr Wang, who does my massage, didn't come until 2 and when she appeared in the doorway I smiled, actually happy to see her. I had begun to enjoy the massages knowing that any discomfort that she might bring about was always accompanied with increases in feeling and mobility. She finished after 40 minutes and I decided to just lie there, content to wait for my next acupuncture treatment.

I didn't have to wait long it wasn't 5 minutes later that Dr Zhou entered with Dr Zhang. I sat in the chair for my customary afternoon treatment. Dr Zhou is a grandfather type figure, distinguished and gray, gentle and quiet, he quickly and skillfully placed the needles and with a gentle smile left the room. 20 minutes later Hong Wen Mei returned to take out the needles. She also had a DVD in hand, she said she has many English DVD's and will bring them for me to watch. It is so encouraging when God goes beyond meeting the needs and begins to meet the wants. I didn't need the DVD but it was a great treat to watch in English. That afternoon remained quiet until Da Gui came for my foot massage and when she finished I decided to call it quits early and watch the DVD that Hong Wen Mei had brought.

Thursday August 5, 2004

There is only one thing more frustrating than a slow recovery and that is, knowing that if I had come here immediately after my stroke it would have been much faster. I've had almost three years to establish habits that now have to be undone. I'm feeling muscles that are weak or in some cases I didn't know existed. I'm fortunate in that I've had no muscle atrophy, I've been careful over the years to do range of motion exercises with the kids help. Now I am seeing where that is paying big dividends. Immediately following my stroke I had my husband massage the affected side when he visited the hospital and when I came home I had him continue to stimulate it with a dry lufa sponge. It varied from feeling numb to experiencing shear pain on the bottom of my foot when he did it but I'm convinced that the constant stimulation helped with maintaining some connection to the brain, making my recovery, or at least the regaining of feeling, faster.

A big part of me used to think that massive amounts of repetition would conquer all. You know, do something enough times and it will make you better. Boy did I have a lot to learn. I've been practicing and repeating the same things for two and a half years with no results so why do they work now? I have found in my experience that repetition only seemed to help when combined with the other therapies. Sure, I experienced a limited return of function to the right side but I got so far and it stopped. For years now, parts of my body had no feeling and seemed to be no more than foreign objects that happened to be attached. When I would attempt pick up something using my right hand I had to see it to accomplish the task. If I took my eye off it for one split second I would drop what I was grasping. It seemed that the only feedback that I had was visual and holding or picking things up came with great concentration and difficulty. When my right hand touched my left side it felt as if it didn't belong. I have also continually fought with the right half of me being physically cold when the left half of me is fine. It was always a challenge but even friends could grab both hands and were appalled at the difference they felt, I was like hot and cold running faucets!

Since my arrival here each of these abnormalities have slowly been corrected and now I am diligently watching and waiting for the rest of me to be fixed. The hand with all its complexities is slowly coming around. I have control over individual fingers and can type (although its hunt and peck) with the right hand. I can hold an ink pen... my writing has much to be desired but it is all returning slowly. Being a patient person before the stroke was never my strong point, after the stroke I was as patient as a saint because everything took so long. Now I have to remind myself to tap into that patient side because total recovery will take some time but the results are worth it.

After only 5 weeks my eyes are beginning to stabilize and the bouncing that I would experience when I moved is now beginning to diminish. Balance is returning and I can now jump up and down on either the right or left leg. One thing that I was hesitant to mention that was critical to me was the restoration of feeling to the bladder and with that control. I cannot begin to help you understand the personal devastation that you feel when that part of your body ceases to respond appropriately. I limited my trips outside of the house and always knew where a bathroom was. I found myself limiting my intake of fluids and if I did drink something I visited the rest room continually out of fear of an accident. In short, you feel like a little child who cannot be potty trained. It's embarrassing!

Two other things to note, the first being cognitive brain factions. I felt most of me seemed to come back after the initial trauma of the stroke. It seemed I could add and subtract ok, or at least I didn't struggle with it when I wasn't stressed or tired and I spoke well enough to get by, but a part of me was missing. Learning, which had always been easy was now extremely difficult if not impossible. I also experienced a constant battle in my head for words, finding the right one or sometimes finding any at all. It was difficult for someone such as myself who always could think on my feet. Now I continually seemed to be mentally and verbally stumbling and when I was stressed or tired things became difficult and almost impossible. With the treatments here both my memory and fluidity of mind are returning, something I never thought possible.

The last thing I have noticed a substantial difference in, is how my emotional state affects my physical body. In the past I have found that under emotional duress my body will begin to "lock-up". Muscles begin to freeze and speech becomes slurred. I have had to literally collapse on the floor into a sobbing heap only to be taken to bed to rest and recover. The events are embarrassing for me who, in the past, was accustomed to having myself "together". Now even after only five weeks, emotional events don't appear to have the devastating physical effect that they had in the past. I still cry at the drop of a hat, but that's ok I think I always will.

Friday August 6, 2004

The day started early enough and I rushed to get through my bath before the phone rang at 7:00. Steve called to check on how I was doing and we confirmed I would extend my trip by at least 30 –60 days. The plan is to return again next June with my daughter for 30 days for my follow up, so she will need a passport before that date. We talked a bit about the storms that came through back home and the branches that now needed to be picked up. We were forced to cut our conversation short when I heard all the dogs barking; apparently someone was at the door.

I quickly called JinWei trying to reach her at an "awake" period after her return to the states, only to be greeted by a groggy voice. JinWei had been sleeping and apparently not changed time zones yet I mean it was 6:30 p.m.! I didn't think she would remember anything I said so I said goodbye and told her I would talk with her when she chose to call.

After I finished with the calls the nurses stopped in on their morning rounds. As I got up I was obviously more than a bit unstable and that's all it took, exercise was cancelled because I was dizzy. I hate it when that happens but I've learned to be honest with how I feel. I can sense dizziness by closing my eyes. If I'm still feeling movement when they are closed then it's not just my eyes but also something more. We checked my pressure both standing up and lying down and there doesn't appear to be any abnormality. The day seems fine sunny and cool with no rain in the forecast and I slept well last night. I wish I knew what caused this dizziness but nothing seems different from yesterday. I suspect the doctor will be concerned with what I am eating but so far it is not different. I guess we'll just take an hour at a time and I'll deal with things as they come.

Professor Shi, Dr Zhuo, Dr Bian, and Dr Zhang gave me my acupuncture and needles to deal with the dizziness. "The box" was applied to needles in my head and I noticed Dr. Bian put several needles on my left leg and foot for balance. I rested the prescribed 20 minutes before Hong Wen Mei came to remove the needles. She was concerned with my dizziness but I'm certain that it will clear up.

After the needles were removed I sat and watched the ongoing construction on the middle school across the street. I think they intend to have it open for the fall so they have been diligently working hard to complete it. It gives me a chance to work on the focus of my vision as I scan the work zone for people. They seem to be making tremendous progress.

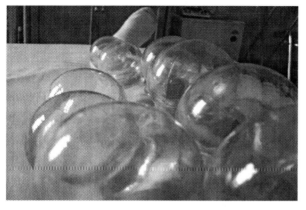

I sat back to do some writing and opened a package of spicy treats that are made in Hunan. I have been warned by the doctors here to limit the spicy food while I'm here. I guess I'll behave and eat right. I only got a 15-minute break before Dr Zhang entered to do my daily "cupping". She was in the middle of placing the cups when Dr Wang entered to give me my daily massage. Dr Zhang was first through the door so we finished up the cupping before Dr Wang got me for massage.

Saturday August 14, 2004

The sun rises a little later so I enjoy sleeping until 5:30. So much has happened in the first 4 to 6 weeks that it has set an unrealistic precedence of sorts. Now that feeling on my right side has been restored my expectations of rapid changes in fine motor skill have been slow to materialize. It is difficult to long to experience rapid change when now only subtle change seems to be occuring. I need to look deep within and examine every aspect of my physical body to determine any changes that might be happening. The doctors all said it would slow down and they, as usual, are right.

The morning started with a quick shower and breakfast and then I entered what has now become my familiar holding pattern until one of the floor nurses can escort me to rehab. It has become rather fun to watch the entire crew of nurses gather in my room during rounds as one grabs my water bottle, towel and room key. They all check me over and straighten my clothes before I'm allowed to leave; today it was Zhang Quan's turn. I noticed she had a sweater on because she felt cold today. The weather has turned cooler but I felt great as we headed to rehab on the second floor and begin my exercise routine.

I began with 50 repetitions on the squat machine lifting 80 pounds. It is enough to stress the muscles and yet not enough to strain them. I've chosen this machine because it works not only on the leg but also the back muscles and since the stroke I've noticed a drop in the shoulder of my effected side. After 25 repetitions I stopped for a water break and examined my muscles. They are definitely becoming

defined again, my lower legs are no longer the flabby and fatty legs I came here with. I still feel a bit of flab on my upper thighs but it is diminishing as well. I finished up my second set of repetitions and took another break while they located the key for the treadmill.

The treadmill has the distinct opportunity of being boring so I spend my time focusing mentally on balance. I spend 15 minutes walking and have found that slower speeds are much more difficult. I have long legs and a big stride so shortening it and slowing it down is extremely difficult. The doctors here have begun to add the challenge of an incline as well. There is a mirror opposite the treadmill so I watch my legs as they swing into place and my shoulders to make certain they remain level. The pattern to my exercise is a familiar one and I've gotten accustomed to having my MP3 player to listen to music during my workout, it plays and helps me stay mentally focused and pass the time. I used to think that if all my muscles were in shape then movement would be easy but it is more complicated than that. I have found that my rehab involves muscles, atmospheric pressure, attitude, emotions, and mental connections. They all work hand in hand and no one is more important than the others. Exercising the muscles is now easy with my feeling restored but forming the connection, rewiring my brain is proving to be the tough part. My attitude is good and I am aware of the atmospheric pressure each day. The challenge comes when I need to control emotions and rewire my brain. The doctors using acupuncture, traditional Chinese medication, and tuina has been invaluable. It seems things that I had been repeating for years hoping for a change are now starting to show change. The treatments are paying off big time and the change, although slow is progress.

My traditional 15 minutes ended on the treadmill and it was time to shift to the machine that works on the muscles in my arms. I have found that I am still extremely strong but that I have a definite tremor on my right side. I have learned to slow my routine and close my eyes to visualize better the connection between my muscles and brain. It has become a very spiritual exercise taking an extreme amount of thought, grace, and patience. Prior to having feeling restored I had no clue without looking where my right hand, arm, or leg was. The first time I remember experiencing this was when I was first hospitalized and the nurse caught me dangling my hand while I was in the wheelchair. If she had not seen it I easily could have caught that hand in the spokes of the chair.

Now I feel like a baby again having to relearn the simplest things. Where my hands are, where my mouth is, what it feels like to walk properly, all these things that half of me can do without any problem is difficult for the other side. I must confess it is harder than I thought it would be. I assumed that everything would come flooding back and just like riding a bike, after a bit I would be fine. Nothing could be further from the truth. Half of me no longer has any idea of how to ride a bike!

Speaking of riding that was the next thing up on my rehab list, the stationary bike. It is becoming easier to keep my foot on and I focus on each muscle group as I push with the left foot and then the right. I am careful not to allow the momentum of the left side to carry me through and not use the right. They have determined that this too is becoming too easy so the machine is set to the maximum resistance to provide me with more of a challenge. After 10 minutes my legs feel like rubber and I'm allowed to take a break.

From here it's on to picking up and placing pegs in a board. They time it but I have become less concerned with the time and spend more of my concentration on my technique. I have been focusing on trying to feel or I should say recognize the feeling of the pegs in my hand and then attempt to hold and manipulate them. I assumed incorrectly that feeling and function went together. If you have one then you have the other. Unfortunately I was missing one vital component, recognition. I need the brain to recognize the peg as a wooden peg, smooth, rounded sides with defined edges at the top and bottom. This is the key to everything! The doctors have been trying to relay that tidbit of information but it was being lost in the translation. Now that I understand the importance of mental recognition I am spending hours holding and feeling things with my eyes closed. I can accomplish many tasks through visualization or looking at the objects involved. It is very different to accomplish them without sight using only feelings. This is where I am discovering the need to re-hardwire the brain.

On my return from rehab I had a few minutes to rest on the bed before the doctors entered for my acupuncture treatment. As each of the needles is placed I am taking new interest in the location, depth and angle of each of the needles and I am particularly interested in their combined effect. I am currently reviewing a book that Dr. Shi wrote about acupuncture. I am reading the translated English version for errors in grammar, but I have been amazed at all I am learning in reading it. The techniques he has developed and that are taught here at the university hospital combine over 2000 years of history and use. I am fining anew that acupuncture and tuina are indeed a science but their practice is more of an art. These combined with the traditional Chinese medications help the body to heal itself.

After my treatments were over and I had a bite for lunch I took advantage of the cool weather to curl up on my bed for a nap. The change in temperature outside has made it much more bearable to open the window and enjoy the air outside. I pulled a light blanket up over my legs and closed my eyes.

I must have needed that rest more than I thought because I slept soundly and was startled when I heard a faint rap on my door. Hong Wen Mei entered with a BP cuff at hand. She smiled gently as I rolled over and managed to pull one of my arms out from under the blanket.

"Good sleep?" she inquired.

"Hen hao (very good)" was my reply.

She finished taking my pressure and rattled off the numbers in Chinese.

"yi bai yi qi shi" (110/70), she noted.

At my request they spoke to me with the Chinese numbers and it helped me to learn. She uttered a simple "bye, bye" as she headed toward the door and I managed to get out a quick "thank you" before it closed.

As she left I stretched my body the length of the bed and gave a big yawn. It seemed like I had just dozed off, but a careful inspection of the clock proved I'd been sleeping for close to two hours. I wiped the sleep from my eyes and focused on the clock. It was just after 4 in the afternoon and on a Saturday, soon my Chinese friend would come to practice his English. It seems hard to believe but someone was actually learning and refining their English from our conversations. I must admit I'd grown accustomed to being able to speak a bit more freely at these times. He seemed to have a good command of the English language and what he didn't know we quickly looked up.

Sure enough as I continued to stretch and take a few steps in the room he knocked and then entered. Shi Xiaolong was almost 15 years old and having two sons myself who were 16 and 17, it seemed quite natural to chat with him. Liang Hui, who is one of the translators, introduced us several weeks ago. He had been coming to chat on Saturdays and Sunday s each week. We talked about everything from language to exercise. He was particularly fond of economics and business and had just finished reading a book about Warren Buffett and his investment strategies.

Sunday August 15, 2004

Today I woke at 5:00 excited that everyone was home and I asked them to call early so I could talk longer. I sat on my bed and listened to Chinese TV and waited for the phone to ring, one hour, then two, and finally three hours passed without a call. I was worried that no call had come and the doctors know I don't exercise on Sunday so they come early for treatment, time was running out. I put all things on hold when I know a call is coming. I limit my fluid intake, don't eat, and stay in the room and refrain from walking. I stop anything that might interrupt my receiving a call, put me in the bathroom or down the hall. I just sit and wait anxiously for the phone to ring. Finally at 8:10 I picked up the phone and dialed our home number. I don't do it often because it's very expensive.

"Hello", my daughter answered.

"Hi" I replied, "its Mom, were you going to call? Did you tell Dad to call at 5:00 like I asked?"

"Yes" was her response. "He went to the store an hour ago and I don't know when he'll be back."

My heart sank; I don't think he realized what an important part of the day this was for me. It wasn't something that I hoped would happen, it was something I planned and made allowances for.

"If there is going to be a call it better happen soon the doctor could be here in 20 minutes." I ended the call with a sad heart. I wait for days to talk in English to my family and the call doesn't come.

I buried my head in my pillow shutting out the world until the nurse came at 8:30. It's at that time they clean the room and I either leave or sit in the corner. No sooner had I shifted to the chair in the corner than the phone rang. I grabbed the portable and answered it. It was Steve.

"I'm disappointed," I said, "I asked that you call at 5:00 so we'd have time to talk."

"Well we had supper and then started talking about the meals for next week and then I went to the store for groceries. Do you want to talk to Elizabeth?", he said as he attempted to deflect my displeasure.

"Yes" I replied, "put her on." Just then the doctor entered and I had to put Elizabeth off as I talked to the doctor. "Tell your dad the doctor just came in." I said as I continued two conversations at once.

"Do you want us to call you back?" Elizabeth inquired.

"No it would be too late by the time I finish all my treatments and I'll be too tired. I asked them if they would delay me by 20 minutes."

"Okay" she replied a note of caution and quiet in her voice.

I hated to ask for the delay because it wasn't one doctor it was four: Dr Bian, Dr Han, Dr Zhang, and Dr Xu. Putting off one was easy but by asking all four to wait I was interrupting the schedule of the entire floor.

I continued my chat with Elizabeth and then rapidly spoke to David, Roy, Yiwei and Andy before the phone returned to Elizabeth. We chatted briefly before I asked her to put Steve on. We were able to talk briefly about dates and upcoming plans; I had to cut short our conversation when the doctors entered again.

Because I was upset acupuncture was a bit painful today, 15 needles in the face, head and neck, another 10 in the hand and forearm and 35 in the leg and foot. Dr Xu attached the box to needles on my leg as the others left. I sat quietly trying to relax and let the treatment have its desired effect, but to no avail. Tears started to stream down the sides of m face and ran into my ears. I would have loved to wipe them away but with needles throughout I had to lie still and wait. After 20 minutes Hong Wen Mai entered to remove the needles. I tried hard to hide the tears and made little of my emotions and laughed it off as just something in my eyes.

A short time later Dr Zhang entered and we began the process of cupping. I was to lie on my stomach and they are applied to my back and the backs of my legs. It is a bit uncomfortable but bearable. I joked with Dr Zhang about how busy she had become lately and not having time to work on her English. I've become very adept at picking up some Chinese and they are very forgiving of my poor use of their language. Ni hen mang – means you are very busy; we'll leave it at that.

After the cupping was finished Hong Wen Mai re-entered to apply my soaks. She entered followed by Dr Xu.

"You're not happy today?" was Dr Xu's question.

That's all it took, the emotional floodgates were open. The one thing that I dislike about the stroke is its ability to keep my emotions on the surface and my inability to control

219

them. They take emotions very seriously here. Your ability to remain up beat and in good spirits helps greatly with the response to treatments. Being upset or overly concerned can wipe out weeks worth of progress. Dr Xu stayed and talked for over an hour and not once did she glance at the clock or act concerned about her time. We finished our chat and she said she would check back with me later.

At that time there was a knock on the door and lunch had arrived. After our conversation I didn't have much of an appetite but ate some to keep up my strength. I've lost a total of 63 pounds to date and I hope to be down even more upon my return. Although the size of my appetite has decreased considerably I know I still need to eat.

Sunday in the western world is a day of rest and it is treated much the same here and my afternoon is intentionally kept free. I have learned to honor one Chinese tradition and that is taking a rest from 1 until 2 each day. I don't always rest except for Sundays. It always seems like a lazy day and it is a way to pass an hour. Today the added emotional energy used up made me feel especially tired so after putting in a DVD I settled back for a rest as I listened.

Monday August 16, 2004

Today started a bit earlier than usual, I found myself wide awake at 4 in the morning. I guess going to bed an hour early doesn't pay off. After lying in bed and trying to go back to sleep I gave up and decided to take a shower. I was clean and dressed before 5 a.m. so I sat back and spent some time writing a few emails. The number of emails coming in has really tapered off, I guess the novelty of my being in China has worn off or people don't consider the results very exciting. Anyway I wanted to be faithful and jot notes to those that had emailed.

The progress had slowed but I am still moving forward after 2 years of no progress and some regression, so I'm thrilled. The phone rang at 6:00 and was a pleasant surprise, Steve was calling early. I guess the email I had sent explaining my frustration the day before hit a soft spot. We chatted briefly before I started making the verbal rounds with the kids. Elizabeth was excited to share about the day's event, they had all just returned from a day at the state fair. It seems they had a good time showing Yiwei and Andy the livestock and other exhibits. Of course plenty was made about the food that they all ate too. David stayed home and was content to pass the time with his video games. It was apparent that he was in the middle of one because he jumped at the chance to pass off the phone. Roy spoke and was a bit more subdued about the events of the day, instead he was looking forward to Wednesday when the entire family would go to the local amusement park and take in the rides. It's at times like these that I miss being home for the "summer fun" and I have to continually remind myself that I am in China for a greater good. I listened intently as Roy described the rides he would and would not go on. As if he read my mind he quickly reassured me that the next time the family went I would go and would be up to going on all rides. With that little bit of reassurance from Roy he passed the phone back to his dad. We chatted a bit about the date for my return and then said our goodbyes. It's always good to hear their voices and be reminded of one of the main reasons for seeking a cure…them!

With that perspective there are only 10 weeks left! That sounds like a short time to better myself, so I'm on a mission to do just that. I sat on the bed doing some stretching exercises and then prepared for rehab. The nurse came in and the made a phone call and I was asked to wait. Obviously something was up but because I didn't speak Chinese I would have to wait to find out.

I didn't have to wait too long there was a knock on the door and Dr Han and Dr Xu entered.

"They want to make a movie of what you can do now with treatments" Dr Xu relayed.

"Oh, okay" I replied

I had gotten used to pictures and videotape documenting my progress, one more was just fine, and after all I was the first American. I lay on the bed and proceeded to get up and put on my shoes. I then used my right hand to hook my MP3 player to my right pocket and proceeded to walk around the room and snap my fingers. They then asked me to walk down the hall and turn and come back. I thought I was done when Dr Han motioned to my computer. With that I started my slow typing with the right hand. When we were finally done we all had a good laugh when Dr Han suggested I dance. I laughed the hardest and told Dr Xu that maybe in a week or so they could tape me dancing but I wasn't ready to go on the video record yet.

After the morning antics were out of the way I headed to rehab. The videotaping had made me late and most of the machines were busy. I started at the squat machine and did my customary 50 lifts and transitioned to the treadmill. The doctor was having fun with me and kept increasing the incline as time passed and I walked. I could feel the added pull in my muscles each time the incline was increased but it didn't dampen my spirits I just walked on and was chuckling when he started to increase the pace of the machine. It was a good workout and I closed my eyes often to focus on each step and the muscles contacting and relaxing. After I finished up on the treadmill all the other machines were busy so I got an extended break. When nothing was free after several minutes the doctor took me to the raised matt at the end of the room, here he demonstrated something he wanted me to repeat. I positioned myself on all fours and then I was to lift the right arm and left legs out simultaneously while keeping my balance. Then rotate to the left arm and right leg. I had attempted this unsuccessfully years ago when I didn't have feeling, so I was intrigued at what would happen now that feeling had been restored. Amazingly enough after several tries I could do it. I rotated back and forth for about half a dozen times and then took a break.

By this time a stationary bike was free and I was escorted to it. I was surprised at how much my muscles ached after the mat exercise. I shifted to the bike and rode my customary 10 minutes. From there I took on the pegs, intent today on rotating each one as I placed it in the hole. It was slow and challenging work but I tried to focus on the task and not the time. Upon finishing I returned upstairs and had a quick respite before the doctors entered for my morning treatment.

Dr Bian was in a particularly pleasant mood and greeted me as she entered the door.

"Good morning!" she ushered in her best English, "how are you today?"

"Great" was my reply. The sweat still clung to my brow from exercise as I looked like I'd just finished a race.

She went right to work placing needles in my head and neck and then motioning to Dr Han to start on my leg as she placed needles on my face. I've gotten used to the slight sting that comes from some of the needles and don't even flinch. I try to pay particular attention to my body as she spins or taps some of them. This is when the combined effect is most obvious. With the placement done Dr Xu positioned "the box", connected the wires and turned it on. Now was my time to close my eyes and focus on relaxing. I must have done a real good job because I was startled when Hong Wen Mei started to remove the needles. Her gracious smile is enough to make anyone feel at ease and the gentleness with which she removes each needle has a soothing effect.

I gestured in her direction and asked, "Would you help me learn Chinese?"

"Me?" She looked a little embarrassed and then with obvious determination in her voice replied, "Yes, I will help you."

I had a lady come up to me on the treadmill and attempt to talk to me and "bu dong" (I don't understand) was all I could say to her. I was determined not to let that happen again. We spoke a bit more and then Hong Wen Mei left saying she would return at 11 for my soak. No sooner had she left when Dr Zhang entered carrying her familiar tray. I have to start thinking about that revolving door, during the morning it is positively hectic in this room. Dr Zhang applied the cups and then we talked about my stroke. I feel blessed having so much attention paid to me.

Hong Wen Mei returned at 11 with a bucket in hand for my herbal soak. It worked out well and while I soaked I practiced my Chinese. She was patient and gracious and carefully pointed out subtleties in tone so I would speak words correctly. After my soak and Chinese lesson I had a quick bite of lunch and stretched out for a quick nap.

I was startled when the nurse entered at three and roused me from a deep sleep to let me know the doctors were coming. The afternoon session of acupuncture went as planned and I was informed that I would be skipping tuina this afternoon. I was obviously tired so I didn't mind a bit. The sooner I had foot massage and supper, the sooner I could get to bed.

Thursday August 19, 2004

It has been several days since I jotted things down but I've notice a slowing in how things happen. It seemed at first that so much was happening. Now that I have progressed to a recognition phase it is much slower. The feelings are there and if I touch any portion of my body I can sense it but now I am having to work at putting feeling together with function. It is extremely difficult to explain but even though I can feel something I can't recognize everything I want to do with it or how to get part A as it were into slot B. It is reconditioning the brain and its connections. Repetition and TCM seem to work hand in hand providing slow and steady progress.

I've had to abandon two pairs of shorts out of fear they would fall off during exercise. That leaves me with two and the one pair are the jeans that I cut off and I fear I won't be in them much longer either. I spoke with Hong Wen Mei yesterday about going out and getting a couple of shorts that fit, she assured me she would look into it. I guess if anyone wants to lose weight this has been a great experience for me. I went from not being able to move much or exercise for long periods to a full 1 hour workout each day with increased mobility, flexibility and feelings I thought were lost forever. I've dropped 35 pounds in about 10 weeks here, not bad at all. I have energy to burn and I feel like I'm starting to look better too. I no longer have high cholesterol and my blood tests looked great! My blood pressure is low and for the first time in a long while I feel great! The Asian diet certainly agrees with my body I only hope I can keep up the habit when I return to the states. Unfortunately we've done a great job of exporting many of our bad eating habits and foods to the young people of China. I fear that they will suffer some bad health problems as a result. As for me I will cook up a storm and learn to enjoy even the "American" foods with more moderation.

Saturday August 20, 2004

I started today out a bit differently. My blood pressure has been getting lower and lower with the weight I have lost and yesterday it was 90/60. So today Dr Zhang asked me to stop taking my blood pressure medication and we would watch it closely.

The nurse came on her morning rounds and at 6:30 it was 110/70 we'll wait to see if it changes during exercise. I stopped keeping a daily log of treatments when the computer glitched and had to go in for repairs but it came at a time when physical changes on a daily basis were harder to detect. Now I have begun a weekly evaluation and I think that although I am aware of subtle change it is much more encouraging for me to view it in this setting.

This week I began to watch for changes in my hand. They seem insignificant to most but for me they are great strides of accomplishment.

- I can drink from my water bottle during exercise without sloshing
- I can point to small circles on a page with only small tremors

- I can hold the phone in my right hand and talk
- I can rotate a round peg between my right thumb and index finger
- I've discovered there is a right pocket that I can place my right hand in
- I can run my fingers on my right hand through my hair

I know they may all seem like trivial things but when you haven't been able to do these little things for years it's a big accomplishment. I think they are having a bit of fun with me in the exercise room. Now that I have feeling restored and movement is returning they're setting up challenges. I've maximized the difficulty on the stationary bike and now they are increasing the incline on the treadmill daily. The one thing I have yet to accomplish is letting go on the treadmill. I mean physically releasing from touching any part of the machine. I think it is in my mind but breaking the habit is proving to be difficult. I don't grip the handlebar; I just have a finger or two touching it. Oh well, that's for future goals I'm just excited for what is happening today.

I continue with my balance exercises on the mat. It has been a challenge to stretch the ankle and a bit painful but I am confident that with time and practice the right leg will mimic the left. I asked Yu Lan, my translator, to come down yesterday and explain my challenges to the doctor. I know what he wants but I can sense his frustration in not being able to speak to me directly. They got extremely spoiled when a Chinese doctor who was a student there interpreted for them; she was followed by Luo Shu Yu who spent several weeks with me. All in all they're doing a real good job.

I've changed my tactics at the peg game and now I pick up the pegs and rotate them into place. I get shaky now and then but the progress is slow and steady. There are only 20 pegs and they are careful to only allow me three rotations of removing and replacing them. I am amazed at how effective that is. I spend time in my room trying the following every day:

Dressing
Putting on shoes
Brushing my teeth
Washing my face
Washing my hair
Typing
Writing
Rotating Chinese balls in my hand
Bouncing and attempting to catch a water filled ball
Throwing a tethered tennis ball
Pointing to circles on a page
Eating
Using the TV remote

Things that each person does without thinking I have had to begin the process of relearning. I thought that everything I had learned when I had no feeling in the right side would just become easier once my feeling was restored. Nothing could have been further from the truth or prepared me for the battle in my mind that I face daily. It seems that everything I had relearned to do I learned to accomplish by sight. In other words close my eyes and I was lost and dropped anything I was attempting to hold.

Now that feeling has been restored I have to reassert my brain and teach it to recognize just what things are, where they are and how to interact with them. The fact that I am doing this almost three years after the stroke offers a bit more of a challenge. I find myself closing my eyes and practicing visualization and rewiring my thought process.

Exercise seemed to go as planned with one exception. I asked the doctors there to keep track of my blood pressure. They unlocked the top drawer of their desk and pulled out a small gray plastic box. When opened it revealed a cuff that went on my wrist and when a button was pressed it would inflate and register my BP. 30 minutes into the work out they pressed the button an the cuff inflated. 110/78 was the reading, not bad considering the intense work out and the sweat pouring from my brow. I continued my workout and asked for one last reading before I left. This time the cuff read 108/72 and I felt good about the reading and the workout.

I returned to my room in time to rest up before the doctors came for my Saturday treatment. When there was a knock on the door I assumed it would be Dr Bian. I wasn't totally wrong Dr Bian was there but I was pleasantly surprised when I saw Professor Shi enter the room. He again had me grip his hand and try a number of finger exercises and seemed pleased with my progress to date. He placed a number of needles in my head and neck as Dr Bian worked on my leg. When they were finished they left and Dr Zhang positioned "the box", turned it on, and left with a smile.

I dozed the 20 minutes before the nurse returned and removed the needles. Cupping was next and Dr Zhang entered carrying her familiar tray. She applied the cups in rapid fashion and then approached my head.

"I'd like to ask a question, I don't know if I can?" She inquired cautiously.

"Go ahead" I said.

"The other day I did the treatment and today..." She paused awkwardly.

Sensing her question I continued, "You'd like to know what I thought, how the treatments were the same or different?"

She smiled. I spent the next few minutes sharing my perceptions and observations. After all, I received treatments from the very best that the hospital offered and the doctors and nurses knew I paid very close attention to any and all treatments and the resulting effects. In the few months that I had been there I had gained a reputation both for my optimism and perception. Now that perception was helping someone gain insight.

When the cupping was finished it was time for the herb soak of my hand and foot. I used to think that this was rather boring but I quickly learned it was a great way to learn Chinese. No sooner had we started than Dr Xu entered and took a seat on the bed. She had some time and was just here to talk. We discussed my treatments and progress and then talked a bit about the letter that I was writing to the President of China.

A letter such as this was quite out of the ordinary but I felt that as a foreigner receiving such remarkable care with such dramatic results, I should share it. I see this hospital, the doctors and nurses, and TCM as a Chinese treasure that can be shared with the world. Exported as it were to other countries. Here is a 2000 year old practice that has been brought into the new century with tested and proven results. This combined with their understanding and implementation of western medicine puts them on the leading edge of medicine.

We continued our discussion as she asked me about my beliefs and what made me so positive and optimistic. "That," she shared, "helps the treatments work better."

I had learned that attitude and emotions played a big part of your treatment and recovery and as difficult as it was at times I needed to maintain an optimistic attitude and remain calm. In fact that is one of the reasons I actually learned to catnap during acupuncture treatments was that it kept me in a calm state and allowed the maximum results to be obtained.

As we talked Dr Xu asked me to talk more about my beliefs and the stroke. I seldom need to be asked twice about my beliefs or the stroke!

"The stroke caused a change in my perception," I said, "not that it changed my ideas. It just brought some things into focus."

"How?" she asked?

"Well" I continued, "I was conceived the night before my father died, survived a bleed and stroke that should have killed me, and I find myself in China experiencing a miraculous recovery! Seems to me I should tell someone about it. I mean you don't survive without a reason. The fact that I had two Chinese students who encouraged me to seek treatment in China and that we found this hospital was not a mistake."

She smiled, "You are a good person, happy and good to be with."

"My mother," I continued, "told me you find what you are looking for. I started looking along time ago for the good and humor in situations as they occurred. The stroke was no different, I just had to look a little harder and deeper."

As we spoke she translated everything that was said to the nurse doing my soaks. I would pause and Chu Jia Qi (my nurse) would nod, smile, and look approvingly in my direction.

Now the challenge, as I saw it, would be not just to share my experiences but have people see and believe what has happened. I guess for that reason I was happy that the changes, although miraculous from my perspective, were slow and not immediate. It made the reality of the treatment more understandable and much easier to accept.

Saturday August 28, 2004

The week got off to a noisy start. They are trying desperately to finish the middle school across the road from the hospital and they stop work at about 11p.m. and start up again at about 5:30. It's been fun to watch and it will be even more exciting when it fills with students – over 2000 of them.

I have experienced a busy week and very surprising in certain aspects. Take my eyes for example. I am staying an extra two months to see them corrected. I don't know what I expected to happen but I was tickled and very amazed at what has begun to occur in them.

First let me digress and bring you up to speed. The stroke caused double vision in my eyes that took some 7-8 months to correct. Then I spent copious amounts of time and money seeking out a specialist that ended up telling me that my right eye and my left eye are perfect, they just don't always play or work well together! There was no surgery or glasses that could correct the problem, it just existed after the stroke and I would have to put up with it. Whenever I would walk things would bounce and move. It made walking, which was difficult anyway, really frustrating. To top it off if I put my head down and raised it, like washing my hair as an example, I had my own amusement ride in my head. Saved a bundle on tickets but it could be a real pain in the….but I digress (even more)! Seems to me I was sharing about a good thing!

Sometimes without being aware of what is happening we do little things, naturally without thought. It is just one of these instances that I am speaking of. Dr Xu brought me a book about TCM knowing that I am trying to learn what makes it so different and special. That's when it happened. Without thinking I picked up the book, which has English on the left and Chinese on the right, and started to read. Yes, I said read! I haven't been able to read a book in 3 years! Not only could I see the words without magnification, they weren't moving, blurred or mixed up. Thinking this was a fluke I enjoyed the book and set it down after a half hour determined to pick it up the next day and have my bad vision back.

The next day came and I picked up the book. I was filled with trepidation as I flipped back the cover to the page I had marked. I slowly let my eyes fall on the page, the words were clear…I could see them! This was no fluke. It felt more like a miracle. Quick, I was busting at the seams and I had to tell someone. Just then my nurse Hong Wen Mei entered my room.

"You won't believe it?" I clamored.

"What?" She looked at me with a big question on her face. Not a question of not knowing but in my excitement she could not understand what I was trying to say.

I paused and took a deep breath, "you understand read, R…E…A…D?' I spelled it just in case. She nodded in agreement. "3 years" I continued, "no read... mei yo" She continued to look intently at me with increasing understanding. "Now I can read! I can see the words clearly in the book." With that I motioned to my eyes and then to the book, her understanding was instantaneous and she flew out of the room.

"Just one minute" I heard her exclaim as she left the room and headed to the nurses station.

She returned just moments later with Dr Zhang in tow. I was sitting in the chair with a cheesy grin plastered on my face as they entered. Hong Wen Mei gestured in my direction as Dr Zhang approached.

"Your eyes" she inquired, "they are better?"

"Yes!" I replied as my smile broadened, "I can read! I haven't been able to just sit and read in 3 years."

"You can see this page, the words, they are clear?" She asked, as she tried to keep a faint smile from beaming across her face.

"Yes!" I bubbled enthusiastically, "They are clear. I don't even need glasses!"

We continued our conversation and I could tell she was amused at my excitement. They had told me months ago that they could restore me and make me as good as new but it was obvious after all they had done my doubts still remained. After all it had been three years and I had tried everything in my power to become "normal" again. Here they were able to accomplish in weeks something I had fought years to attain. Once again I was humbled by their approach, technique and confidence. I really don't know why I worry or doubt, they have assured me of the outcome. I guess I just let my past failures try to dictate their outcomes. I'm shutting up now and enjoying that humble pie.

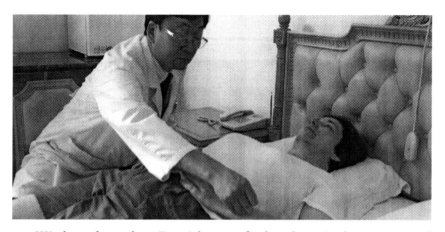

Wednesday the President of the hospital sent word through Dr Xu asking if I would be videotaped for their 50 year anniversary. It was the least I could do for people who had given me so much. Thursday brought a flurry of activity when the video cameras arrived. There were 8 doctors in attendance and the entire atmosphere was one of fun. Two different cameras shot pictures while Dr Han (the President of the Hospital) spoke with me through Dr Xu and did my acupuncture.

He had come on several occasions to do my treatment so this was not out of the ordinary. The cameras did, however, take some getting used to. When all was said and done we all had a good time and the appropriate pictures were taken. I hope to get a finished copy of the video even though I won't be able to understand it.

The week ended on a good note. You know you never know the people you touch unless they are revealed to you. This was the case for me this week. A young Chinese woman of 39 approached me in the hall and we exchanged pleasantries. Ni hao! Or good day, how are you. It seemed simple enough until I saw her again in the exercise room and then in the elevator. She spoke with my nurse and after learning of her interest in my stroke I was determined to meet and talk with her. Here that is quite an undertaking. The nurses and I can maintain a pretty good dialog with their limited English, my limited Chinese, my electronic translator/dictionary, and a good sense of humor. Speaking to a Chinese patient is quite a different endeavor. The nurses warned me that I was a happy person and she seemed very unhappy. I think they were worried that she might discourage me.

I had learned through first hand experience that a stroke is devastating and many times we take out our frustrations on those closest to us. We assume because we could not control the stroke and we have lost control over our bodies so we need to try to control people through our attitudes and actions. After all it's the last form of control we have left! It often is expressed in attitudes of negativity or coldness, anger and resentment but deep down we are afraid, afraid of the unknown. It is that fear that, until met head on and conquered, is really in control.

I coaxed one of the nurses to broach this woman and ask if she wanted to meet me and talk with a translator. Her answer was a resounding yes and with that Dr Xu graciously offered to go with me. We met at half past three in the afternoon in her room. She has a woman who stays with her and helps her with her daily needs. We were seated opposite her on the bed and she started the conversation by asking how long it had been since my stroke. She wanted to know everything. What I suffered from, why I came to China, what treatment I was having, if anyone was here with me. The list seemed endless. But with Dr Xu's help I answered all her questions one by one. She shared how much she was impressed by my strength, my determination, and my attitude. I in turn got to share with her how that had developed and that your beliefs and attitude are what keep you going when nothing else feels possible. After 40 minutes I was forced to cut our time short but we both agreed to talk again. I headed back to my room comforted that God could work and use me even in a different country where the person I'm communicating with is speaking a different language. He has a way of making the insignificant, significant and the impossible, possible!

12

Final Stretch

Friday, September 3, 2004

Today began like all of the other days here, filled with treatments and time off now spent reading , watching a DVD, or my new sport - giving grief to the nurses. There is a joke on the floor now that Ruth has an infectious disease – that of happiness and laughter! As the day wore on I was tempted to become tired, the weather was dreary and damp and not exactly good for balance or eyes. I've learned that my physical body is very much connected with the outside world and on dreary days it is best to not push too hard. I was tempted to curl up with a blanket and the remote when I received a call from Yu Lan. It was regarding the group from England she said that the leader of the group wished to meet with me in about 30 minutes if I agreed. I saw nothing that stood in the way and it seemed like a perfect way to keep myself busy late in the afternoon.

I'm so glad I did! I met with a fascinating woman, Ms Harriet Lansdown who is the Pathway Leader for Traditional Chinese Medicine at the University of Salford,

England. She was a joy to speak with and had brought over a number of individuals to study and learn about TCM. I finally feel after 3 months of treatment like I am my own self again, we had quite a lively discussion talking about my stroke, subsequent condition and affects and the treatment I had received in the states. And why I came to China to seek treatment. I shared with her that it had become the recurring question of all of the international visitors that spoke with me.

"I really can't fault any treatment that I had there in the U.S.," I stated, "but I had come to the end of the line and was beginning to regress instead of progress. I had gone beyond their expectations and they seemed thrilled."

"Well," she replied, "once they treat the initial stroke and stabilize you they look for the underlying cause and treat that. Little is done for the actual stroke other than rehabilitation therapy."

"Exactly!" I remarked. "Here they are treating the brain and making changes at that level. Certainly there is also rehabilitation therapy but the results are amazing. I actually made several of the rehab tools to use at home and was doing all I could with little results for the past two years. What they have done here in a small amount of time is remarkable."

"And it is reproducible" she continued, "I was amazed and excited with the documentation and the awards that their research here has. It's one thing for someone to have remarkable, and some might call miraculous results and quite another to make those results teachable and reproducible."

"It's been difficult" I added, "to convey to others that my treatment here and the results are normal and not something that, even though it seems so to me, is not miraculous. I feel like I am on a mission, a quest as it were to take this information to others. This is too good to keep quiet about."

We continued our conversation and only ended our discussion when Harriet had to leave. I encouraged her to let those who were with her know I would be happy to speak to any of them at any time.

After our talk I was more determined than ever to get a hold of any and all information that the hospital had regarding TCM and its implementation and effects.

Saturday September 4, 2004

This week I spent time down the hall speaking with the woman (Deng Zhen Hong) whom I met last week. It is a bit of a challenge because I need to arrange to have either my translator or Dr Xu available to translate Chinese to English and vice versa. I was amazed in talking with her how much she wants to gain control over her own attitude. Many people who suffer strokes resign themselves to life as an invalid, and I am not simply speaking in terms of the physical body. They set mental and emotional limits for themselves, determined not to cross them for fear they might be hurt. While I acknowledge and understand the fear (far better than you can realize) I also know that it can be mentally and emotionally paralyzing, keeping you from reaching your full potential.

It was obvious that Deng Zhen Hong was a woman who understood the trials that lay ahead of her. I challenged her to see the stroke as a means to learning new things and that she could take the lessons she learns and help someone else the same way I was helping her. This helps to keep a focus beyond self and gives you a reason to live. You do not just exist for your own sake but to help someone else. So many people have asked me if I am getting help for my own sake, so I'll feel better? Certainly not! I mean I don't want to discourage those that get better or seek treatment because they are doing it for themselves but I found that you need a lot more to motivate you during the tough times. And trust me when you've suffered a stroke there are more tough times than you would care to admit.

Deng Zhen Hong shared with me that she very much wants to be happy but that with the stroke it's hard. I understand, that on top of the physical challenges that were thrust on her without warning, she also has mental and emotional challenges to face. A severe stroke tends to be all -inclusive and doesn't leave much alone.

At least she has had the benefits of the herbal medication that Professor Shi developed. It has amazing effects on the brain including helping to stabilize the emotions. I used to struggle with controlling emotions after the stroke, it was as if the floodgates were opened and couldn't be closed. I've been taking the medication since I entered the hospital here and I am amazed with the results. My cognitive functions and my emotions are back to pre-stroke levels.

On Tuesday I met with and spoke to the leading physician from France in stroke treatment and research. Our conversation was quite enjoyable and informative. She wanted to know all the details regarding my bleed and stroke from the moment of its onset thru my hospitalization and rehab and finally my motivation for coming here to China. We talked at length about the medical aspects and the type and amounts of time spent in rehab and she asked what part of my treatment here and subsequent recovery was psychological.

My immediate response was that you could not separate my attitude from the results in TCM. Each of the therapies works together with the others and a good positive attitude was necessary. I reminded her that I was the quintessential patient in all my treatments in the states over the past 2 1/2 years. In fact, I shared, I actually had one of my physicians remark that even if there wasn't anything she could do for me I always made her feel better about herself. Although I had to agree that attitude and expectations tended to go hand in hand, I reiterated that I had spent 2 1/2 years doing all that I could do to "fix" myself after the stroke. It wasn't until my treatment here that I was able to do tasks that I had only dreamed possible after years of trying. So "what" I challenged her was different?

I understand the medical and scientific side but I shared two questions with her that I asked myself upon my arrival:

- ❑ Why would a country practice a form of medicine that is 5000 years old and has a written history of close to 3000 years?
- ❑ Why, when people have to pay for their own treatment, are hospital and the outpatient clinics full?

The answers to both questions are the same - *the treatments and the therapies here work!* When I came here I left my expectations in the dirt, meaning they were as low as they could get. The doctors had to prove to me that TCM worked; I had spent years trying everything with no results. It took weeks of positive results before I started believing them and truth be told part of me still can't believe what is happening to my body. I won't be the one to tell someone

243

they should or should not seek treatment here. I only know I'm kicking myself for not coming sooner.

On Wednesday the international flurry continued as I met a delegation from Italy that included the Under Secretary of Health, Cesare Cursi and a number of physicians and professors from leading Italian medical schools. They asked what has become a recurring question, why did I seek treatment in China? I am the first to admit I'm no physician but whether it is a little stroke, big stroke, hemorrhage or clot, the patient is only concerned about one thing… recovery. Could I do tomorrow what I had done yesterday? I had "recovered" in the U.S. and had bested my physician's wildest hopes but I was not satisfied. I still suffered from an absence of feeling on the right, balance problems, vision problems, and no fine motor skills. I had done the best that I could and was told that I should be happy with what I had recovered. He was impressed with my current recovery status and I challenged him to take this knowledge back to Italy.

China seemed to offer me a chance to regain more of what I thought I had lost forever and in 3 months they have turned a skeptic into a believer. As s result I am probably their biggest advocate now, not just because of what they are doing for me, but also for the thousands of other patients that I see them help every day. It's easy for people to say, 'Oh I'm gad for *you*" but keep themselves out of the picture. If there is one thing I have learned it is that I am not alone and there are plenty of "miracles" happening everyday.

I have been so impressed with my treatment that I wrote a letter to the President of China, I don't know if he will get it or if he'll read it but this is what I said:

Dear President Hu Jin Tao

I realize you are a very busy man but I hope this letter or the message it contains reaches you.

I am a mother of 3 and a survivor of a severe stroke three years ago that was expected to kill me. I have exceeded the hopes of my physicians in America and was convinced I could be better. I was fortunate enough to have a Chinese exchange student who suggested I look in China for my answer. With her help I found the First Teaching Hospital of Tianjin University of Traditional Chinese Medicine. As a result I have become the first American to seek medical treatment in China.

I wanted to take this opportunity to express to you what a wonderful treasure this hospital and traditional Chinese medicine are to China. I have only been here 8 weeks and in that time they have restored all feeling to my right side (I had no feeling for 3 years), restored my balance, I am seeing fine motor movement return and restored clear vision. The results are miraculous to say the least. I serve on the American Heart Association Iowa Advocacy Committee and they are watching my treatment here in China with great excitement. Strokes are still the leading cause of disability in America.

I have found first hand that this hospital and the doctors using TCM, with a 5000 year history, are on the leading edge of medicine incorporating both eastern and western methodology and taking it to new heights. Professor Shi Xuemin, the academician of the Engineering Academy of China; has directed my treatment and he together with Dr. Bian Jinling have successfully combined acupuncture, tuina, and traditional Chinese medicines to begin a restoration process that no one in the U.S. dreamed possible. I hope, as I share my story, I will be the first of many who can reap the tremendous benefits that China has to offer to the world.

Thank you.

As is evident in my letter I feel very strongly about this hospital, these doctors and TCM. They are giving me back physical function and more importantly an increased understanding of my body. They will be the first to admit their own limitations and as such offer no "miracle cures." They have completely embraced and utilize western medicine but their ability to combine traditional Chinese medicine with the western medicine gives them answers to many questions we are still asking.

Tuesday, September 7, 2004

Yesterday I was pleased to meet a woman from Germany, her name is Kerstin and she is only 28. She was recently diagnosed with multiple sclerosis and before starting any "western" treatment she came here on the advice of her acupuncturist. She checked in Sunday for about three months stay and came with her boyfriend. I shared with her that she was wise to bring someone with her but he can only stay with her for a few weeks so I am certain that she and I will become good friends.

I studied German in high school but that was many years ago and I'm glad that her English is quite good. She brought her laptop computer for the stay and I explained that she can hook up to the internet from her room. She was thrilled! She had lots of questions and wanted to know all about me, my condition following the stroke, my rehabilitation, and finally my decision to come here. I tried to answer all of her questions and provide her with as much information as I could regarding the day-to-day events here. At the same time I wanted to know about her, her diagnosis, prognosis, and decision to come here.

We talked about everything, the doctors, nurses, treatments, tests, time off, food and even laundry. It was enjoyable being able to speak to someone in English other than my translator! We had such a good time talking that I was surprised when Da Gui stuck her head in to let me know it was time for my foot massage. I left and we agreed to continue our conversation later.

I began my foot massage with Da Gui only to be interrupted by my nurse who came to trim my fingernails, nothing slips their attention. She and Da Gui enjoyed talking while I played visual tennis between the two of them and watched as the conversation went back and forth. Every now and then I caught a word I knew but most of it was too fast to understand.

While we were all together Dr Bian and Dr Xu entered. Dr Bian was happy that I had met the new patient and hoped that I would explain some of the treatments in more detail. They chatted quite a bit and then asked what I had planned for dinner. When I responded and said nothing, I wasn't hungry another discussion ensued. It was decided that Dr Xu would run to the store and pick a few things up for me to eat. Dr Bian does not like it when I skip a meal so Dr Xu ran to the store and picked up some fruit and vegetables for me. Da Gui finished my foot massage and before I knew it night was here and I was more than ready for bed.

Friday, September 10, 2004

I've begun to notice what were subtle changes in my right hand are now becoming more pronounced. The shaking or tremors still exist but I am able to exert more control over them. I have gone from simply grasping objects to being able to manipulate them. The process is slow but I am seeing progress. I still play the peg game everyday inserting wooden pegs into a base but now I am rotating and manipulating the pegs. The process that started with sight, I am now slowly beginning to transfer to actual brain activity and recognition that does not require sight to complete.

In the exercise room I have been moved over to machines that work specifically on the hand. It amazes me that they did not put me on these machines sooner but I have learned that their methods, although a bit different, have far reaching results. I am able to use the right hand to carry anything without watching it for fear that I might drop it. Being able to feel things has definite advantages. I've found by using several machines that there are a few muscle groups needing a lot of attention. I am hoping that over the next several weeks here I can correct that weakness.

The changes have made quite a difference in the things that I am able to do. I now do several things with my right hand, such as use the TV remote, hold the telephone, drink bottled water, shake hands and open and close doors. Recognition is slowly increasing and in time I hope there is little noticeable difference between right and left hands.

I spent more time getting to know Kerstin from Germany and learning a bit more of her signs and symptoms. TCM is unlike basic western medicine in its root philosophy and does not treat symptoms specifically. TCM is a complex system in which the doctors begin with the understanding that we are products of our total environment and their treatment is reflected in that. It is definitely different in that they expect the body, when stimulated, to heal itself. I guess this is not as far fetched, as it might initially seem. After all, when we get a cut we expect the body to heal it!

Sunday, September 19, 2004

It has been another exciting week and one full of still more changes. I noticed a pain in my right lower back. It is different to sense pain after so many years of feeling nothing. It felt as if it were a pinched nerve or a pulled muscle. Again, the mind is guessing. The doctors discovered that not only is there a pain in my back but it extends down the leg and into the heel. It follows the sciatic nerve; they began treating it with acupuncture needles and heat. As it has been treated it is slowly increasing the feelings in my foot. I am at a "prickly" stage and the affected area is slowly diminishing and being replaced with normalcy. It is really quite exciting!

This weekend the excitement continued with a move. The doctors asked if I would be willing to shift from room 1202 to 1209 so that I could be next door to the gal from Germany. Her boyfriend went home on Thursday and they wanted to keep her happy. Because she speaks very good English, I will suffer (Ha, Ha) and endure the move down the hall. It has been a real joy having her here on the floor, it has been more than 30 years since I studied German in high school but it is all coming back. I escorted her to the massage room downstairs and spoke with the Chinese attendants for her. At one point she asked me a question and I answered her without missing a beat. Not until you consider that she asked the question in German does it mean much. We both got a big laugh when we realized what happened.

My husband called and said that several friends and relatives had asked why I had moved.

"Isn't it obvious?" I asked

"Not really!" he replied.

"Well just tell them I got into trouble, that before the move I was only two doors away from the elevator. Now I am across from the nurses' station! That should answer their questions!" I said laughing

"Oh yea so the nurses can keep an eye on you! Those treatments must be having a greater impact than I thought." He boldly remarked

I must confess the move did take energy to accomplish but I am happy to act as an encourager to someone else. After all, I have about 40 days left and if I can help while I am here it is a good use of my time. The only hitch is it will take a day before the Internet is connected through my phone but I guess I can handle that. Kerstin was diagnosed in May with Multiple Sclerosis and she is only 28. I am impressed that she followed the advice of her acupuncturist and sought treatment here. They have had great success with the people who have come even in late stages of MS, it is not a disease that they can cure but their treatments are very effective at putting the disease into a remission. She has been a joy to get to know and I have one more place to put my head the next time I'm in Germany!

The "pain" in my back has added another treatment to my very busy morning schedule. Now it looks something like this:

6:30	Nurse takes Vital Signs
7:00	Breakfast
8:00	Nurses on Rounds

9:15 –9:45	Acupuncture
10:00 – 10:40	Heat and Herb Salve Treatment
10:40 – 11:00	Foot and arm soaks
11:00 – 11:45	Tuina
11:45 –11:55	Cupping
12:15	Lunch
3:15 – 3:45	Acupuncture
4:30 – 5:30	Foot Massage

This week I will not exercise while I have heat treatments (shen deng), normally I have a work out in rehab from 8:00 – 9:00. I think I'll enjoy a little break, Ha Ha!

Overall, I'm excited about the progress that is being made. At times it seems slow but when you consider that I have gone nearly 3 years without feeling and only limited mobility it is very exciting. The feelings of "normality" in my anatomy are quite overwhelming in my mind. I keep thinking I will wake up and things will return to numbness. As deep feelings within the body take on a level of normality, I am shocked even further. TCM focuses a lot on how the body interacts with the surroundings. I have noticed a big link here with weather and as a result lower my expectations on those days but I'm thrilled with all that is possible even on bad days!

October 3, 2004

I know I am not noting my everyday adventures as frequently but progress appears to be slow and steady and I am spending much of my free time with Kerstin. As Sundays go I thought today would be pretty typical, my standard therapies followed by time to relax. Nothing could have been further from the truth. Everyone here in China is celebrating a national holiday from October 1ˢᵗ through the 7ᵗʰand as a result the doctors are only here in the morning for acupuncture and the nursing staff is reduced to give people time off. Based on this it is easy to see where I would get the idea for a relaxed day, I've actually enjoyed the holiday because it keeps my afternoon to a minimum of activity.

This morning I felt as if the doctors were "surrounding the wagons" for a big attack, after they placed the needles they were all smiling and encircled my bed.

"What?" I asked cautiously. "You all look like you've swallowed the proverbial canary." I don't quite know if Dr Xu understood my statement but she smiled broadly just the same.

"The doctors would like to take you somewhere this afternoon. Will you feel rested enough to go?" She inquired.

"Sure. If they finish my IV in time." I replied cautiously.

"Good, they would like you to go to a wedding with them." She continued, "One of the doctors on the 11ᵗʰ floor is getting married today."

With that they all smiled and exited, content that they had accomplished their task. In the meantime my mind was racing. This all sounded like fun but what time, what would I wear, when would we get back, and what exactly is a Chinese wedding like? I was determined to corner my nurse when she returned to remove the needles.

The 20 minute wait seemed like an eternity but the nurse finally entered, smiled and began to remove each of the needles as I began my extensive "wedding" interrogation. She smiled with each of my questions and let me know that I would be ready to go at 3:30 and Kerston (the German patient) would go too. Great, at least I wouldn't stand out as the only foreigner there! Come to think of it she really didn't answer my questions but diverted them beautifully. Just then Kerston popped her head into my room.

"I understand we are going to a wedding." She remarked.

"Yes." I replied, "They surrounded me when I had needles in so I figured why not, it beats sitting in my room."

"You too?" She smiled, "They sure know when to ask!"

I filled her in on the details that I had gathered and we were both thrilled that we were going together. She headed back to her room when the nurse came in to find her. I continued with treatments, first shen dong (heat therapy), then zhen xi (herb soaks), followed by ba hao guan (cupping). As soon as cupping was over it was a brief visit to the bathroom before I got my daily IV medication. It took about 4 hours and kept me sitting in bed focusing on a DVD. I guess I should be thankful for the diversion of the DVD, without it the time would go really slow.

This was definitely not the typical Sunday that I had back home. Before the stroke we would attend church in the mornings and after the stroke it became next to impossible for me to attend. Between the dealing with no feeling in my bladder and falling asleep without direct interaction, it kept me home. Here in China my days were always filled with treatments and the progress I had made would be most appreciated when I got back to the states. I could hardly wait to attend a Sunday service knowing that I wouldn't be plagued by any of the medical problems that had been once created by the stroke.

My treatments seemed to click by until it came time for the IV. It was boring and slow and sitting still has never been something that I have appreciated. I sat watching the

DVD as the medication dripped into the vein in my arm. The nurses switched bags after 2 hours and I was in the home stretch with one to go. I glanced up when I heard a knock on the door, expecting to see a nurse entering to remove the IV. I was not prepared to see Dr Han enter wearing "street clothes" prepared for the wedding. The nurse followed and removed the IV and I hurried into the bathroom to change out of my shorts and T-shirt into long pants and a blouse. I forgot to mention that I had on a holter monitor until 10:30 that morning and back-to-back treatments prevented me from taking a shower or washing my hair. I exited the bathroom looking a bit disheveled as Dr Han grabbed my brush and proceeded to run it through my hair.

I was sorry the wedding wasn't 1 week later, and then at least I would have one outfit that fit. As it stood the clothes that I had were way too big and hung on my body. I had lost 8" off my waist and over 40 pounds since I had been in China. It had been fun for the staff to joke with me about and I must admit I didn't have a problem with it until now. Oh well, I could hide in the back and watch the proceedings and no one would notice. I stood at the nurses station and waited for Kerstin.

As soon as she appeared we headed to the elevator with Dr Han. This can be tricky if you stopped to realize that Dr Han spoke no English, fortunately my Chinese is much better than when I came. When we got to the ground floor Dr Han motioned to a row of chairs and asked us to have a seat. With that she disappeared. Kerstin and I realized that we had been left alone, if even for a moment and laughed about making a run for it! We wouldn't have gotten very far our Chinese was rather poor and I doubt that the taxi drivers would have understood anything we were saying.

Moments later Dr Han reappeared with Dr Bian and then they both disappeared again. Kerstin and I sat discussing what we thought might happen at the wedding. Neither of us had any idea of what to expect and spent the time talking about weddings we had attended in the past. I shared with her the events surrounding my own wedding and how the pastor joked after the ceremony that his fee increased when it was time to sign the certificate!

"It wasn't legal until we all signed!" I remarked, "or at least that was the impression the pastor gave us as he smiled."

A short while later Dr Han reappeared and we followed her to the main door. It seemed that they had been waiting for Dr Lu to arrive with a car. He pulled up and hopped out and opened the doors as we all piled in and started the trip. We passed another wedding procession on the way and noticed the long stretch limo with flowers on the hood. A van was in front of the car with the back open and a man videotaping the limo. Dr Lu maneuvered the car passed the procession and we continued on. We finally pulled up to a large restaurant where we got out of the car just in time to see another limo pull up and hundreds of firecrackers being lit. The sound was deafening and went on for what seemed like an eternity. This is a tradition in China and required at weddings.

We made our way upstairs where there were throngs of people. Kerstin and I made our way to the back of the room and tried to remain hidden

there. I felt very secure on the back hall, looking the way I did. The doctors and nurses decided to help me and before I knew it I was a guest of honor at the wedding. Normally this would have been an honor but in China the honored guests sit in front of everyone else. Remember I had left the hospital looking more than a bit disheveled. As a result, I was to find myself sitting next to Doctor Bian and two other employers and sited across from the bride and broom's parents. This alone would have been enough to embarrass me but to my surprise the doctors informed me that at the end of the ceremony I was expected to bless the marriage "in Chinese." I rapidly requested that they write down exactly I was to say so that when my time to speak occurred I would not look dumbstruck. The blessed event took place and I survived! It was worth the suffering that I endured because following the wedding was an enormous meal. It was fabulous!!

I returned to the hospital and my normal, boring routine. It was nice to have had the experience but I honestly have to say I am glad it is over and I survived.

Sunday, Oct 10, 2004

I only have 18 days left in my stay here in China and I want to make the most out of every moment that I have left. So much has happened to and for me during this stay that I am still trying to absorb it all. As I rolled over on my right side in bed I was reminded that it is something that I haven't been able to do for 3 years. Lying on my right side was extremely uncomfortable and sleeping on that side was impossible, so it's hard to believe that is in my past.

The discomfort that I have felt in my right back has slowly subsided with the treatments and mobility to that area is increasing daily. I told my daughter that I now felt like I could shoot baskets with a basketball again, something that after the stroke I never dreamed possible. Jumping is going to take some work but my right hand is gaining control and dexterity each day. My balance is wonderful and although I still feel a bit off at times I am able to steady myself in the most unusual situations. I had fun yesterday riding on their flat escalator that travels between the floors at the department store. I was practicing holding on with the right hand and maintaining balance while slowly walking forward. Again, something that was difficult if not impossible just 6 months ago. Simply getting on a moving escalator took an extreme amount of thought, balance and guts

Walking has taken on new vistas. Not too long ago it was something that I did for short distances and with great difficulty. I can now meander through a shopping mall or department store and not worry about falling into someone or something and I don't spend my time trying to locate seats or bathrooms.

I actually went shopping at a department store here in China for shoes, something I haven't done in 3 years. The tennis shoes that I have worn since the stroke are large and use Velcro to fasten them. I hadn't realized what I was missing until I tried on a pair of shoes that fit! They were wonderful. It will take a little getting used to but I'm excited. I actually bought a pair of shoes that look good! It is a strange feeling to have a right foot and leg after years of not feeling them.

Now I am looking forward to having clothes that fit. I am not quite 6 feet tall and I have very long legs and with the massive weight loss that I have experienced I treated myself to having a suit of clothes hand tailored for me. It was cheaper than buying if off the rack and still possible in

China. The clothes should arrive Monday or Tuesday of this next week.

Monday, October 11, 2004

This morning I was able to return to exercise. I must admit I was a bit apprehensive because the doctors would not allow me to go to the rehab gym during these past 3 weeks while they were determining the reason for one of my abnormal lab results. Only one blood test was elevated and it registers an enzyme that is typically elevated after a heart attack. Because of my own fathers death at 42 from a massive heart attack they were particularly cautious about me. They had noticed that since my departure from the blood pressure medications that I had taken since the stroke my pulse had decreased greatly. It was now about 56 and that was down considerably from the rate of 74 that it had been. Knowing that when I was in shape years ago it was not uncommon to see it remain in the 50's during rest, I was not surprised, I had lost a total of 70 pounds over the past 7 months and I expected some change. The elevated CK could also be attributed to a release of enzymes by skeletal muscles. Because many of the muscles were now being felt and utilized for the first time in 3 years and I could feel the "burn" of many of them, I attributed the lab result to use of unused muscles. The doctors, however, wanted to be certain so over the course of the past 3 weeks repeat blood work was done, EKG's were set and done every 2 days, and exercise was out. I am happy to report that I am in excellent shape after all the tests have been completed!

After three weeks I thought that I would have gone backwards and exercise would be difficult but the acupuncture has actually kept me on track. I picked up like nothing had happened and was thrilled at how good it felt. Prior to my stroke I was always on the go and after the stroke it was a different story. I knew it would take time to "get back to normal" but I was not prepared for what normal was. My energy level was a 4 on a scale of 1-10 (10 being greatest) and that was a good day. On a bad day I was lucky to make it to 1, sure I did a real good job of trying to hide the results of the stroke when I was in public. But I paid dearly for everything I did and things that I wouldn't have given a second thought to in the past would drain me. Family and friends who were closest to me could tell the difference. I would save up energy if I had an event for one of the kids at school or had an appointment to attend. Going out became the exception rather than the norm. I was able to "keep it together" for the kids but it took a tremendous toll on my marriage. The only person that I felt I could share with was the one whom I was closest too.

Steve! He didn't just get one or two things dumped on him it was truckloads! Feelings of frustration, anger, resentment and fear all came out at his feet. He was a dutiful husband and stuck by through it all but struggled constantly. It wasn't until a counselor friend of mine shared some wonderful insight that it all made sense.

"He wants to fix you." Kevin shared, "Men like to fix things and if they can't fix you then you must not be broken. After all, they are men and they can fix anything that is broken!"

It was as if I had been smacked in the head by a block of wood, of course this is why he focused so on what the doctors said. He along with them wanted me to "do" all the "right" things. It didn't matter if they worked or not, just going through the motions seemed to place a check in some invisible box in his head. To him the stroke was a massive list of things to do and when I reached the end, well... I'd reached the end and that was that! Logical isn't it! It didn't seem to bother him that my neurologist couldn't give me a name of anyone who had survived this type of stroke because no one else existed. They said be content with what returned and he was able to take them at their word.

The rub or friction in our relationship occurred because I could not be content. I was constantly pushing and stretching myself, blind to the fact that in the process I was pushing and stretching him. And this was a man who was content with life just where he was. The analogy of a bull in a china shop doesn't quite compare to the purpose or direction that I had but the energy and the results are about the same. The more I pushed, the more damage to our relationship I caused. Because he had not personally experienced the frustration of the after effects of the stroke he could not comprehend its impact. The experts said, "be content" so he was. I was the one with the problem!

I learned one important lesson from the stroke and that is how to play the shoe game. For those of you who don't know what I'm talking about let me explain. It is extremely important that we learn how to step out of ourselves and put ourselves into the shoes or place of someone else. Truly understand what they are experiencing with their physical senses, mind, and emotional being. Typically we step into someone else's world and envision how it would affect us and how we would respond. Although we can learn a lot about ourselves in this scenario we know and therefore understand little about the person whose' shoes we are standing in. Each person is made up of a complex history of ideas and experiences and it is important that we take those into consideration when we are trying to gain understanding. A while back there was a TV program called "The Pretender" where an individual became different personas. He was a master at the "shoe game" and as a result could out think his adversaries while righting the wrongs of the world. While I in no way expect you to go that far it is a good picture of what we need to do in order to truly understand another person.

My life experiences have taught me how important it is to play the "shoe game" and how important it is to challenge others to partake as well. There are numerous saying that share the importance of walking in someone else's steps but I have learned that it is crucial that we go further and see with their eyes and hear with their ears.

This is the piece of the puzzle that I needed to make my relationship with Steve grow. I needed to understand how the stroke affected him and his understanding and reactions to it. I also needed to challenge him to play the shoe game and see the world through my eyes, not how he would do things but how I have dealt with things. When we were married the pastor remarked that we were two distinctly different individuals embarking on a life together. At no time in our past 18 years together have we been tested as we have with this devastating stroke. The fact that Steve has allowed me to spend months in a different country enduring medical treatment and "chasing a dream," as many have called it, is a testament of his love and faith in my vision and me.

I have been blessed to find a hospital that seeks answers unlike any I have ever seen before and those answers have restored me physically, emotionally and spiritually. Now I am on a mission to share that love, hope, and vision to others who are seeking answers for themselves or their loved ones.

Monday October 18, 2004

Reality is beginning to set in today, I faxed my husband the final cost estimate for my remaining 10 days and sent out the last email update to those tracking my progress. This afternoon Dr Bian pulled me aside and asked to have a talk. As both she and I walked into my room we were followed closely by Dr Xu. I felt a bit like a kid who was called to the principal's office, I sat down as Dr Bian took a seat opposite me. Hmm, I thought, she seldom sits to talk and as a woman on the go we typically talk while she stands in my doorway or at the foot of my bed. Today she pulled up a chair and sat. I glanced at her and observed that she had an unusual firm look on her face, I really didn't know how to read her. I sat smiling, trying to hide any emotions as she talked to me in Chinese. I watched her carefully and then waited patiently for Dr Xu to translate.

"Dr Bian wants to know if you want a party with all of the doctors and nurses?" She said with a smile.

I learned along time ago that here they assume nothing and they wouldn't presume to hold a party in my honor without first asking me.

"Certainly!" was my response, "they've done so much for me, I would love an opportunity to see them all one last time and thank them."

Next Monday October 25th was selected as a good date and Dr Bian wanted to know if there was any food in particular that I wanted.

"Anything is fine," I said.

It was obvious that there was a great deal of emotion involved that was being contained. For the first time going home took on a stunning reality. All the Doctors and nurses had become like family to me, I had many new brothers and sisters and daughters and sons!

Something wonderful had happened during my stay and treatment, I was not viewed so much as a patient but as a friend. They were all ready talking about my return trip and how much time I would need in order to sight see a bit more. Dr Bian and Dr Xu continued as we talked about my travel home, my bags, flights, time enroute, and who would meet me. I assured them both that although it was a long flight I would take it easy and my family would all be there to greet me. Dr Bian seemed content with my plans but this was the first time I had even slightly seen a deeper emotional side to her. As my plans were shared and met with approval, the date for the party was confirmed and both doctors exited to the nurses station to announce the plan. I followed smiling and accepted praise from Dr Han who kept remarking how good I was looking with my weight loss.

The evening continued as I pulled out my bags and began the tedious job of packing, rearranging and weighting to make certain that I would be within limits. I decided that I would leave all my now over size clothes behind to provide more room and lighten my load. I packed and repacked to disperse weight and make the bags easy to handle. I'm certain for all the work I've done I'll end up changing it at the last minute.

Chang Quan, my evening nurse, came in to take my evening blood pressure and noticed the bags on my bed. She helped me move the bags off my bed and onto the floor and then looked up at me with sad eyes. She had worked the night I went out with all the nurses so I asked if she would be able to attend the party on the 25th. She lit up brightly with a smile.

"Yes" she replied with a sense of confidence in her voice, "I do not work and I can come."

She reached out and took my hand as she smiled. Chang Quan had become like another daughter to me and I was touched that she would be able to attend. I was even more thrilled when she informed me she would be working on the night/morning that I left for the airport. It was as if God put icing on my cake, knowing she would be one of the last faces I would see on my departure from China gave me a warm feeling deep within.

As night began to envelope my room I curled up on my bed, pulling the blanket up tightly. I couldn't help but thinking of the morning before my stroke and how I snuggled up under the blanket then. It seemed so much had happened since then and now for the first time in three years I could curl up again comfortably. So many changes had taken place since the first day I arrived in Tianjin and was met with a swarm of physicians. I had changed on the outside for sure but it was the inner peace and confidence that to me was the most noticeable. God had worked 10,000 miles from my home and I was reminded that just like being a foreigner in a foreign land as a Christian I am an alien in this world and here only as a temporary assignment. One question remained unanswered in my mind, would my treatment and subsequent return to normalcy go unnoticed or would it have a dramatic effect of opening people's minds to new possibilities and solutions? Thoughts continued to flow through my mind. Having met with so many people from so many different countries around the world, what would be the affect? I drifted off to sleep contemplating the results that my visit and treatment might have throughout the world. Whatever the outcome I knew that this entire episode in my life was much bigger than me and would therefore require a greater power to oversee it.

Thursday October 21, 2004

It doesn't seem possible but next week at this time I will be on the road headed toward Beijing. Yesterday I met a group from Russia followed by a group from Australia. I have become rather well versed in being able to share my story in a short period of time and highlight those areas of interest. The group from Australia asked a number of pertinent questions that I was happy to answer. I have been giving the nurses and doctors here a hard time about their English. They have become much more proficient since my arrival and I said I would have to send more American patients over so they don't forget what they have learned. I have already told both JinWei and Yiwei that they will need to speak to me in Chinese so I can continue in my learning.

Later in the day Liang Hui returned to take me to one of the other floors to meet some of the Chinese stroke patients. We met Dr Bian and Dr Han as we walked to the elevator and Dr Bian was concerned that I might get cold. You see since my arrival I have worn shorts and although it makes for easy access during treatments it has also been a major focus of the doctors. As the weather has gotten cooler they continually ask me: "Leng, bu leng?" which means cold or not cold? I always reply "bu leng!" (not cold) but it has become somewhat of a running gag.

As we continued on to the elevators we passed the head nurse who smiled, pointed at my shorts and laughed. We only had a short wait before the doors on the elevator opened and we were ushered inside. All of the elevators are continually staffed and the women who staff them have gotten to know me very well. They tend to look out for me making certain that I am given clear access on and off and communicating in Chinese to others on my behalf.

"Ni hao Ruthie!" The elevator operator offered as I boarded. I could tell by her smile and look that she too was concerned that I was wearing shorts.

"Wo bu leng, ni hao ma?" I said in my best Chinese both answering her unasked question and asking her how she was.

"Hen hao" was her reply!

All of the people in the hospital call me Ruthie the doctors, nurses and staff alike all treat me as a family member and have made my stay here most memorable. The elevator attendant and Liang Hui exchanged words in Chinese and although I could not understand all of the words it was quite obvious that I was the source of their conversation.

"She says that your Chinese is very good" Liang remarked.

"Only the small number of words that I know" I replied.

It was obvious I spoke very little. Over the months I had become quite good at listening and understanding much of what was being said around me. It was quite obvious when I was the cornerstone of the conversation but more challenging when they were simply chatting amongst themselves.

Before I knew it the elevators opened on the eighth floor and Liang motioned to exit. I stepped out and allowed Liang to lead. I had no idea where we were heading and I've become a good follower since the stroke. We briskly walked

down the hall as I realized that Liang was looking for a doctor. I stopped as she apparently met with success and then we proceeded behind the doctor to another room down the hall. Upon entering Liang held a brief conversation with the first doctor as she made a quick introduction, smiled and then headed back out the door. Liang continued speaking with the new doctor and then we all headed back out into the hall. I would later learn that the first doctor we met was the director of several floors.

We proceeded into one of the rooms that was lined on one side with occupied beds surrounded by family members of each patient. I had learned early on during my stay that family is extremely prized in China and it seemed that each of these patients had at least one person present. I had been told that if an individual did not have any family then neighbors would help. It was apparent from the numbers of people that this was not just a good story to be told but a reality in their culture. Something that I think we would do well to emulate!

It was apparent that as an American I stood out and we were attracting quite a bit of attention. As we approached the bed of the first patient the doctor began speaking to Liang who in turn translated for me. Apparently he was a 46 year old male who had suffered a brainstem bleed as well and as she shared the doctor pulled out the MRI. I glanced at it as the doctor held it up and the spot of the bleed was very apparent. I spoke with Liang and asked what kinds of signs or symptoms the patient had before his stroke. It seemed that he had a history of hypertension and a severe headache just prior to the stroke. He had been transferred within days of his stroke from a western style hospital to this one. The only lasting effects from the stroke appeared to be some minor facial paralysis that I was told was responding well to the acupuncture.

We passed through several rooms and the families and patient were quite amazed when they learned that I was also a stroke survivor who had come here for treatment. I remarked to Liang that this trek through the hospital was definitely not something I would have attempted 5 months earlier! It was apparent after seeing numerous patients that those who received the treatments and therapies early in their rehabilitation phase were responding much quicker than those who were transferred after several months.

We continued on seeing patient after patient and the doctor informed me that approximately 90% of the patients that she treated on her floor were stroke cases. I was encouraged to hear that they received much the same treatment as I did and it was apparent that the families of these patients were directly involved daily in the patients well being and rehabilitation.

We completed our tour and I was able to convince Liang Hui that I would enjoy the walk up the stairs to the 12th floor. This was something that I would not have welcomed just 5 months earlier! We arrived at the 12th floor just in time for my foot massage.

As I lay on the bed the flurry of the days events were at the forefront of my mind. It seemed that there was so much to do and yet little time remained. Dr Xu entered with my camera in hand having been gracious enough to take some pictures of the outside of the hospital. The fact that in a matter of days I would be packing up and heading home was increasingly apparent with the faces that greeted me at each turn.

The staff was going out of their way when I found out that the party they had planned for me was going to be held at the hospital on the 26th. It seems that no one wanted to be left out or miss it. I was indeed honored and yet I got a lump in my throat each time I thought about it. I would have to ask them to provide boxes of tissues for the party and my last day. The fact that I would be leaving the hospital at 5 in the morning when no one was around except one nurse, now offered me a degree of comfort.

Thursday October 21, 2004

As the days here become fewer and fewer I have been focusing on what things I have learned that I can take back and share with others. I have been honored to have 8 of the best doctors care for me and provide me with a schedule of treatments and acupuncture. They have treated everything from my lack of feeling to a common cold, and very effectively I might add. I got an unexpected visitor that day, Yiwei's father was in Beijing and hired a car to bring him to Tianjin for a visit, we only had 30 minutes together before he had to leave but it was a good indicator of what is in store when I return to the states.

My translator, Yu Lan arrived just as he made it to my room. I looked up as one of the doctors ushered him to my door. Startled was my first response after all it was not someone I expected, especially coming all the way from

Changsha. My initial tendency quickly turned to elation when I realized he had come from Beijing just to see me.

He took a moment to gain his composure as I stood and turned to face him. He made a comment to Yu Lan as I uttered my brief "ni hao". She relayed that if he hadn't seen me for himself he would not have believed the change that had occurred. Sure I had lost weight but what he noticed was the speed and way in which I moved. It is difficult when you look at your self each day to comprehend the dramatic change that others will see after 5 months. I was thrilled to see a familiar face and when he was so startled at the changes that they had made in me it reaffirmed that the investment in time, money and labor was well worth it. We continued our conversation and talked about the treatments, my plans after returning and his daughter at college. It seemed as if we just got started when he had to go to catch a flight. I assured him I would visit again in Changsha next summer and asked him to pass on my progress to JinWei's parents. We parted with a simple bye and I was left to talk with Yu Lan.

She had visited Beijing the day before and confirmed that I would have assistance from Beijing through Tokyo. I would spend 30+ hours on planes and in airports and they wanted to make certain that I would have wheelchairs and assistance all the way. They wanted me rested after my long flight and although I could walk I knew the stress of the trip would take its toll so I went along with my doctors plans. She returned my passport and plane ticket and assured me all was in order for my flight home. It's nice to have people who will look out for me, I guess I am accustom to doing things on my own and its nice to be spoiled for a change.

I had just finished up with Yu Lan when Dr Xu entered my room.

"Dr Bian says you will have an herb bath today okay?" She informed me.

"I guess so?" was my response, "if that is what Dr Bian has said I guess I won't argue."

I had learned log ago that Dr Bian looked out for my welfare as if I were her own flesh and blood and she had never steered me wrong. If she said I was having an herb bath then I was having an herb bath and there was no question about it. I just wondered where mei rong and zu liao were going to fit in. Mei rong was a face massage and with the number of needles that I had in my face head and neck each day I really looked forward to it each week. Zu liao was my regular foot massage and it was having a dramatic effect on my overall body. Dr Xu assured me I needn't worry and that she and Dr Bian would escort both Kerstin and I downstairs after 3:00.

Three o'clock came and it was Yu Lan and Dr Bian who ended up leading the way. Both Kerstin and I were totally blind when it came to seeing what awaited us. We ended up going to a secluded area in the first level of the hospital just beyond the foot massage and face massage area. The room we were led to was lined with lockers and we were asked to disrobe and enter the bath area. I learned long ago that modesty was something that others seemed to have because after having 3 kids and a stroke, mine was gone. We were wet down with warm water and allowed to soak in a hot herb bath for 20 minutes. It was wonderful! Then the attendant began using a coarse gloved hand to aggressively massage my entire body and remove all layers of dead skin. I was finally rinsed off and lead out to the dressing room where they had clean attire for me to wear. I waited as Kerstin followed and we both were then taken to the face massage area.

Talk about relaxed, as we lay there getting the face massage I had a hard time staying awake. From there it was time for the foot massage. We moved out of the face massage room back into the front entry room for our foot massage. This room is filled with at least 30 overstuffed chairs that envelop you when you sit. Foot massage in China is a standard and you can get them just about anywhere. I have found that their technique is both invigorating and pleasant and the results are wonderful. The foot massage starts out with the 10 minute herb foot soak and while that is happening the therapist begins a hand and arm massage. By the time they got to my feet I was so relaxed you could have held me in a bowl. When all was said and done and it was time to walk back to my room it was difficult to motivate myself to move.

I managed to get to my feet and make the trip upstairs were I finished my supper and found my way to my bed and a nice warm blanket. Sleep came easily that night and I was forced to admit it was times like these that I will really miss!

Saturday October 23, 2004

Yesterday seemed to come and go so quickly that I almost didn't have time to notice that it was my last Friday in China for quite some time. I managed to call my son at 8:20, which was 7:20 a.m. his time and wish him a happy birthday. It's at moments like these that I miss home. I assured him I would be back soon and he went over the gifts he received as I heard a game running in the background. I was assured that he was just checking it out prior to school, having just received it. Content with his answer I let it pass, games were strictly prohibited prior to school but in this case I would make an exception.

The kids had done so much growing up in the 5 months since I left for China. It would be good to see them and yet I kept wondering what I would see. I reflected on the fact that only 3 years ago there was a strong chance that I would never see them again. I mean we begin dying the moment that we are born. Our days are numbered. We just do not keep that reality in the forefront of our minds. It is not until some outside force acts as a reminder of our mortality or vulnerability that we stop and take stock of our lives. And it seems that many people are content to live day by day not considering where they have been or where they are going.

It seems cliché, but just as the stone that is thrown into the water causes ripples on the surface, so top our lives affect others. Too often we don't think about the stone that now sits on the bottom of the lake, we only see the ripples that it created. If we did, we would realize that although it is small it is having an effect on its surroundings. It is displacing water, moving sand, providing a spot for algae to grow, acting as a refuge for small fish, any number of things. In fact if enough stones were cast into the water the lake would be filled. Seems to be a bit far fetched but that is the insight that visionaries have, they may be one person but they see, realize and hold fast to the fact that they have the ability to effect 10's of thousands and ultimately millions of people.

That is the hope that leads me, pulls me, and ultimately guides me. God isn't finished with me yet! He fully intends to use my life to impact hundreds and thousands of lives. That may seem arrogant to some but in reality I am just a person like so many, who has suffered greatly. But I have chosen to overcome that suffering and so many more obstacles placed in front of me. How? Through a mindset on things that are bigger than me. My life here on earth is temporary, meaning any and all challenges and obstacles that I face are temporary. If I truly believe that my spirit is eternal, then the body is simply a vessel that I inhabit to use to learn and serve others.

Hence the words that I am always sharing with others: "it's not what you know that matters, but what you are willing to learn" and "life is a gift… but living is a choice!" Both of these are things that I have learned and I challenge anyone and everyone to take them to heart and ask themselves what kind of impact they and their life is having on others?

13

The Homecoming

The day started early and at 4:00 a.m. I began by changing clothes and packing my bags for the long journey ahead. I didn't have much to try and fit in, mainly toiletries and sleep

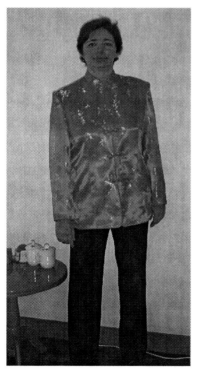

wear. When everything was stowed for the trip I began the process of burning CD's for the nurses. It was something that I had begun the night before and stopped to take a rest. Now I began anew by dragging pictures onto the blank CD and burning enough copies for all the doctors and nurses. (I don't know what we did before digital photography. It certainly has made sharing memories much easier) While that slow process began I quickly washed my hair and checked the clock. When en 5:00 a.m. came I debated checking on my nurse but only a moment later she popped her head in to see if I was ready.

At 5:10 Yu Lan showed up ready to begin the drive to the airport. After the CD finished in my computer we packed up my carry on bag and headed to the elevator. Kerstin, who had sleepily pulled herself out of bed, briefly stopped me. We tearfully exchanged goodbyes and vowed we would stay in touch. With that, Yu Lan and I rolled the suitcases into the waiting elevator and the nurse gave me a final wave goodbye. I assured her I would return next year and with that the doors closed and we began our uninterrupted descent to the first floor. Upon exiting the elevator we were greeted by our driver who had parked immediately outside the door. He and the elevator operator loaded my bags into the back of the car and he graciously opened the back door. I climbed in and Yu Lan asked if she could sit in back with me. I assured her I thought it was a great idea and would make speaking to her much easier.

We began the long trek to the airport talking about family, friends, China, America, and different cultures and languages. This was the first time that we had an opportunity to just talk at length about trivial things. Before I realized it we were pulling up to the Beijing airport. Yu Lan hopped out and got a cart for the bags and I followed as the driver headed off to park. We made our way to the China Air information desk where Yu Lan began a discussion in Chinese. These are the moments that I treasure having a native to the country with me. She paused only once asking me for my ticket and passport and then continued her discussion. She emerged and said we could leave the bags as we headed upstairs to find the restroom.

Returning to our original location after finding the restrooms, we were greeted by a young woman with a wheelchair. I had agreed with Yu Lan to pay the extra fee and be escorted through the departure process and to the flight. It would be a long day and I didn't mind the added assistance. I took a seat and Yu Lan followed until we parted at the entrance. With her gentle wave goodbye I proceeded through security without incidence. The attendant took me all the way to the gate and waited with me until we boarded. Because of the chair I was the first to board and given a seat on the aisle immediately inside the door of the plane. It was in the front providing me with easy access to the bathroom and ample legroom. The plane was not full so I had an empty seat next to me as I settled back for the 3 hours trip to Tokyo.

I guess the reality of going home was beginning to hit but right now the entire episode felt a bit surreal. It didn't feel like I'd spent 5 months in China! The fact that the staff at the hospital treated me more like family than a patient made the time there more than rewarding. Seeing the change that they have made in me was exciting. I actually considered walking through the airports but I'm enjoying the wheelchair and added help. I think the biggest thing I've notice today apart from regaining my feeling is that my body doesn't lock up under emotional stress, like the stress of heading home.

The flight to Tokyo was uneventful and I actually got to catch a few winks and relax. When I landed in Tokyo and I was greeted by a wonderful Japanese man with a wheelchair. We zipped through the airport and he transitioned me through another security area where we sat and waited for a bus to take us to the other international terminal. I sat patiently waiting as a bus pulled up and a young Japanese woman got out and stood at the doorway in front of me. She said the name of the airway and several people stepped forward and exited. Several others shouted out their airlines and started asking her if that bus took them too. I had only just arrived but it was obvious that the bus only went to one section of the terminal and it was not their section. They seemed very angry and frustrated and it was at this time that I contemplated how the young woman felt. Everyone was shouting out their airline and in a language that was not her own. You could tell by her body language that she was feeling a bit overwhelmed. Several of the men close by spoke to the man that was waiting with me. He repeated what she had said, "just wait for your bus." If these people could have stepped back and seen themselves I think they would have seen things differently.

The woman re-boarded the bus and left with the passengers for her airline. I could tell from the behavior of several around me they were not happy. Just then another bus pulled up and I could see the disabled stickers on it. My attendant began heading toward the bus and I could tell a number of the passengers wanted to get on board. Apparently they hadn't caught on yet. Oh well! I hope they do and realize that they are in a foreign country and are ambassadors whether they like it or not. I guess that is the one thing I realized being abroad in China Other people would gauge the United States based on my behavior, so it better be good!

After we boarded the bus we made the short drive to the next terminal. The attendant wheeled me to the American Airlines counter where we waited in line. All I could envision at this moment was a group of people fighting for the remaining spot on a bus only to arrive to a long line of people. That's not what happened but it was a fun vision I replayed in my head!

We slowly progressed in the line and at last it was my turn to offer up my passport and ticket. She checked me through and then the attendant wheeled me to my gate.

"Domo Aregato" I said in my best Japanese. I made it a point years ago to learn "Thank-you" in several languages. I guess I never dreamed I would use it!

"Sayonara", he replied. And with that I was left sitting to pass 3 hours while I waited for my flight to Chicago to board. I pulled out my laptop and noticed that they offered wireless Internet for 500 yen per day.

Now is when I am discovering again what a blessing my little iBook computer is. With the wireless card I can log on to the Internet and send messages. It was only $5 so it was cheaper than a phone call. I logged on and got my email and sent off a message home and to the staff in China, updating them on my progress and location. I guess it's just a matter of time before access will be offered aboard international flights as well. Technology certainly has made the process of communication faster.

The flight from Tokyo to Chicago was full and it wasn't until later in the flight that I felt that things were quiet enough to approach one of the flight attendants.

"My hand writing is terrible since my stroke and I was wondering if you could help me fill out my customs form?" I implored.

"Certainly!" she said as she dug for her glasses. "I knew you had experienced something but you are moving so well," she added, "I wouldn't have guessed you had a stroke."

As she helped me fill out the form I filled her in on the past 5 months and the results I'd gotten. She asked me to share my story with another attendant and so we continued our conversation. It was exciting to share with someone who seemed to appreciate all that I had been through. It had been three years getting to this point and yet I was certain that in the midst of this "enlightened" individual. Dark days and minds lay ahead. I was simply glad to be going home to friends and family who would be happy to see me.

My lay over in Chicago was long and uneventful. I didn't want to fall asleep for fear I would miss my flight, so I stayed awake and made small talk with others as they waited for their flights.

As I chatted and listened I was amazed and reminded at how just hours before I was in a different country with a different language. I was reminded again of something that Joe, a good friend shared with me years before.

"Communication" He said, "is shared meaning and shared understanding!"

The question welled up within me. Could I truly communicate what had happened to me? Would I be able to help people understand exactly what I had experienced and that it wasn't meant for me alone? Just as I started to ponder these thoughts my flight was called and I was wheeled to the plane. I was very grateful that I had the wheelchair. It was becoming quite apparent that the long trip was taking its toll.

After I boarded I used the short flight to Iowa to contemplate the thoughts that I had started. I had promised my kids that I would keep out of the limelight and lay low for at least 6 months. After being gone I felt I owed them that much. At the end of that time I figured it would be obvious to me how I should go about sharing my story.

It was a short flight to the Des Moines airport and I waited on board until all the passengers filed out before I made my way to the front of the plane. A young man met me with a wheelchair ad I smiled.

"You must be Ruth" he said.

"Yes, as a matter of fact I am" I replied.

"There's a whole lot of people waiting for you downstairs" he continued.

"I guess I better not disappoint them then, huh?" I stated.

And with that I chose to follow him and not use the wheelchair for the walk toward the passenger meeting area. I only had to walk about 400 yards before I arrived at the top of the escalator and stepped on. As I slowly moved down, faces of family members, friends and signs were there to greet me. I stepped off the escalator to open arms, handshakes, and hugs. Boy it felt good to be home! The throng of well wishers urged me forward, as we moved toward the baggage area. It took so long that we were met by the young man I had followed who had graciously collected my bags from the baggage area. Steve ran ahead and got the car as I said my hellos and goodbyes. It was all a bit overwhelming but encouraging just the same. The trip home was filled with questions and when we finally arrived at the house my bed and sleep were beckoning. Tomorrow would have to be soon enough for the story.

14

Why Traditional Chinese Medicine?

Once upon a time in a land far... far... away,
there lived a...
... well, isn't that how stories are supposed to begin?
Oh, I guess that only applies to fairy tales!

Well, the story you have read is real, the names are real, the people are real, events and emotions are real. This was done to prevent anyone from having any doubts about the validity of what has happened. This story was composed and written over a course of four years and in that time I have run into those who doubt or think that my experiences are somehow unique. Nothing could be further from the truth! Currently someone suffers a stroke every 45 seconds and someone dies from a stroke every 3 minutes. It is the third leading killer of people in the U.S. ranked behind heart disease and <u>all</u> cancers combined! It is not, as many would think, an "old persons" disease. It affects all ages, races, and sexes and is the leading cause of disability in the U.S.

Why mention this? I guess it is to help you understand that it could happen to you and I guarantee that you know someone who has been affected by a stroke. I am unique only in the fact that after my stroke I refused to give up and chose instead to take control of my disease and was blessed with having a family that stood behind me. As a result I became the first "westerner" who dared to look east for answers that I have now learned have been here for centuries. In that respect I am unique and yet I hope I am the first of tens or even hundreds of thousands who benefit from the experiences I've had.

When I began my search into different avenues for the solutions for the physical problems that my stroke left me with I was open minded and had no clue of what to expect. I started looking for answers and educating myself shortly after I returned home from the hospital. Online searches were tedious and challenging because after the stroke the mind did not always work correctly and I kept typing the wrong letters in the web addresses. Part of the problem was my left hand still lacked coordination and the remaining problem was as much as I tried to hide it my brain was definitely confused about the things I thought I saw and how I interpreted them.

I received a tremendous amount of information from the American Stroke Association, statistics and risk factors and more information than I could digest. After prolonged searching I felt there was little real help to be found except information that I found regarding acupuncture and studies involving different types of physical rehabilitation. Those seemed to be the only avenues left open to me. I continued my extensive physical therapy efforts at home after insurance money ran out. I even invested in a treadmill to allow my walking to continue during inclement weather. I looked for and found an acupuncture practitioner in my local area and after about 6 months of physical therapy I visited him. He was pleasant and we spoke at length during my first visit. He wanted to learn about my symptoms and me. After that initial visit I began seeing him 2 times a week and receiving treatments. I felt as if my balance was improving some and total numbness in my right side was replaced with numbness and intermittent pain on the bottom of my foot. Pain is typically viewed as a negative feedback mechanism. To me this was something I saw as good. It beat numbness and gave me a sense of hope that something was there. I continued to see him for another 6 months before finances became a major factor and it became impossible to continue. Acupuncture wasn't covered by insurance so I had to pay out of pocket. It amazes me that the only thing I felt was addressing the real problems that I had and not masking them was the one thing ignored or limited by my insurance.

It wasn't until I began to experience other health issues that I began my search for answers with a new intensity that bordered on desperation. This time my search continued with more fervor and aggressiveness convinced that if I didn't find the answers I was looking for I would be destined to go down a path of physical deterioration. I must confess that most people around me although verbally supportive were a bit confused as to why I didn't just fall in line with the powers that be and be content with where I was. I had toyed with the idea of seeking treatment overseas 1 1/2 years after the stroke, but the summer of 2003 there was a SARs scare so I abandoned my idea. It wasn't until I had Yiwei start the search in Chinese that I began to become intrigued with the information offered on the web. She found abundant information online in Chinese about strokes and it all seemed to point to one hospital. The First Teaching Hospital of Tianjin University of Traditional Chinese Medicine.

I was intrigued by this Traditional Chinese Medicine and a teaching hospital peaked my interest even more, I began doing as much research and learning as much as I could about TCM and this hospital.

TCM it appeared was a very ancient form of medicine with a history dating back some 5000 years. Unlike our western form of medicine, which I might add only has a short scientific history; TCM was built upon real people finding real solutions to everyday problems, something that the scientific medical community often likes to refer to as anecdotal evidence. 5000 years in my estimation was a long time to develop a history and pattern of what works so although it differed greatly from everything I had been looking at I decided to look further. I was encouraged to find that not only a long history but documentation also existed supporting their methodology and modes of treatment and therapies. The more I looked the more I found and the more impressive the findings were. Several friends approached me to ask why I would consider a trip to China rather than seeking treatment in the United States. My response was rather simple:

"If given a choice of the student, the teacher, or the master," I would reply, "who would you seek treatment from?"

I felt that I had one shot at this and that I would invest my entire being to make that the best shot possible. It had not escaped me that I was conceived the night before my father died, survived a stroke that should have killed me, was plagued with almost every physical challenge, and given an opportunity and connections to seek treatment in China.

I do not believe in "chance." Things happen for a reason and I was going to take this opportunity and embrace it.

It didn't take long after I arrived at this hospital to begin noting the differences. I quickly discovered that it was  the best in China for stroke treatment, something that they specialized in. It was the first hospital of its kind to combine not only Traditional Chinese Medicine but Western Medicine as well.

Their approach to disease is quite different. Rather than looking at and treating symptoms they focus on the entire body and look at syndromes and differences in them. They have found that a problem that is manifested in one part of the body is usually caused by something elsewhere and it is important to view and treat the patient as a whole. Having spent years learning and practicing in the western medical ways, this was an extremely foreign concept. Over time I have begun to see the "specialization" that we practice in the west as almost a detriment to be overcome. We are so busy at trying to specialize on smaller and smaller issues that we often miss the "big" picture. I know numerous patients that have numerous doctors treating them, each for a different malady. It doesn't take a rocket scientist to tell you that any breakdown in communications between "specialties" and you have a potentially deadly situation.

Much of this "communication" relies heavily on the patient's shoulders to pass on. Medications prescribed by Dr

A may conflict with those prescribed by Dr B and unless the pharmacist catches it or it is flagged by a computer program as a problem it goes undetected. This scenario also depends on the patient going to the same place for their medications, if a patient visits 2 or more doctors and gets their prescriptions filled at different locations there is a strong chance that potential drug interactions will be missed. For this reason it is important for people to be well educated about their own health and take responsibility for their own bodies.

After spending only a week in this hospital I was forced to ask myself two questions.

- Why are they practicing a form of medicine that dates back over 2000 years?
- Why are the outpatient clinics full when people have to pay for their own medical care?

When I began looking into the history of "western" medicine I was inundated with volumes of information that listed numerous writings about and studies of the "medical forefathers." It seemed anyone who wanted to make a name for themselves academically wrote about others who had made breakthroughs or compiled comparative studies of them. I was intrigued to find you could trace most medicine back to the early Greeks who established a written form of the medicine they practice. I guess I was not as amazed at what I found as what I did not seem to find.

In all of my research little, if any, find any mention of the volumes of medical knowledge that was accumulated over the centuries in China. In searching for medical information the earliest information I came up with dated back to the 5th and 4th Century B.C. regarding the *Hippocratic Corpus* which consists of some 60 medical writings. In contrast, the

Classic on Medical Problems was written before the Han dynasty (206 B.C – 220 A.D.). It outlines a principal base for TCM and covers physiology, pathology, diagnosis, and treatment. I realize that is only a start. The book entitled The Herbal was the earliest I can find and it summarizes the pharmacological knowledge known prior to the Han dynasty. It covers in great detail some 365 drugs discussing their actions and how to make up each prescription. Huang Fumi (215 – 282 A.D.) put together his book ***A-B Classic of Acupuncture and Moxibustion*** which lists over 349 points on the body.

China began its medical reach beyond its borders when in 713 A.D. the Japanese stipulated that ***The Tang Materia Medica*** (written in 659 A.D.) was a required textbook for medical students. This book listed some 850 drugs, complete with descriptions and illustrations.

It seems unique that from a country that has given us silk, paper, and yes even gunpowder, we are quick to embrace some of what they have to offer but not all. I clearly am not an expert on Traditional Chinese Medicine. There are doctors and professors here that can talk me under the table, and in Chinese no less. But I found that they were quick to embrace the technological medical advances of the west and combine them as needed with traditional Chinese practices and medicine. Together they offer solutions to problems that we still fight to conquer in the west. We are throwing millions if not billions of dollars at problems that have already been solved. I have found no reason to return to the states and a "study" when I have already been given the solution.

Contrary to what many people are already telling me: 'that's nice for you', 'we're so happy *you* found an answer to *your* problem', 'well.. *your* stroke was different,' I'm not out of the ordinary and not different! Everyone who has a stroke can be treated this way. It works! That's why I found the outpatient clinics full. Sure their methods are different but their results are stunning. Here I learned people have to pay for their treatment so you know they won't waste hard earned money on something that doesn't produce results. Everyday I passed groups of people who lived at home and came in for treatment. Some walk dragging a leg while being supported by friends or family members, some use canes, while others come in wheelchairs. All of them come for treatment and to regain feeling and function. Those with the most severe cases are hospitalized. Those who can afford to stay in a hospital do! But not alone, friends or family members stay and assist with their care. They help them in their rooms and in getting from one floor of the hospital to the next for therapy or treatment.

I was different there not in my physical stroke but in the fact that I speak English and I am here alone. The doctors, nurses and translators have been wonderful. They see to my every need and meet many needs that are not even apparent to me. Because of the fact that I am the first American to seek treatment, at first I thought they had gone out of their way to be kind but I am finding that this is just the way they are. Family is extremely important and because mine is in the U.S. they have more or less all adopted me. I laugh and tell the nurses that I feel like their mascot. (Now try explaining that one through a cultural and language barrier – it took some doing but I did it!)

I chose to seek treatment in China after several years of conventional treatment and limited alternative treatment. For those thinking about Traditional Chinese Medicine I encourage you to look carefully into it and speak openly and honestly with your personal physician and get their advice. Keep in mind that it is your body and you will have to decide what avenues you will take. I can only share my experiences and choices and challenge you to take control of your own life.

While in China I was visited by a man from Sweden and he interviewed me for many people that he has direct contact with: doctors, nurses, acupuncturists, professionals, just to name a few. One of the questions that he asked toward the end of my interview was this:

"What advice or words do you want those seeing this to be left with?"

"Well," I responded, "People need to take control of their own lives. There are plenty of people who will control your life for you if you let them. I have found that if you are not finding the answers that you are looking for then you are not asking the right questions."

15

Living In The Light

I just recently returned from China and was on top of the world. I had continued to see great improvement while I was there, and even more exciting was the fact that several other stroke survivors that I had taken to China were also making tremendous progress. Of course I was brimming with energy and feeling like anything was possible. I was thrilled with all that was happening but at a loss to continue that same level of change at home.

Now that more people were going and seeing remarkable results there had to be a way for me to continue that process here at home. There had to be something else I could do. I continued with acupuncture and massage in the U.S. but something big seemed to be missing. I thought about everything that touched me, air, water, food, everything. The air in Iowa is as good as China, maybe a little humid in an Iowa summer, but good. The water seemed fine, so what was different. The more I thought, the more frustrated I got. Then it hit me like a bolt of lightning! I had lost 50 pounds while I was in China the first time. 50 pounds in 5 months was very impressive but I had regained almost 30 pounds in the 7 months since I had returned! Why? What was so different about what I had been eating in China?

Here at home I tried to cook wisely and buy good and healthy foods, so what was different? In thinking more about it I had to admit that I shop *weekly* for groceries and buy a lot of packaged food or frozen with plenty of shelf life. I had to admit that in China, most of the food I had consumed was bought fresh and cooked that day. Could it be that simple?

With more questions than answers I began intense research. I had received my nutrition training years ago in college and I knew from ongoing reading that the "old food pyramid" was greatly flawed. I realized too that the science of nutrition was only a short course in most doctors training, but there had been a lot of exciting research in the last 15 years. Anyone who did much reading would be aware of the amino acids and antioxidants needed, the necessary vitamin, minerals and essential fatty acids. After all these had been a staple in most homes for decades. The press was full of omega 3 and omega 6 fatty acids a few years back. But to my dismay there was something obvious that I had been overlooking. I uncovered a group of scientists and doctors who were doing everything they could to get the word out about essential monosaccharides.

Monosaccharides? I dug a little deeper and a friend directed me to a web site www.glycoscience.com, it explained what the essential sugars were and how they worked. According to recent studies every cell with a nuclease in our body is covered by structures or "things" that bring nutrients into the cell or communicate "talk" with surrounding cells. The key to the whole process are "glycoproteins".

During the 1960s, research first began to appear on "glycoproteins". These "glycoproteins" as they are called are simply protein molecules bound with carbohydrate molecules. It seems that they talk to other parts of the body through "simple sugars". Now don't jump ahead of me! I'm not talking about the sugar you put in coffee or bake with. These simple sugars (monosaccarides) combine to form *thousands* of unique patterns for communications.

This was explained to me rather simply. Let's look at the English language, we have 26 letters in the alphabet and when combined they can form tens of thousands and even millions of words, right? Well, each of those letters is only made up of four shapes: a short line, a long line, a small curve, and a big curve. These simple shapes combine to become words.

Let's take the word:

H E L P

If you simply remove the long line you get:

— — ⊐
 —
— —

The word is totally lost and miscommunication occurs! Science has found that our cells communicate through those simple sugars and that out of the numerous chains (words) that are formed by the cells, they are all made up from just 8 shapes or "simple sugars"

By 1996 scientists had identified the eight sugars found on human cell surface "glycoforms" that are involved in cellular communication processes. Of the eight sugars needed for cellular communication, only two are found in any abundance in the American diet.

We know that the fruits and vegetables in the supermarkets are picked green, shipped and held until needed, ripened chemically, and delivered with remaining shelf life. It is a great convenience for stores and makes sense economically, but means poor nutrition.

I know this seems hard to believe but the science backs it up and in 1996 Harpers Biochemistry, one of the leading medical textbooks, was rewritten to include this science. I knew that if I continued to follow this research it would lead me to a logical conclusion and I was startled to see the following:

In the 1900' s only 1 autoimmune disease was present

- 1911 Solidified Shortening Product introduced
- 1920 Commercial White bread
- 1924 Frozen foods
- 1925 Cooking Oil

By 1950 there were 7 autoimmune diseases

- 1956 Margarine developed and sold
- 1950's Fast food establishments
- 1954 TV Dinners introduced
- Introduction of the first food pyramid

Now after 2005 there are over 80 autoimmune diseases!

(For a more complete list of the years when foods were added see www.strokesurvivors.net)

It became apparent to me in my continuing research that I found a trend of decreasing nutritional value in the foods that we eat and conversely a "sicker" society. I found that our body was designed for raw fruits and vegetables and we now eat a majority of highly processed, refined, frozen and preserved foods.

Intake of Carbohydrates*

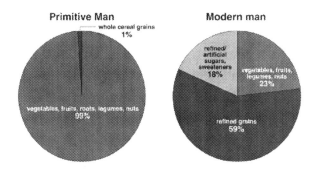

Primitive Man

whole cereal grains
1%

vegetables, fruits, roots, legumes, nuts
99%

Modern man

refined/
artificial
sugars,
sweeteners
18%

vegetables, fruits,
legumes, nuts
23%

refined grains
59%

Certainly we live longer lives but I found there has been a stark increase in the numbers and kinds of cancer, heart disease, stroke, diabetes and autoimmune diseases

The answer seemed too simple! I mean diet and nutrition? I knew that disease was often referred to as an iceberg. We only see the tip, while something much more dreadful lays just beneath the surface. I was shocked to discover that in nutrition studies over the last 30 years, the amount of specific nutrition available has decreased markedly. While one serving of broccoli would have supplied more than the current RDA of vitamin A for adults in 1951, one would have to eat more than two servings today to obtain the same amount of vitamin A. In 1951 two peaches would have supplied the current RDA of vitamin A for adults. Today you would have to eat almost 53 peaches to meet your daily requirements! Another study compared data collected in 1930 and 1980 for 8 minerals in 40 fruits and vegetables. The author reported significant losses of calcium, magnesium, copper and sodium in vegetables, and magnesium, iron, copper and potassium in fruits. The true shocker comes when you realize that the RDA (recommended daily allowance) is what is required to sustain "life" and not the "health" of an individual.

I discovered the last few days in the field are when the final (necessary) nutrients are developed within each plant. With "green" harvesting much of the nutrition that we seek is missing. This is the problem; it's like trying to drive a car while missing the wheels. The engine may work but you won't go very far! Based on my research, if I add all these things to my diet from a natural source then my health should improve right? I mean that's what I was searching for wasn't it, a way to continue to stimulate my body in healing itself?

The next several weeks and months proved to be the most exciting in my life. Once again, just like venturing to China, I set myself up as a test case. I was already taking the vitamins but they were synthetic so I switched and added the following to my diet:

❑ Natural Vitamins and Minerals
❑ Anti-Oxidants
❑ Amino Acids & Fatty acids
❑ Glyconutrients

The first thing I noticed was, within days I saw my energy level reach and maintain the "China" level I so enjoyed. Within the first week I felt an overall increased strength and stability. After two weeks I noticed the clarity of my skin returned to my "China" level. Although this was good and encouraging, I wanted to see progress with my stroke.

That's when it happened! Things that were once so automatic with my right side and had been replaced with my left now started becoming automatic again. To my surprise I found myself reaching for things with my right hand. To the ordinary observer this is nothing new, but to the stroke survivor this is powerful. In the past I had to continually remind myself to try and use my right hand and although it was unsteady it was now useable. Now I discovered even my stability in the right hand was beginning to improve. I could walk barefooted and stay balanced. The "weird" feelings that I still had on the bottom of my foot were slowly being replaced with feelings of normalcy.

Over the weeks that followed I found myself acting less like a stroke survivor and more "normal". The continued progress and level of increasing health that I had been searching for was found! Traditional Chinese Medicine focuses on stimulating the body to heal itself. Now at last the healing that I had been looking for had been found in, of all places, China and the way to continue that healing was staring me right in the face: "Glyconutrients."

My husband likes to describe our health like a boat. In good health, we are riding high and safe from the waves. When we don't have the nutrients our bodies need, it is like springing a leak. Our bodies can cope with some, but start riding lower and lower in the water. We slip from good health to minor illnesses, to chronic illness, to severe distress. This leaves us in the position where a minor ripple can swamp the boat and sink us. Most of us are content to ignore the little signs and signals that our bodies give us. You know, being tired, indigestion, aches and pains. Our bodies need the proper materials to repair the leaks so we can bail ourselves out and get back to good health.

I had to wait until I experienced a tragic health crisis before I saw the light. For those of you who are, or know, stroke survivors don't wait! I have answers now! It doesn't matter if you are 25 or 75 the solutions to "disability" are there. Never say never!

For those of you who are *seemingly* okay or "healthy" don't ignore the "little" signs and symptoms of disease; being tired, indigestion, aches, and pains and things we attribute to "getting old". Remember icebergs (like diseases) reside primarily under the surface. I won't take the time here to share with you the numerous stories of individuals who "felt fine" just before they were diagnosed with cancer, had a heart attack, suffered a stroke, were diagnosed with diabetes or Multiple sclerosis or some other disease.

We worry or take the time to make certain we have "health" insurance, when actually it should be called "sickness" insurance because that seems to be one of the only times we use it. True health insurance is what we choose to put into our bodies. Grandma was right we are what we eat!

I pray and hope that those who read this book or watch the numerous interviews that I have given will see my experience as motivation for taking action of their own, not simply a good story that happened to someone else. Now you know and have the information, what you do with it is up to you!

To obtain more information on stroke survivors and China or simply to learn about what Ruth is doing visit www. chinaconnection.cc

For more information about health and diet visit www. strokesurvivors.net

16

Reflections

For those of you that want to know a little bit more about Ruth and just who she is read on.

As is the case with most children, I was born at an early age and I should have realized then, that I was destined for fame and greatness. My mother was the first to recognized that I had a gift...

okay I admit it...

it was for running into doorknobs.

Face it, (no pun intended) I was a klutz and was continuously tripping over my own two feet and as a result always seemed to have the proverbial black eye. Nowadays teachers would think something was happening at home. The fact was I was just a clumsy and rambunctious kid! That seemingly haphazard and yet purposeful drive became the force that would constantly spur me on. It is said that what we are as adults, or I should say what we become, is determined by the experiences that we have as children and how we are taught to respond to those. So in order to truly understand what I have experienced as an adult we need to go way back, you know... before color TV, and DVD's. You see, in order to begin to comprehend my thought process in overcoming challenges you must first appreciate my upbringing and the family I was blessed with.

As I said, I was born at a very early age into a family with six, yes I said <u>six</u> girls... I was number seven! Of course everyone in the family was hoping for a boy.... and ...well, what can I say... they were blessed with me. When I was brought home my then four-year-old sister threatened to send me back from whence I came, but Mom quickly dispelled that idea. Don't get me wrong, being the seventh girl has its benefits, after all, hand me downs were never in short supply. But with twenty years spanning the age from the oldest to youngest it limits the numbers of times you can alter an outfit because after awhile there is nothing left worth sewing. Fortunately Mom was a whiz with a needle and thread, after all she got her college degree in home economics and I'll bet she never knew then how practical it would be in her future.

As the seventh girl I was raised just a bit different... expectations being what they were I was encouraged to be a bit of a tomboy. The frills and lace of many of the hand-me-down clothes didn't hold up well to the ruff and tumble life I chose to lead. Dressing up took a back seat to blue jeans and climbing trees and if mud or water was anywhere close by, I would find it.

Being number seven did have a few advantages. I was so small I could hide well and blend into the background and it took forever to get to my name on the "list".

What is the list you ask? Well, the "list" was a recited list of names of children that my mom would verbally go through while trying to find the appropriate name that matched the child in front of her. The key to "winning" at this game was to escape visual sight before your name was called. If you managed to escape before a match was made you "won". However, Mom quickly caught on to the hidden rules of this game and out of extreme frustration and (I feel) a deep desire to win herself, she often just pointed and used the expletive YOU! Game, Set, and Match... you'd been caught, and she won!

As the baby of the family I had distinct possibilities and I was just getting the hang of it when...

...oh there I go getting ahead of myself again. Let's back up.

Life for me started out in the fast and rough lane, my father died of a severe heart attack before I was born. In fact, I was conceived the night before he died! This was something that my mother finally shared with me when I turned 17. I must confess I had my own questions in my mind, I mean I could count backwards and 9 months was cutting it close. Today I would probably have found myself in a basin as an aborted fetus but I thank God daily that my mother, in the midst of her anguish, pain, and responsibilities... carried me to term. When I showed up I was what you might call a mixed blessing. A constant reminder of the man she no longer had in her life, but a reminder that life goes on even in the midst of loss and pain.

I'll never forget hearing how Mom described it: she was a schoolteacher when Dad died and when the school principal found out she was expecting a baby he remarked that he didn't know whether to offer her congratulations or condolences. Think about it, having six children in the 1950's without a husband is daring enough, she found herself with all of this *and* pregnant. I'll never really know the heartaches that she was forced to deal with during those 9 long months leading up to my birth. I just happy that she chose to have me!

The blessed event, that is... I came into the picture screaming at 8:16 p.m. on May 18th 1959! I think it is important to know and understand that there have only been a limited number of times since my birth when I *haven't* been loud, voicing my opinions. At least I had the consideration to show up late in the school year so Mom had the summer to work me into a schedule. (Like I had anything to do with it) I should have realized then that I was meant to be and would have a positive impact on those around me.

In the book of Psalms in Chapter 139 it says that God formed me in my mothers womb. That Gods work in forming me was wonderful and I was not hidden from Him even in the secret place of her womb and God knew that at that time each of the days and events of my life. Little did I know then what God had in store for me over the years that would come to pass? Hindsight has taught me that God's plans are in-depth and involved and He always allows me to use my free will, He, however, has already seen far in advance the very end of my story.

When I was born my mother was already receiving the maximum government check for assistance because my father had been a veteran retiring from the Air Force after he served more than 20 years. They reshuffled her check to include me and my portion of her stipend came out to a whopping $2.64. I dare you to try to raise a kid on $2.64 a month. Even in 1959 it was more than a challenge. It was at this point that her home economics degree danced between fantasy and stark reality. One and one, no matter how much you stretched it, didn't add up to four. I am amazed how she survived with seven girls. I know it was not always the happiest of times. Each day for her was a challenge that seemed to require a miracle for her to exist let alone carry on, and yet each day passed and we stuck together as a family.

After I turned three my mother remarried and a year later my brother was born. Happy day! Hold on a minute… I just lost my baby of the family spot! Oh well at least I gave it up to a boy. That's right, a boy was born and would live under our roof. Just think of it, such far reaching implications, as he got older we were going to have to totally rethink the morning bathroom schedule.

It was at this time that should be surrounded with happiness that life reared its ugly head. My stepfather celebrated the new birth by getting drunk and the honeymoon was over. Life came crashing down and Mom discovered to her shock and dismay that this wonderful man who came into her life to save her and her brood of seven (now eight) was indeed an alcoholic. The life that she dreamed of living just took a dramatic turn for the worse.

Of course this wasn't the end of the marriage but the beginning of a new chapter that came filled with challenges, heartaches, headaches, joys, victories and disappointments.

I could spend countless hours and an endless amount of paper rehashing the life of the child of an alcoholic… but I won't. I lived and I'm better for it.

God knew what was before me long before it came to pass and later in Psalm 139 it says that God has searched and known me. He knows when I sit down and when I stand up. He understands my thoughts and watches over me, and He is intimately acquainted with all my decisions. In short, God is looking out for me!

I think it was at this early point in my life that I learned, or at least realized life, or at least circumstances, were not always kind or fair, in fact often it appeared to be just the opposite. I did an okay job at growing up and my mom was always there, keeping her eyes peeled and offering guidance along the way. It was through these tough times that humor seemed to offer not merely an escape, but a path through the horror of a temporary predicament to the joy and contentment learned on the other side. I hadn't learned yet that there was one who could take all those hurts and pain and turn it into pure joy.

I was blessed to have had my mother as a teacher in seven different subjects in school: American history, world history, government, economics, psychology, sociology, family living and most importantly a teacher in Life 101 at home. She served as the high school guidance counselor preparing me for my college days but more importantly she was an example of determination and strength that would guide my life outside of her home. She saw early on that awkward and rambunctious child and nurtured and encouraged me.

I did not understand then what a good job she had done and the true inspiration and blessing that she would become in the years ahead! I remember fondly the "first official advice" that she offered me as I left home to face the wonderful world of college:

"Now always," she said in her finger waving mode, "Always… maintain your sense of humor." Her lips began to curl into a smile, "Circumstances may not seem funny now… but sometime… sometime in the future, a day, a week, or a year… it will be. You'll be able to look back at some point, smile, laugh and see things for what they are… bumps and not mountains."

It's amusing to look back and realize that with each major event in my life; college, my marriage, the birth of my first child (check that - I married my first child and gave birth to the second), our move overseas (I was 7 months pregnant at the time), the birth of my next child, and even when she discovered she was fighting breast cancer at age 70, she offered me that same advice.

"Look for the humor in a situation and you will surely find it." She would say. I have now come to understand that you will find whatever you fixate on. Joy, sorrow, happiness, grief, pain, relief... it is all there, you just need to chose what to focus on. You are offered a choice of things to pin your hopes and dreams to, the challenge comes in making wise choices and determining what exactly to look for and focus on.

I remember sitting with her and laughing hysterically about the people and events she faced in dealing with her cancer; the surgery, recovery and radiation therapy. Her visits to the doctor became events we bet on; the length of the wait, number of people in the waiting room, the tests ordered, the prescriptions ordered, and the like. Each event became a challenge, an opportunity that we got to embrace and explore for hidden treasures. She is the one who taught me to treasure challenging events and to hold on to them and squeeze them for every ounce of good that they would bring <u>out</u> of you. She didn't know Christ until just before she died but she understood and knew Gods principals and how we as flesh and blood individuals learn. She taught school for over 30 years and her method is now as clear to me as ever... her concern was not **if** you knew the answer going into a test... but could you **discover it** during the test and **learn it** and **apply it** when it mattered most?

Those lessons became the cornerstones for my life: discovery, absorption, and application. I think Mom would be proud, it has taken awhile but I have learned to uncover the truth, take it to heart and apply it when it mattered the most. I hope and pray you will too!

About the Author

Ruth Lycke is a wife and mother of three. Not necessarily an accomplishment until you consider she is one of ten children (the youngest of seven girls), has been a host Mom to more than seven international students, a stroke survivor, patient advocate, and the first American stroke survivor to seek treatment in China.

After the stroke Ruth found herself living what she had so often taught, "It's not what you know, but what you are willing to learn that matters!"

Through the support of her husband and kids, and the use of Traditional Chinese Medicine and Nutrition she has overcome:

- Lack of Balance
- Total Numbness on Her Right Side
- Double Vision Problems
- Mobility Problems
- Loss of Fine Motor Skills
- Cognitive Problems

She has definitely learned first hand to 'Never' say 'Never'.

Find her online at www.chinaconnection.cc

Printed in the United States
58563LVS00004B/1-24